The Compromise of Return

PRAISE FOR *THE COMPROMISE OF RETURN*

"In an engaging, thoroughly researched study, Elizabeth Anthony reveals how and why Jewish returnees came back to 'their' city, Vienna, but not to Austria. They persisted in reclaiming their familial, professional, and political homes, as they compromised with ongoing individual and governmental antisemitism, including the refusal to return their property. Elegantly written, Anthony's book highlights the hardships and disappointments of Jewish survivors as they settled back 'home.'"

—Marion Kaplan, author of *Hitler's Jewish Refugees: Hope and Anxiety in Portugal*

"With *The Compromise of Return* Elizabeth Anthony brings history alive. She paints a vivid picture of the life of Jewish Austrians who chose to remain in or returned to Vienna after the fall of the Nazi regime. Through poignant personal interviews coupled with meticulous archival research and in conversation with international scholarship, the author convincingly argues how their unique Jewish-Viennese identities allowed them to remain in an anti-Semitic society that presented itself as Hitler's first victim. *The Compromise of Return*, the first comprehensive English-language study on the topic, constitutes a major contribution to post-war Austrian and Holocaust histories."

—Jacqueline Vansant, author of *Reclaiming* Heimat: *Trauma and Mourning in Memoirs by Jewish Austrian Reémigrés*

"Deeply researched and beautifully written, this book tells the poignant story of Jewish survivors' return to Vienna, really for the first time. Brimming with insights, it gives voice to the returnees; it is they who stand at the core of this history."

—Dirk Rupnow, Institute for Contemporary History, University of Innsbruck

THE COMPROMISE OF RETURN

VIENNESE JEWS AFTER THE HOLOCAUST

ELIZABETH ANTHONY

WAYNE STATE UNIVERSITY PRESS
Detroit

© 2021 by Elizabeth Anthony. All rights reserved. No part of this book may be reproduced without formal permission.

ISBN 978-0-8143-4838-3 (paperback); ISBN 978-0-8143-4813-0 (ebook)

Library of Congress Control Number: 202094884

Cover image: Mayor Theodor Körner welcomes Austrian Jews returning from Shanghai at Vienna's Wien-Meidling train station. (US Holocaust Memorial Museum; courtesy of the US National Archives and Records Administration, College Park, MD)

Published in association with the United States Holocaust Memorial Museum

UNITED STATES HOLOCAUST MEMORIAL MUSEUM

The US Holocaust Memorial Museum's Jack, Joseph and Morton Mandel Center's mission is to ensure the long-term growth and vitality of Holocaust Studies. To do that, it is essential to provide opportunities for new generations of scholars. The vitality and the integrity of Holocaust Studies requires openness, independence, and free inquiry so that new ideas are generated and tested through peer review and public debate. The opinions of scholars expressed before, during the course of, or after their activities with the Mandel Center do not represent and are not endorsed by the Museum or its Mandel Center.

Wayne State University Press
Leonard N. Simons Building
4809 Woodward Avenue
Detroit, Michigan 48201-1309

Visit us online at wsupress.wayne.edu

For my mother, Susan Lillie Anthony, and in loving memory of Joseph Peter Anthony, Jr., and Lisa McCloskey Georgules

CONTENTS

Acknowledgments	ix
Introduction	1
1. Historical Context: Prelude to the Holocaust in Austria	15
2. The First "Returnees," 1945	43
3. *KZ Rückkehrer*: Coming Home from Concentration Camps	84
4. To Reclaim *Their* Austria	125
5. (Re)establishing Careers in Vienna	164
6. Emerging Identities and Enduring Challenges	190
Conclusion	236
Bibliography	243
Index	259

ACKNOWLEDGMENTS

This book represents not only a decade's worth of work but also a synthesis of distinct phases of my life. It signifies a logical progression from one stage to the next and incorporates my past professional life working with Holocaust survivors, my private and professional experiences of growth in Vienna, my scholarly life of research and writing about survivors, and my current and continuing path as a Holocaust historian. With the weight of such significance, both personal and professional, I struggle for a proper expression of appreciation for the numerous people and institutions that showed immense confidence in my research. I grasp for appropriate words of thanks for the extraordinary generosity of time and expertise shown by colleagues and friends over the past ten years.

Perhaps the most difficult to articulate is my gratitude for Debórah Dwork, founding director of the Strassler Center for Holocaust and Genocide Studies at Clark University, my doctoral adviser, and my friend. From the moment we met in her living room to discuss my application to the Clark University doctoral program, it was confirmed; she was the scholar with whom I wanted to work. I wanted to learn from *her*. Debórah's tireless support and unwavering belief in me has shaped the Holocaust historian and professional I am today. Without her, this book simply would not be. I am deeply grateful for her guidance, mentorship, and, above all, friendship, throughout the process of bringing this project from a seed of an idea through to publication.

The Strassler Center and Clark University also provided me the unmatched and inspired support of Taner Ackam, Thomas Kühne, Olga

Litvak, Robert Melson, and Mary Jane Rein, as well as Margaret Hillard, Jean Hearns, and Tatyana Macaulay. Colleagues and dear friends Alexis Herr, Jody Russell Manning, Christine Schmidt, and Raz Segal have been with me and this work from the start, and I appreciate the hundreds of hours of discussion and debate they enthusiastically provided. I am also grateful for input and encouragement from Clarkies Sara Brown, Sarah Cushman, Emily Dabney, Mikal Brotnov Eckstrom, Mike Geheran, Adara Goldberg, Stefan Ionescu, Natalya Lazar, Khatchig Mouradian, Ilana Offenberger, and Joanna Sliwa.

Atina Grossmann and Marsha Rozenblit generously read and advised on my dissertation committee and helped me keep consistent, accurate, and on task with "Return Home," the earlier incarnation of *The Compromise of Return*. Dirk Rupnow knew I was embarking on the correct path with the right topic and has supported my research and me from the start. For contributions tangible and otherwise, I am also indebted to Thomas Barth, Tracy Brown, Julien Carabalona, Tim Corbett, Barbara Grell, Gabor Kadar, Marion Kaplan, Katharina von Kellenbach, Barbara Kintaert, Eduard Kubesch, Hannah Lessing, Alexandra Lux, Susanne Ogris, Katrin Paehler, Maggie Peterson, Binh Pok-Carabalona, Markus Priller, Karin Quigley-Draxler, Dan Roberts, Gayle Scroggs, Leslie Swift, Susanne Urban, Johanna Webster, Greg Weeks, Anna Wexburg-Kubesch, and Jenn Wood.

Many archivists, reference librarians, scholars, and experts around the world deserve special recognition for assistance they provided. At the United States Holocaust Memorial Museum, many thanks are due to Diane Afoumado, Michlean Amir, Suzanne Brown-Fleming, Ron Coleman, Kierra Crago-Schneider, Jo-Ellyn Decker, Krista Hegburg, Samantha Hinckley, Lisa Leff, Megan Lewis, Noelle Little, Alexandra Lohse, Jürgen Matthäus, Geoff Megargee, Vanda Rajcan, Tracy Rucker, Paul Shapiro, Vincent Slatt, Suzy Snyder, Anatol Steck, and Wendy Lower. I would like to acknowledge Misha Mitsel and Shelly Helfand of the JDC Archives in New York, as well as the reference and reading room staff at the Leo Baeck Institute, the Center for the History of the Jewish People, Yad Vashem, the United States National Archives and Records Administration in College Park, and the Library of Congress in Washington, DC. Elisabeth Klamper at the Dokumentationsarchiv des österreichischen Widerstandes (DÖW) has shown unparalleled kindness and munificence, both as an archivist and as a friend. Thanks to Brigitte Bailer and Winfried Garscha, also of the DÖW; Shoshana Duizend-Jensen at the Wiener Stadt- und Landesarchiv; and to the former and current staff at the Israelitische Kultusgemeinde Wien, especially Lothar Höbling, Susanne Uslu-Pauer, David Forster Winterfeld, and Ingo Zechner. The advice and support of Ed Serotta, Tanja Eckstein, and their team at Centropa helped me to shape the direction of my research from the beginning and provided many crucial introductions to survivors in Vienna. I am grateful for all they have done for me, as well as all they do for our field.

A number of institutions showed confidence in my work through the provision of research fellowships. These include a fellowship through the U.S. Fulbright Program and the Austrian-American Educational Commission; a Sharon Abramson Research Grant from the Holocaust Education Foundation of Northwestern University; a travel grant to attend the 2011 German Studies Association conference from the Austrian Culture Forum; a Leo Baeck Institute-DAAD fellowship to conduct research in the archives of the Leo Baeck Institute in New York; the Memorial Foundation for Jewish Culture; and the Claims Conference, the Fromson family, and the Rose family for their support during my time at the Strassler Center. This book was also made possible through a Barbara and Richard Rosenberg Fellowship at the Mandel Center for Advanced Holocaust Studies, United States Holocaust Memorial Museum. I am particularly grateful to Professors Carola Sachse and Oliver Rathkolb for sponsoring me at the Institut für Zeitgeschichte at the Universität Wien during my Fulbright year, along with Lonnie Johnson, Irene Zavarsky, and Molly Heidfogel-Roza of Fulbright's Vienna office.

I would like to thank the members of the Publications Subcommittee of the Mandel Center's Academic Committee for approving this work as a copublished volume by Wayne State University Press and the United States Holocaust Memorial Museum. The statements made and views expressed, however, are solely my own and my responsibility. I am also grateful to the Emerging Scholars Program at the Mandel Center for Advanced Holocaust

Studies for its support in the preparation of the manuscript and of the book proposal.

I appreciate the commitment and encouragement I have received from Wayne State University Press throughout the publishing process. Special thanks are in order to Kathy Wildfong, who first expressed interest in publishing this book and pursued my proposal with dedicated enthusiasm; Annie Martin, who shepherded me through to signed contract; Andrew Katz for remarkable copy editing; Carrie Teefey and Kristin Harpster for bringing all the pieces together; the design team for making everything look as it should; and Emily Nowak and Jamie Jones in the marketing department for their support and advice.

I have had the good fortune to meet exceptional people at important times in the course of my studies and career. Two in particular had profound impact on me and my work early on and deserve special recognition. Professor Björn Krondorfer saw something in me that I had not yet seen myself during my undergraduate years at St. Mary's College of Maryland and invited me to take part in the 1995 Interfaith Council on the Holocaust's summer exchange program. That experience set me on this course, and for more than two decades he has continued to mentor and encourage me. Martin Goldman gave me the opportunity of a lifetime when he hired me in the United States Holocaust Memorial Museum's Office of Survivor Affairs. We were a "dream team," and he modeled a proper ratio of reverence and joyfulness in our particular workplace and with our extraordinary constituency.

Indeed, survivors make up the heart of this book. I am indebted to Paul Back, Paula Bizberg, Hannah Fischer, Eva Kallir, Walter Kammerling, Fritz Koppe, Susanne Lamberg, Erich Lessing, Anny Mandl, Jonny Moser, Robert Rosner, Leo Schaechter, Ruth Schauder, Kitty Suschny, Otto Suschny, Lilli Tauber, Max Tauber, and Hansi Tausig for sharing so much with me in formal interviews and informal exchanges. The English conversation group at the Tagesstätte at the Maimonides Zentrum in Vienna provided me weekly inspiration and immeasurable insight. The group of survivors who volunteer at the United States Holocaust Memorial Museum first moved me and continue to motivate me and my work. I owe so much to those whom we have unfortunately lost—Bob Behr, Leo Bretholz, Erika Eckstut, Frank Ephraim, Manya Friedman, Jack Godin, Henry Greenbaum, Werner Katzenstein, Willie Luksenburg, Michel Margosis, Margit Meissner, Morris Rosen, Charlene Schiff, Flora Singer, Regina and Sam Spiegel, Charles Stein, Herman Taube, and Rabbi Jacob Wiener—as well as those from whom we are fortunate to continue to learn: David Bayer, Fritz Gluckstein, Nesse Godin, Helen Goldkind, Inge Katzenstein, Louise Lawrence-Israëls, Helen Luksenburg, Kurt and Jill Pauly, Halina Peabody, Pete Philipps, Esther Starobin, Charles Stein, Susan Taube, Marsha Tishler, Irene Weiss, and Martin Weiss.

Along with survivors, "home" and different concepts of it are central to this work. I am privileged to have enjoyed home in a few places and with very important people. First and foremost, my parents, Joe and Susan Anthony, showed me constant and steady support for all my endeavors, academic, professional, and otherwise. My mother started me on this journey years ago when she accompanied me on my first explorations of Holocaust history. I am grateful to my sister, Leah Anthony Guidry, and to Chretien Guidry for their enthusiasm and encouragement, as well as their understanding when I was not always accessible. My nieces, Rachel and Ellie, and my nephew, Nathan, provided much-needed hope and laughter while I worked on this disheartening topic.

Insight and understanding resulted from enjoying Vienna as my second home and the opportunities it offered as I conducted long-term research while immersed in the city. I am particularly fortunate to be a part of a most wonderful and loving family in Vienna. Margit, Jimmy, and Philip Engel, I am so grateful for your interest in and support of this project from start to finish. Despite the dismal history I have portrayed in *The Compromise of Return*, I also know the beauty, love, and goodness in the city and among the Viennese, and the Engel and Grell families are the best examples. I am also lucky to have a loving Worcester family. Lisa, Stefan, and Elly Georgules took care of me throughout my residence at Clark and offered their home to me as my own. Uncle Chris Lillie and Aunt Kathy Rose have been by me through thick and thin, both for intellectual discussion and to provide strong shoulders on which I can always lean. Aunt Brenda Partain has cheered me along and made the crucial Lillie-Partain family connection to my adopted aunt and dissertation editor extraordinaire, Barbara Muller. And finally, and most importantly, there is Roland Engel. He is steadfast in every way, and I can imagine no partner more supportive, no fan more enthusiastic, no friend more loyal.

INTRODUCTION

Hansi Tausig fled Nazi Vienna in 1938. Like many German and Austrian Jewish women, she escaped to the United Kingdom after securing the necessary paperwork and support to take a domestic position. She lived in and around London for nearly eight years, and throughout she connected with other young Austrian émigrés—most of them Jews—through the Austrian Centre, a cultural organization established by and for Austrians living in London. In addition to providing social and cultural opportunities, however, the Austrian Centre served as a cover organization for the Free Austrian Movement of the Austrian Communist Party. Indoctrinated through the party's youth arm, Young Austria, a young and idealistic Hansi eagerly returned to Vienna in the spring of 1946 with a number of other members. The party had promised that their return was not only welcome but also eagerly awaited, and they planned to take an active part in the rebuilding of an independent, democratic Austria—*their* Austria. But Hansi and her colleagues were disabused of such idealistic notions almost immediately upon their arrival. Once home, they found a population living in a partly bombed-out city and, along with everyone else, they too suffered hardships that included a housing crisis and food shortages. They also met with enduring antisemitism and contempt from gentile Viennese who already identified as part of the collective Austrian "first victim" of the Nazis. The Communist Party ultimately failed to gain much footing in the government, and, over years, Hansi and many others became disillusioned with and finally left the party.

I met with Hansi in the living room of her Vienna apartment more than sixty years after her return. She served me slices of *Apfelstrudel* and poured countless cups of coffee as she related her experiences of return and resettlement in her hometown. After hours of discussion and many examples of her disappointment and frustration, I still felt her connection to and love for the city. In an effort to prompt her assessment and explanation of this curious incongruity, I asked her for a quick and instinctive response to the question, "*Why* did you return?" She replied with a touch of bitterness and a wry smile but without a moment's hesitation: "Because we were naïve!" But when I asked why she stayed, why she had not returned to the United Kingdom or emigrated elsewhere, she looked at me, sincerely bewildered. "Why would I do that? This is my home!"[1] Nonetheless, and despite it all, Vienna was *home*. Austrian Jews and those with a Jewish family background that rendered them targets of Nazi "racial" persecution numbered more than two hundred thousand before the Anschluss united Nazi Germany and Austria in March 1938. Almost all of them lived in Vienna. A little more than seven years later, at the time of the Red Army's conquest at the end of the war, less than 3 percent remained alive in the city.[2] Some of them had survived as *U-Boote* (literally, submarines) in hiding, while others had endured under different levels of protection due to marriages to so-called Aryans, because of a mixed "racial" heritage, or as employees of the Viennese Jewish community that operated in some form throughout the Nazi regime. Approximately 1,727 concentration camp survivors had joined them in Vienna by the end of 1945,[3] and by April 1947, about 2,000 had returned from exile abroad.[4] Most of these Jewish returnees chose to stay and reroot in the post-Nazi society of their hometown, all with eyes wide open to their charged surroundings and the city's recent past. They knew that their fellow

---

1. Hansi Tausig, interview with author, Vienna, Austria, December 13, 2010.
2. Jonny Moser, *Demographie der jüdischen Bevölkerung Österreichs 1938–1945* (Vienna: Dokumentationsarchiv des österreichischen Widerstandes, 1999), 55.
3. F. Wilder-Okladek, *The Return Movement of Jews to Austria after the Second World War* (The Hague: Martinus Nijhoff, 1969), 114.
4. Evelyn Adunka, *Die Vierte Gemeinde: Die Geschichte der Wiener Juden von 1945 bis heute* (Berlin: Philo Fine Arts, 2000), 56.

Viennese had embraced the Nazi takeover and unification with Germany and regularly confronted the society's tight adherence to a mythical identity of "first victim" of the Nazis in the aftermath of an Allied victory.

Two years after the end of World War II, approximately forty-five thousand Jews lived in Austria, but about thirty-five thousand of them were among the tens of thousands of displaced persons (DPs) from other European countries who streamed into DP camps, primarily in Germany and Austria, as they sought to begin their lives anew in third countries.[5] The percentage of the prewar Jewish population living again in Vienna had reached about 5 percent.[6]

The city's remaining and returned Jewish residents were first and foremost *Viennese*, and many survivors remain insistent in their identification as such, not "Austrian." They had been socialized in a city with a long history of antisemitism but were accustomed to the hardships that entailed and knew how to nimbly maneuver discrimination and hostility. The same sensibility of ambiguity that enabled gentile Viennese to enthusiastically embrace the Nazis also allowed their quick shift to assume the role as the Nazis' first victims, just as it enabled their wholehearted belief in both. It also allowed Viennese Jews to conceive of a return to a place in a society with indistinct and evolving guidelines of belonging in which they trusted they could still fit, even after the devastation and loss of their families and community. They expected that they could refashion fulfilling lives in the city they loved by employing a level of discretion and relying on well-honed skills of peaceably living among antisemites. The understanding of the vagueness involved

---

5. Postwar Joint press release, July 30, 1947, translation of a July 16, 1947, press release, from Information Office in Jerusalem, AR 45/54-143, Records of the New York Office of the American Jewish Joint Distribution Committee, 1945–1954, Archives of the American Jewish Joint Distribution Committee, New York, NY.

6. This figure includes formal members of the Jewish community as well as those defined as "Jews" by Nazi racial policy. Herbert Rosenkranz stated that a total of 185,028 Jews were in residence in Austria on March 11, 1938, which corresponds with the membership numbers of the Israelitische Kultusgemeinde Wien (IKG; the Jewish community of Vienna). See Rosenkranz, *Verfolgung und Selbstbehauptung: Die Juden in Österreich, 1938–1945* (Vienna: Herold Verlag, 1978), 13. Jonny Moser further calculated that 201,000 Austrians were targeted as Jews by Nazi racial policies. See Moser, *Demographie der jüdischen Bevölkerung Österreichs*, 18–19.

in a "Viennese way," of flexibly fitting into the city's culture, permitted the acceptance of conceivably living next door to a convinced Nazi, for example. They had pegged the Viennese population as opportunistic and could assume a corresponding adaptation to the Allied occupation. With that, Jewish returnees could feel confident in the possibility of a safe and secure life in their hometown once again.

Jewish returnees were *Viennese*, not just in thought and identification from afar but in the action of their return as well. Language and literature scholar Jacqueline Vansant has argued that, with their return and reclamation of their home, Austrian Jewish reémigrés sought to reconnect to an Austrian "we."[7] Although some still may have thought in terms of an Austrian collective, I would argue that a further-honed and particular *Viennese* "we" represented that which they sought to rejoin. These returnees still conceptualized Vienna as *home* and wanted to go back and reengage. Different but sometimes overlapping ideas of home guided them there. Some sought to salvage a *familial home*, with surviving relatives or at least in the place that they had last enjoyed family life. Others strove to reclaim a *political home* with the support and guidance of their political parties and comrades. And some looked to resume life in their *professional home*, the place where they had trained and gained experience or where they had once—and now again—aimed to form careers.

The vast majority of Austrian Jews, most of them Viennese, however, remained abroad after the war in the various locations around the globe to which they had fled to safety. They had created new homes in new places, although often with a nostalgia for and connection to what they had left behind. Many exiles' homes in other countries still felt and looked like Viennese domiciles decades later, transported across time and many national borders.[8] They had found a home by re-creating one, retaining what they wanted or what they needed of the old, and fitting it into the new. They had either a new home or a distinct sense of having lost "home" altogether.

---

7. Jacqueline Vansant, *Reclaiming Heimat: Trauma and Mourning in Memoirs by Jewish Austrian Reémigrés* (Detroit: Wayne State University Press, 2001), 15.

8. See Diana Gregor, *heim.at.home* (Vienna: Metroverlag, 2012).

But the few thousand who chose to go back and to stay to reestablish lives in their hometown could still see Vienna as home. Because they kept this sense of belonging and being in the city, they could go back. And once there, even when circumstances turned out differently than expected, a Viennese awareness helped them identify the compromises required to stay.

Why did some Viennese Jews still envision homes and lives in a country that had shortly before robbed and then either expelled or deported them? Why choose to live among those who months or years before had sought their annihilation? The short answer to "why"—to go home—fails to explain the overall phenomenon in its complexity and nuance and requires an examination and analysis of "how." Many Jews and gentiles living outside Austria even today consider the return to the former Nazi country inconceivable, yet so many Jews living there cannot imagine their home anywhere else. Both on an emotional level and in an actual sense, *how* did survivors return? How did they organize a place to live, sustenance, and an enduring livelihood? How did they cope with living among their relatives' and friends' murderers, or at least the supporters of their murderers? And how did they manage to coexist with so many of their former friends and neighbors who stood by during genocide?

The majority of European Jewish Holocaust survivors either remained abroad or emigrated onward after the war, but some did go back to their prewar homelands. Germany's Jewish population in 1933 had exceeded 523,000, but only 12,000 to 15,000 lived there in 1947, most of them returned camp survivors along with "reemerged" former *U-Boote* and the spouses or children who had been protected by mixed marriages.[9] By the end of the 1950s, some 12,500 (of 278,000) German Jewish émigrés too had gone back,[10] to comprise a native Jewish population of a maximum of 27,500, just 5 percent of its prewar total—a percentage similar to the Austrian case. Jews from

---

9. Michael Brenner, *After the Holocaust: Rebuilding Jewish Lives in Postwar Germany* (Princeton, NJ: Princeton University Press, 1997), 42.
10. Ibid., 138.

countries that had been conquered and occupied by the Nazis returned home in greater percentages than did German- and Austrian-born Jews. In the Netherlands, of a prewar population of some 135,000 Dutch Jews,[11] about 21,000 returned. Just 5,000 of the 110,000 Dutch Jews who had been deported—mostly to Auschwitz and Sobibor—survived and went back,[12] where they joined about 16,000 Jews who had endured in hiding.[13] In Slovakia, just under 23 percent of the prewar Jewish population returned after liberation.[14]

But some Jews did return to Vienna. A good number found nothing awaited them, but a few regained homes, businesses, and careers. Those who stayed to reestablish their lives also took part in rebuilding European Jewish and secular life. *The Compromise of Return* utilizes contemporary archival documents and newspaper articles, testimonies, and oral histories to illuminate and analyze the experiences of the Austrian Jews who chose to live in Vienna again after the Holocaust. It focuses on the immediate postwar period and population and the ongoing politics of a national blind spot that has left the events of this time largely unexamined. It illuminates the collision of wartime experience with the fierce struggle of postwar identity politics and traces the early years of the reestablishment of a strong and vibrant—albeit small—Viennese Jewish community. This book's analysis of the postwar history of Holocaust survivors who returned to Vienna explores their motivations for laying down roots anew in a hometown and a homeland that had expelled them and did not expect them to return and investigates the issues and problems they confronted in doing so.

---

11. In January 1941, the German occupiers forced Dutch Jews to register as Jews; 159,806 individuals did so, including 19,561 children from mixed marriages. This total also included about 25,000 Jewish refugees from the German Reich. Thus, of a prewar Dutch Jewish population of nearly 135,000, some 15 percent returned. United States Holocaust Memorial Museum, "The Netherlands," accessed March 18, 2019, https://encyclopedia.ushmm.org/content/en/article/the-netherlands.

12. Dienke Hondius, *Return: Holocaust Survivors and Dutch Anti-Semitism* (Westport, CT: Praeger, 2003), 55.

13. Ibid., 31.

14. Yehoshua R. Büchler, "Reconstruction Efforts in Hostile Surroundings—Slovaks and Jews after World War II," in *The Jews Are Coming Back: The Return of the Jews to Their Countries of Origin after WWII*, ed. David Bankier (New York: Berghahn Books, 2005), 257.

This book follows patterns of return. In the course of research and examination, it became clear that Jews who went back to Vienna could be seen as members of distinct cohorts, each group sharing similar wartime experiences and locations, motivations for return, and postwar arrival dates in the city. Those who survived within the city limits reemerged to "return" to society first, followed in the first few months of peacetime by those who came back after internment in concentration camps. These first two groups arrived in Vienna within the first hours, days, or months of the war's end and mainly harbored ideas of reclaiming their *familial home*. Jewish émigrés who survived the war abroad with their political parties in exile returned in the next wave, which started at the end of 1945 and continued through 1946, and—like Hansi Tausig—sought to take part in rebuilding an autonomous and democratic Austria; they aimed to reclaim their *political home*. A fourth group of returnees mainly began their remigration from locations abroad about two years after the end of the war and did so seeking to regain or begin anew careers they could only imagine in their *professional home*.

To be sure, returnees had manifold and complicated reasons for their postwar (re)settlement, and sometimes those overlapped. Those who returned from living in exile in Shanghai, for example, held the same hopes for a familial home but came back a few years later than the first, immediate postwar cohort. Some politically affiliated returnees had designs on recovering a career in their hometown, even if it was primarily their work on behalf of their party and country that carried them there. The possibility of multiple and intersecting incentives for return notwithstanding, a general pattern of common experience and timeline emerges.

The particular context of Vienna, Austria, and Austria-Hungary underpins this history. Jews had a long presence in the region and enjoyed the liberal policies and restrictions in the Habsburg Empire. They remained loyal and supportive of the monarchy through World War I and the bitterly disappointing defeat of the Central Powers of Germany and Austria-Hungary. Despite freedoms greater than those of Jews in other parts of Europe, antisemitism was pervasive in the empire and then in German-Austria after

World War I. But Austrian, and in particular Viennese, Jews knew how to traverse such discrimination as a part of the landscape of their beloved Vienna. The interwar rise of a homegrown Catholic fascism, Austrofascism, and an opposing and illegal Nazi Party fueled a buildup to the Anschluss, the unification of Germany and Austria into one German cultural nation-state. The concept of Anschluss had predated the Nazis and Hitler by many years and seen together with native antisemitism helps to explain the large part of the population that embraced the March 12, 1938, arrival of the Germans, as well as the wanton violence perpetrated against Jews and their homes, businesses, and religious institutions. The Viennese Jewish community responded as it was forced to but also as it saw best. That is, Viennese Jews could only cooperate with their Nazi oppressors to administer a forced emigration program. Of a pre-Anschluss population of more than two hundred thousand Austrian Jews, the vast majority of them Viennese, about two-thirds fled the country after the Nazi takeover, after suffering persecution and spoliation, and most of them left thanks to the extreme efforts of the Viennese Jewish community. When Nazi policy shifted to deportation and annihilation, hopes of escape were all but lost, and by the end of the war some sixty-five thousand Austrian Jews had been murdered.

The Soviets conquered Vienna in April 1945, and as their troops advanced through the city, the retreating Wehrmacht (Nazi German army) and Waffen-SS (combat units of the Schutzstaffel, or SS, that fought alongside the general army) continued to fight and terrorize Jews to the bitter end. Fighting broke out in the streets, and the city center became the front line. The Red Army took the city, and Jews who survived the war under different levels of protection or in hiding cautiously emerged as a part of the first wave of returnees to Vienna. They joined those who were still there who were married to so-called Aryans, the children of such unions, and the employees of the few remaining Jewish institutions that served them. Another estimated eight hundred also had survived in hiding in the city. All reemerged and reentered the society from which they had been thrust. Without a choice or even a thought, they were the first Austrian Jews to "return" to Vienna, with the only ambition of survival in their familial home, a place they physically had never left.

The second group of Jews to return comprised concentration camp survivors. They employed varied processes and journeys as they too followed their impulse to return to a familial home. Liberated in camps across Europe, their only thought was to again be in the last place that they had been with family. Their intentions may or may not have been to stay permanently, but they certainly planned to return, and many reestablished lives in Vienna. By the time of their arrival, just weeks or months after the war's end, the postwar government's embrace of the so-called victim myth had taken hold and shaped a developing postwar national identity that viewed the Anschluss as an aggressive military invasion and occupation and Austrians as victims. Camp survivors met with little sympathy or understanding for their wartime trauma and suffering from their gentile compatriots, as they struggled along with the small but strengthening Jewish community to get back on their feet.

Austrian Jews who were affiliated and active with their political parties in exile abroad formed the next group to return to Vienna. Their parties shaped their motivations and expectations to return home while they lived abroad after fleeing from the Nazis. Both the Communist and the Social Democratic Parties told their members that Austria and Austrians wanted them to return, an overall message that involved a certain level of acceptance of the victim myth. They mistook the departure of Germans from postwar Austria as an overall departure of Nazis, a concept that served to encourage Jewish Social Democrats and Communists to go back to take part in the political and physical reconstruction of their country. Upon arrival, however, the reality they encountered quickly disabused them of their idealistic notions. They too confronted their neighbors' refusal to face what had transpired, along with gentile Austrians' self-pitying narratives of victimization. Notwithstanding an environment hostile with lingering antisemitism and Nazi sentiment, these politically affiliated returnees stayed and did indeed help to rebuild their country. They sought to regain their *political home* and did, even if it did not develop as anticipated.

Returnees from exile abroad looking to regain a *professional home* began to arrive shortly thereafter. Doctors and lawyers whose training and certification were tied directly to Austria, for example, saw Vienna as their one and only place to make a career and thus a home. Many writers and performers who felt tied to the language held the same ideas. All returnees felt many of the same challenges in the course of launching their lives again in Vienna. Antisemitic hostility included official discrimination and deprivation of victims' welfare benefits, and a cemented victim myth ensured a lack of empathy and understanding by gentile neighbors. A series of restitution laws quickly proved ineffective. Reaction to such legislation included the formation of advocacy groups to protect the so-called Aryanizers and to try to ensure that they retained Jews' property acquired under Nazi "Aryanization" policies. Political parties vied for the electoral support of former Nazi Party members, while Cold War tensions between occupation forces shaped the postwar Austrian government and a new and emerging Austrian national identity. And at the same time, Viennese Jewish identity developed and adapted to the postwar situation.

A number of particulars to the Austrian and the Viennese setting require specific attention. The unique context of postwar Austria and the victim myth are fundamental to understanding the specific experience of Viennese Jewish returnees. The Allies' wording of their 1943 Moscow Declaration gave credence to and shaped an entitled attitude of victimhood that guided the formation of a new Austrian national identity after the war. This statement, issued on November 1, 1943, by US President Franklin D. Roosevelt, British Prime Minister Winston Churchill, and Soviet leader Joseph Stalin, elucidated their plan for the postwar treatment of Austria. It proclaimed the Anschluss null and void; called for the establishment of a free Austria, specifying it as "the first free country to fall a victim to Hitlerite aggression"; and declared the Allies' intention to liberate the country from "German domination."[15] Postwar politicians utilized this statement for political gain and took advantage of rising Cold War hostilities to seal Austria's victim status.

---

15. US Congress, Senate Committee on Foreign Relations, and US Department of State, *A Decade of American Foreign Policy: Basic Documents, 1941–49* (Washington, DC: Government Printing Office, 1950), 11.

The victim myth thus sets both the context and the tone in which this book presents the experiences of Vienna's returned Jews. The choice of language in this particular setting is important. For example, in the postwar decades, everyone from scholars to the average person on the street referred to the German "occupation" that began with the Anschluss in March 1938 and ended in April 1945 with the Red Army's "liberation" of the city. The most conservative and right-wing even spoke of "seventeen years of occupation" to mean that Austria first suffered seven years under the Nazis, followed by ten years of the Allies. The Anschluss, however, was neither an aggressive military invasion nor an occupation, and therefore the Soviets did not liberate the country but, rather, conquered it. For this reason, I decline to use either term. This choice becomes tricky with regard to survivors' testimony, as many do refer to their "liberation" by the Red Army. For Jews alive in Vienna at the end of the war, this description was indeed true, but I argue that it is definitively incorrect to use the term *Befreiung* (liberation) in most cases related to Austria. The fact that many survivors employ the term, however, indicates a certain perspective and milieu in which they lived after the war and one we must consider. They were Viennese, after all.

Nazi language presents a unique challenge, and I have made every effort to indicate that such terms are not my own, either through the use of quotation marks or with reference to a "so-called" concept. In other cases, I have declined to use terms that are otherwise commonly accepted. For example, the use of the word *Kristallnacht* has fallen out of fashion in Austria because of its Nazi origin and use. One writes rather of the *Novemberpogrom* (November Pogrom) or *Reichspogromnacht* (Night of the Reich's Pogrom). The Nazi term *Mischlinge* (persons of mixed "Aryan" and Jewish heritage; literally, mongrels) poses obvious problems with its negative canine connotation, but I have used it with indication. I have treated "mixed marriage," "Aryan," and "race" and "racial" in the same way, with an acknowledgment of the associated issues, and have used each with care.

I have specifically avoided the somewhat untranslatable German word *Heimat*. It connotes something deeper than "home" or "homeland" and involves a feeling and atmosphere (*Stimmung*) with a connection to landscape and a link to other elements of a culture. Survivors have indicated (during interviews that I conducted and those I have read) that Vienna is their home (*Zuhause*) but not their *Heimat*, something that was lost to them. And Austria certainly does not represent *Heimat*, seemingly because of the Nazis' corruption of the word. If they have a *Heimat*, some have said it could be Israel, although they do not live there and may never have. In identifying Israel as a land to which they are connected in a way that defies description, they convey a love and relationship associated with a geographic location that they cannot feel for Austria or Vienna—although Vienna, nonetheless, was and is home.

To add another layer of difficulty, the Nazis used *Heimat* as they did words like *Volk* (also difficult to translate but something like "ethnic group" or "people of a national group") and *Stolz* (pride) and in such a way that they came to connote and indicate National Socialist sentiment. Such words are employed today with care and specificity but retain these colorings of German nationalist ideas.

Finally, I would like to clarify that I employ the term "Holocaust survivor" as the United States Holocaust Memorial Museum does in its exhibitions and literature. That is, a survivor is "any person who was displaced, persecuted, and/or discriminated against by the racial, religious, ethnic, social, and/or political policies of the Nazis and their allies between 1933 and 1945. In addition to former inmates of concentration camps and ghettos, this also includes refugees and people in hiding."[16] Thus a Viennese Jew who fled Nazi oppression after the Anschluss is a "survivor," just as were those who endured concentration and death camps. Those who survived in their hometown under different levels of hiding or protection, too, are Holocaust survivors.

Much like Hansi Tausig, the world-renowned psychoanalyst Sigmund Freud felt a paradox in his commitment to Vienna. He encapsulated the

---

16. United States Holocaust Memorial Museum, "Who Is a Survivor?," accessed March 15, 2018, http://www.ushmm.org/remember/office-of-survivor-affairs.

incongruous yet faithful nature of Viennese Jews' relationship to their city in a conversation with the writer, producer, and director Ernst Lothar shortly after World War I. The two met in Freud's Berggasse apartment in Vienna's ninth district, where they lamented the fall of the dual monarchy and dismemberment of Austria-Hungary. Freud remarked, "I don't want to live anywhere else. For me, emigration is out of the question. I will just live on with the torso and delude myself into thinking that it is the whole body." Neither man could have known that in less than two decades they both not only would emigrate but would be forced to do so. Freud closed their discussion that day by observing, "Austria is a country that annoys you to death but where you want to die anyway."[17]

Author and journalist Eva Menasse noted that this statement could be Lothar's life motto.[18] Fortunate to flee shortly after the Anschluss that united Austria with Nazi Germany, Lothar, his wife, and their daughter made their way via Switzerland and France to the United States. After an initial struggle, he reestablished himself as a writer in his land of exile but finally returned home in 1946 as a theater and music officer of the US Department of State.[19] Lothar permanently resettled in Vienna in the late 1940s, and his struggle with national identity, his experiences in exile, and the effects of National Socialism on his homeland and hometown inspired much of his work over the course of his career.

Freud and Lothar had been born in Moravia in Austria-Hungary, but their families had migrated to Vienna when both were young. Most Jews in Vienna at least stemmed from families that originated in other parts of the empire, if they had not actually migrated to the imperial capital themselves. Although some spent summer months in the Ausseerland (a mountainous lake region in Austria) and others may have enjoyed winter sports in the

---

17. "Österreich ist ein Land, über das man sich zu Tode ärgert und wo man trotzdem sterben will." See Wolfgang Wiesmüller, *Eine Schwierige Heimkehr: Österreichischen Literatur im Exil, 1938–1945* (Innsbruck: Institut für Germanistik, 1991), 345.

18. Eva Menasse, "Eva Menasse über Ernst Lothar: In einem einzigen Leben," *Der Standard*, January 23, 2016, http://derstandard.at/2000029559024/Eva-Menasse-ueber-Ernst-Lothar-In-einem-einzigen-Leben.

19. Vansant, *Reclaiming Heimat*, 18–19.

Austrian countryside and alpine regions, it was the capital city in which they lived and to which they were dedicated. For most—including Freud and Lothar—Vienna *was* Austria.

And so, to paraphrase Freud, one might say that *Vienna* annoyed Lothar, but he wanted to die there anyway. And in fact, he did. But he also wanted to live there. It was home, nonetheless.

I

HISTORICAL CONTEXT

Prelude to the Holocaust in Austria

The first section of the book *Wie wir gelebt haben*[1] (How we lived) looks and feels like a handsome family album or scrapbook. These first hundred pages are full of beautiful photographs with personal captions, nostalgic anecdotes, and happy memories. Leafing through without knowledge of the title, one might consider the faces and families to be a typical cross-section of the general population of early twentieth-century Austria-Hungary. Photos from those years show families from places across the empire and many rooted for generations in the imperial capital. World War I soldiers pose for group photos, school classes smile for cameras, and families enjoy the outdoors. Shopkeepers stand in front of their stores, little boys sport lederhosen, and young women wear the fashionable hairstyles of the 1920s.

Little in the pictures reveals that the subjects are Jews. A few shots of children and young adults in costume indicate Purim celebrations, but otherwise these are simply frozen images of families in the first decades of

---

1. Tanja Eckstein and Julia Kaldori, eds., *Wie wir gelebt haben: Wiener Juden erinnern sich an ihr 20. Jahrhundert* (Vienna: Mandelbaum Verlag, 2008). The full title translates literally as *How We Lived: Viennese Jews Remember Their Twentieth Century*. The English translation of this book is titled *Vienna Stories: Viennese Jews Remember the 20th Century in Words and Photos*.

the twentieth century. With a more careful read of the captions and stories, however, particulars of the Jewish experience in Austria-Hungary come to light. A portrait of young Gizela Brück is positioned alongside a later photo of her with her young husband, Josef Kocsiss. Their daughter, Gisela Eva, provided family background for the publication and explained that her mother had been only twelve years old when she and her family fled the Russians during World War I. Like many other Galician Jews, they sought refuge in Vienna and never returned to Poland. The caption of the second photo indicates that Josef was a gentile; like many Viennese Jews, Gizela had intermarried.[2]

On another page, Edith Landesmann's parents pose in Brünn (a city in Moravia, now called Brno), passengers of the ubiquitous cartoon airplane of early twentieth-century studio photography. The caption explains that they first met at the Maccabi sports club.[3] Pages later, Gerda Feldsberg's grandfather Josef Stadler gives the camera a puzzled look as he stands in front of his shop window. He and his wife, Emilie, ran a store in Vienna's second district while they lived in the ninth.[4] As was the pattern of Viennese Jewry, home and business focused on the Leopoldstadt—the traditionally Jewish second district—and, once a level of financial success had been achieved, the newly prosperous moved their residence to the ninth to live among many other middle- and upper-middle-class Viennese Jews.

The book contains the family photos of Austrian Jews who returned to or stayed in Vienna after the Holocaust and includes their memories as gathered in the Jewish historical institute Centropa's extensive interview collection. Contributors shared pictures and told stories to help editors portray their families' experiences. The collection clearly depicts the variety of origins from which so many Jews living in Vienna came. At the start of the 1900s, Jews from across the empire migrated to the capital city, where

---

2. Ibid., 26.
3. Ibid., 37.
4. Ibid., 56. For more on Jewish neighborhoods in Vienna, see Marsha Rozenblit, "The Jewish Neighborhoods in Vienna," chap. 4 in *The Jews of Vienna, 1867–1914* (Albany: State University of New York Press, 1983), 71–98; for information specific to Jews living and working in Vienna's second and ninth districts, see 85.

their families may have lived for decades. Some came to pursue a university education and gain professional training; others fled antisemitic Russian troops during World War I. Their diverse backgrounds combined to reflect the multiethnic and multinational tapestry of the greater population of the Habsburg Empire.

In many ways, Austrian Jews were—and had been—typically Austrian. Joseph Samuel Bloch, rabbi, member of the Imperial Parliament, and publisher of the Jewish newspaper *Österreichische Wochenschrift* (Austrian weekly), had argued as early as 1886 that Jews were the most loyal citizens of the monarchy and represented the ideal Austrians in a multiethnic society facing a rise of nationalism. "If one could construct a specifically Austrian nationality, then the Jews would constitute its foundation,"[5] Bloch observed just nineteen years after Jews were accorded full emancipation and citizenship rights.

Jews had lived in Austria for centuries. After the Revolution of 1848, the monarchy lifted settlement restrictions, and Jews from Bohemia, Moravia, Hungary, and Galicia migrated to the capital with a feeling of safety in a modern Vienna. They finally received full emancipation in Austria following the Ausgleich (the reorganization of the Habsburg Empire into the dual monarchy of Austria-Hungary) in 1867, and such movement continued and intensified.[6] But as the Jewish population of the city increased, antisemitism neither disappeared nor diminished, and the issue of nationality and nationalism grew across the Habsburg lands and among its citizens. Jews were blamed for the May 1873 stock market crash,[7] for example, and increasing prejudice gave rise to politicians with particularly antisemitic philosophies. The late nineteenth century saw the rise of Georg Ritter von Schönerer's

---

5. Joseph Bloch, *Der nationale Zwist und die Juden in Österreich* (Vienna: Gottlieb, 1886), 41, as cited in Lisa Silverman, *Becoming Austrians: Jews and Culture between the World Wars* (Oxford: Oxford University Press, 2012), 6.

6. Rozenblit, *Jews of Vienna*, 5.

7. William O. McCagg, *A History of Habsburg Jews, 1670–1918* (Bloomington: Indiana University Press, 1989), 156.

Pan-German Party and its platform based on German nationalism, popular antisemitism, and a larger unified German state, of which Austria would be a part through Anschluss with Germany and German-speaking regions of Europe. By blaming Jews for all societal problems, the Pan-German Party helped propel antisemitism into the realm of racism.[8] Antisemitism also played a significant role during Dr. Karl Lueger's term as mayor of Vienna (1897–1910).[9] Lueger, a Christian Social Party member, was not a German nationalist, however, but rather an Austrian patriot, loyal to the monarchy.

Austrian sentiment in the years leading up to World War I focused largely on loyalty and a dedication to maintaining the monarchy but included no specifically "Austrian" national feeling. Most identified with a particular Austrian province alongside an allegiance to the empire, and many identified with a German cultural nationality.[10] The idea of the political organization of independent German-speaking states, however, had roots that dated back to the fall of the Holy Roman Empire in 1806. With the 1848–49 German Revolution, these deliberations intensified into the *Großdeutsche/Kleindeutsche Debatte*. The Habsburg Empire had favored a *großdeutsche Lösung* (Greater German solution), which would in its understanding include the German states and the entire empire under Habsburg leadership. The *kleindeutsche* (Lesser German) solution, promoted by Prussia, sought to unify just the northern German states and did not include Austria. Prussia opposed the integration of the non-German portions of the Habsburg Empire, and the *kleindeutsche Lösung* prevailed.[11] Although the concept of Anschluss had this long, popular history, only a small minority hoped to split the empire to unify with Germany at that time. Certainly no

---

8. Andrew Gladding Whiteside, *The Socialism of Fools: Georg Ritter von Schönerer and Austrian Pan-Germanism* (Berkeley: University of California Press, 1975), 61.

9. John W. Boyer, *Political Radicalism in Late Imperial Vienna: Origins of the Christian Social Movement, 1848–1897* (Chicago: University of Chicago Press, 1981), 217.

10. Barbara Jelavich, *Modern Austria: Empire and Republic, 1815–1986* (Cambridge: Cambridge University Press, 1987), 146–47.

11. See Imanuel Geiss, *The Question of German Unification, 1806–1996* (London: Routledge, 1997), 16, 40–41; William W. Hagen, *German History in Modern Times: Four Lives of the Nation* (New York: Cambridge University Press, 2012), 139–40; and Michael Hughes, *Nationalism and Society: Germany, 1800–1945* (London: E. Arnold, 1988), 89–90.

one anticipated the post–World War I dissolution of Austria-Hungary and the creation of a separate, small Austrian state.

Despite antisemitic hostility, Jews in Vienna found their way through the challenging environment. According to historian Marsha Rozenblit, Jews' propensity to work with other Jews and the establishment of their own professional organizations helped protect and insulate them from the discriminatory climate, although it also served to inhibit total assimilation into Viennese society.[12] Most lived in the first, second, and ninth districts of Vienna, along with their coreligionists of varying social classes, where they also socialized with and mostly married one another.[13] Jews both maintained a separateness and distinction and also contributed to and took on significant roles in Viennese society, culture, and professions through the career and educational opportunities that opened to them in the some sixty years following the Ausgleich and the attainment of equal rights of citizenship. They integrated into society with enthusiasm, and many enjoyed great success, leading to a common misconception of widespread conversion to Catholicism and overall assimilation in that short time.

The pervasive presence of antisemitism notwithstanding, by the turn of the century Vienna's Jews identified as thoroughly Viennese. Survivor Helen Herz recounted that her family was Jewish by religion only and that "one had nothing to do with the other."[14] Marsha Rozenblit's theory of Habsburg Jews' tripartite identity helps explain this phenomenon. Bolstered by the protection and acceptance they felt under Emperor Franz Joseph in the years leading up to and through World War I, Austrian Jews considered themselves to be politically Austrian, culturally German, and ethnically Jewish.[15] In addition, Rozenblit explains that in Vienna "Germanization" did not require melding to or with a German *Volk*, or concept of an ethnic

---

12. Rozenblit, *Jews of Vienna*, 49.

13. Ibid., 71.

14. Helen Herz, interview 903, Visual History Archive (VHA), USC Shoah Foundation, Los Angeles, CA, accessed at the United States Holocaust Memorial Museum (USHMM), March 27, 2015.

15. Marsha Rozenblit, *Reconstructing a National Identity: The Jews of Habsburg Austria during World War I* (New York: Oxford University Press, 2001), 4.

"people," as the Viennese were less preoccupied with German national identity.[16] In addition, I posit that a *fourth* aspect of identity emerged in the specific case of the Jews of Vienna, one to which Rozenblit alludes: a feeling of being socially and aesthetically *Viennese*. The possibility for that layering in self-identification was (and is) possible in Vienna in particular. Gentile or Jew could be Austrian and also distinctly—and perhaps more importantly—Viennese, which speaks to the ever-present ambiguities typical of the Viennese mind-set and way of life. One could feel both Austrian and German while remaining a loyal monarchist, while others felt both Austrian and German but favored Anschluss, the joining of Austria and Germany to unite Germans living in different but neighboring lands. With similar intersection and potential contradiction, Jews could be 100 percent Viennese but also Austrian, German, and Jewish at the same time and in different ways.

Jews supported the waging and fighting of World War I, which Rozenblit has characterized as a Jewish holy war that provided the possibility for Jews to focus on Russia as an enemy both of their country and of themselves as Jews. It also gave rise to the opportunity to show fidelity to the empire *and* solidarity and support for their coreligionists who suffered oppression and brutal, deadly pogroms in other lands.[17] Tens of thousands of Jewish refugees fled the Russians and the war to Vienna, where the Jewish community and the Austrian state supported them. This influx of Jews from the east compounded wartime hardships, such as food shortages and increased black-market activity, which conspired to raise antisemitism among the general public.[18] With the dissolution of the Habsburg Empire at war's end, Jews and other minorities suffered in newly defined nation-states, and common belief held that Jews were unable to maintain any national loyalty.

Contrary to outside perceptions of a unified body devoted only to itself or a larger concept of a Jewish "nation," divisions marked the Jewish community and its members. Viennese Jews found no one amalgamating political stance, and the Israelitische Kultusgemeinde Wien (IKG; the Jewish

---

16. Ibid., 33.
17. See Rozenblit, "A Jewish War," in *Reconstructing a National Identity*, 43–58.
18. Ibid., 78.

community of Vienna) suffered struggles between Western Jews and Ostjuden (Jews from the eastern parts of the former empire), the religious and nonreligious, the modern and the traditional Orthodox, and between assimilationists and Zionists.[19] While some Jews turned to Zionism, others rejected the idea of a particular Jewish nationalism and clung to hopes that the shrunken post–World War I state would permit them the possibility of identifying as both Austrians and Jews, even if they were unable to consider themselves a part of a German *Volk*.[20] Still, they realized that the days of their tripartite Austrian-Jewish-German identity were over and that their future in the First Austrian Republic was uncertain.

The end of the empire was particularly difficult for Austrians. Many remained loyal to the lost monarchy, but its dissolution fostered a focus on identification with a larger German cultural nation.[21] By February 5, 1919, all political parties in Austria were in favor of Anschluss with Germany,[22] despite the Versailles peacemakers' prohibition on the unification of the two countries. And, save for the Social Democratic Party, antisemitism remained pervasive in politics in Vienna.[23] The Social Democrats held majority-governing power in the capital from the end of World War I to 1934, and their policy making in Vienna was taken as a model by the Socialist *Internationale* and around the world.[24] The party did not enjoy the same success in other parts of Austria, however, and resentment grew in the provinces. Hostility focused on liberal spending on the social welfare system and

---

19. For an in-depth analysis of this topic, see Harriet Pass Freidenreich, *Jewish Politics in Vienna, 1918—1938* (Bloomington: Indiana University Press, 1991).

20. Rozenblit, *Reconstructing a National Identity*, 156.

21. Bruce F. Pauley, *From Prejudice to Persecution: A History of Austrian Antisemitism* (Chapel Hill: University of North Carolina Press, 1992), 75.

22. Rolf Steininger, "12 November 1918–12 March 1938: The Road to the Anschluß," in *Austria in the Twentieth Century*, ed. Rolf Steininger, Günter Bischof, and Michael Gehler (New Brunswick, NJ: Transaction, 2002), 90.

23. Rozenblit, *Reconstructing a National Identity*, 168. Also see Bruce F. Pauley, "Political Antisemitism in Interwar Vienna," in *Jews, Antisemitism and Culture in Vienna*, ed. Ivar Oxaal, Michael Pollak, and Gerhard Botz (London: Routledge and Kegan Paul, 1987), 152–73.

24. Wolfgang Maderthamer, "12 February 1934: Social Democracy and Civil War," in Steininger, Bischof, and Gehler, *Austria in the Twentieth Century*, 58–59.

the party's alleged control of organized labor. These views yielded the city's moniker, Rotes Wien (Red Vienna).[25]

Jews in Austria felt uncomfortable with the newly defined state and worried about their status within it. Most Jews in Vienna grieved the end of the monarchy, even while some anticipated greater democracy in the new political constellation; and Galician Jewish refugees in the city feared that they were doomed to remain foreigners in their adopted home.[26] The community remained strong nonetheless, and by 1934, the Jewish population of Vienna totaled 176,034.[27]

At the same time, Adolf Hitler and the National Socialists were rising to power in Germany. With the end of the Weimar Republic and President Paul von Hindenburg's appointment of Hitler as chancellor on January 30, 1933, the Third Reich launched and began to assert power with the arrest and detainment of political opponents. Official anti-Jewish practice began with a state-sponsored boycott on Jewish professionals and Jews' businesses, followed by antisemitic legislation with increasing restrictions on Jews. Austrians knew what was unfolding in neighboring Germany. The Tausend-Mark-Sperre (Thousand Mark Tax) imposed on Germans crossing the border into Austria brought home some economic realities that clarified Hitler's awareness of Austria's dependence on German tourism and effectively showed his control and impact.[28] In addition, mass unemployment and wage decline, inflation, and industrial problems followed by a banking crisis colluded to foment dissatisfaction in the Austrian provinces and led some to the growing National Socialist movement. The Alpine regions' newly impoverished middle class, which depended on German tourism and demand for agricultural goods, applauded the possibility of unification with Germany and provided grass-roots support for the Austrian Nazi Party, the

---

25. For more about Red Vienna, see Helmut Gruber, *Red Vienna: Experiment in Working-Class Culture, 1919–1934* (Oxford: Oxford University Press, 1991).

26. Rozenblit, *Reconstructing a National Identity*, 134–35.

27. Jonny Moser, *Demographie der jüdischen Bevölkerung Österreichs, 1938–1945* (Vienna: Dokumentationsarchiv des österreichischen Widerstandes, 1999), 7.

28. Werner Dreier, "Doppelte Wahrheit: Ein Beitrag zur Geschichte der Tausendmarksperre," *Montfort* 37, no. 1 (1985): 63–71.

Deutsche Nationalsozialistische Arbeiterpartei (German National Socialist Workers' Party, or DNSAP).[29] Chancellor Engelbert Dollfuss and his Christian Social Party, however, opposed Anschluss and favored a specifically "Austrian" identity. They did not aspire to join Greater Germany because they recognized Austria as a "second German state" and, as a Catholic one, the better of the two.[30]

Dollfuss merged the conservative Catholic and Austrian nationalist Christian Social Party in 1933 with other like-minded groups and the paramilitary Heimwehr (literally, Home Guard) to form the Vaterländische Front (Fatherland Front). With the support of Italian fascist dictator Benito Mussolini, the Front sought to maintain a distinct and separate Austria, protecting the nation's Catholic nature from influence by Protestant Germany and the Nazi Party. Dollfuss outlawed both the Communist and Nazi Parties, and political struggles between the Heimwehr and the Social Democrats evolved into violence in the streets. After a short but bloody civil war fought in February 1934 between the paramilitary troops of the two parties,[31] Dollfuss declared the Social Democratic Party illegal as well.[32] In July, he fell victim of an attempted Nazi putsch. Although unsuccessful in the move to take over the government and initiate Anschluss, Nazi revolutionaries assassinated the chancellor. Karl von Schuschnigg succeeded him

---

29. Maderthamer, "12 February 1934," 49.

30. Rolf Steininger, *Austria, Germany, and the Cold War: From the Anschluss to the State Treaty* (New York: Berghahn Books, 2008), 7.

31. For more about the 1934 civil war and surrounding events, see Irene Etzersdorfer and Hans Schafranek, eds., *Erzählte Geschichte: Der Februar 1934 in Wien* (Vienna: Autorenkollektiv, 1984); Günther Schefbeck, ed., *Österreich 1934: Vorgeschichte—Ereignisse—Wirkungen* (Vienna: Verlag für Geschichte und Politik, 2004); Josef Fiala, *Die Februarkämpfe 1934 in Wien Meidling und Liesung: Ein Bürgerkrieg, der keiner war* (Hamburg: disserta Verlag, 2013); Helmut Konrad, "The Significance of February 1934 in Austria in Both National and International Context," in *Routes into Abyss: Coping with the Crises in the 1930s*, ed. Helmut Konrad and Wolfgang Maderthaner (New York: Berghahn Books, 2013), 20–32; and Anson Rabinbach, *The Crisis of Austrian Socialism: From Red Vienna to Civil War, 1927–1934* (Chicago: University of Chicago Press, 1983).

32. Rudolf Neck, Adam Wandruszka, Kurt Peball, and Isabella Ackerl, *Protokolle des Ministerrates der Ersten Republik, 1918–1938* (Vienna: Verlag der Österreichischen Staatsdruckerei, 1980), xvii.

Austria, 1933 (US Holocaust Memorial Museum)

and continued to lead the Fatherland Front, staving off National Socialism for another four years.

Sometimes described as Catholic fascism, the Austrofascist dictatorship eschewed Nazism altogether. Modeled on and aligned with Mussolini's form of fascism, the Austrofascists looked to Italy as their closest ally, a relationship that Austrian leaders miscalculated. Italy could not help Austria escape increasing German pressure and impending Anschluss, a point on which the Austrian Communist and Social Democratic Parties' positions differed—the Communists opposed unification with Germany, and the Social Democrats endorsed it. In fact, Dr. Karl Renner, the Social Democratic chancellor and minister of foreign affairs for Austria from 1918 to 1920 and president of Parliament from 1931 to 1933—later, the first postwar president of Austria—was a vocal supporter of Anschluss with Germany in 1938.[33] Weighed against the Austrofascist dictatorship's oppression of his

---

33. Evan Burr Bukey, *Hitler's Austria: Popular Sentiment in the Nazi Era, 1938–1945* (Chapel Hill: North Carolina University Press, 2000), 38.

party, unification with Germany seemed a viable option that might favor the Social Democrats' political and strategic position.

An agreement signed by Schuschnigg and German ambassador Franz von Papen on July 11, 1936, helped to strengthen Austria's illegal Nazi Party with its release of Nazis imprisoned in Austria and the promise of Germany's respect for Austria's sovereignty. After Schuschnigg's humiliating meeting with Hitler at Berchtesgaden in 1938, where the German dictator demanded the legalization of the Nazi Party in Austria and the admission of more Nazi representatives into Austrian government, Schuschnigg called for a plebiscite to be held on March 13. His plans foiled by the Anschluss, he resigned on March 11, 1938. He had spent the preceding years trying to prevent what became the inevitable, including a last-minute effort to hold a vote on the question of Austrian independence. In anticipation of the referendum, devotees painted political slogans in favor of the Fatherland Front on streets and sidewalks around Vienna, graffiti that just a few days later would play an emblematic role in the particular Viennese persecution of Jews. Hitler ended Schuschnigg's talk of a referendum with a telephone call to inform the Austrian chancellor of what was to come, and Schuschnigg stepped down with a farewell radio address that he concluded with, "God protect Austria." Austrian National Socialist Arthur Seyss-Inquart assumed power immediately, and German troops rolled in on March 12, 1938, to seal the Anschluss—the union of the two nations into Greater Germany.[34]

The Nazis maintained the ban on the Social Democrat and Communist Parties and increased pressure against and the persecution of their members, as well as the leaders of the Schuschnigg government. Arrest as a political opponent of the Nazis meant deportation to concentration camps, where Social Democrats and Communists were imprisoned side by side with their former Austrofascist oppressors. Schuschnigg himself survived incarceration as an enemy of the state. Arrested and jailed in Gestapo headquarters on March 13, 1938, he remained in Nazi hands through the end

---

34. Dieter A. Binder, "The Christian Corporatist State: Austria from 1934 to 1938," in Steininger, Bischof, and Gehler, *Austria in the Twentieth Century*, 84.

Anschluss, March 1938 (US Holocaust Memorial Museum)

of the war, including more than three years in the Sachsenhausen concentration camp and shorter stints in both Flossenbürg and Dachau.[35] With the Nazis also came increased antisemitic measures and rhetoric, and many Jews as well as both Jewish and gentile Communists and Social Democrats looked to leave Austria.

POST-ANSCHLUSS REALITIES

Few Austrian Jews had yet realized the importance of fleeing to safety by the time of the Anschluss. Despite their awareness of what was unfolding in Germany, many still thought such maltreatment and oppression impossible in their country. How wrong they were: for Jews, Austria in spring 1938

---

35. Tracing and Documentation file for Dr. Kurt Schuschnigg, 1.1.5.1/98922135/ITS Digital Archive, USHMM, Washington, DC. In 1947, Schuschnigg emigrated to the United States, and from 1948 to 1967 he taught as a professor at Saint Louis University. In 1967, he returned to Austria and lived the next ten years near Innsbruck.

proved much worse than Germany. With the quick change of power came anti-Jewish violence, plunder, and persecution on a massive scale. Nazi Germany absorbed Austria into Großdeutschland (Greater Germany) and renamed the new province composed of the former country the Ostmark (literally, eastern march). Most individuals and certainly the IKG recognized the need to leave immediately. Austrian gentiles enthusiastically welcomed German troops and quickly turned against their Jewish neighbors, along with—and with scant need for encouragement from—the government and the police. Historian Gerhard Botz has argued that in addition to Austrian antisemitism, the material interests of the Viennese fueled the persecution of Jews, a pattern similar to that which emerged in east-central and eastern Europe.[36] Many Austrian gentiles stood to benefit greatly from the subjugation and exploitation of their Jewish neighbors.

Historian Paul Schatzberg referred to the violence and bedlam after the Anschluss as "The Vienna Pogrom of Spring 1938,"[37] a reference to the November Pogrom, the commonly accepted turning point of state-sponsored persecution of Jews in the Third Reich. If the public destruction and anti-Jewish violence of November 9–10, 1938, constituted a new level of radicalization in the persecution of Jews in Germany, it was a marker of continuity in Austria.[38] Anti-Jewish violence had begun with the Anschluss, along with so-called wild Aryanization, which occurred when gentile members of the general public forcibly took their Jewish neighbors' property outside of the state-structured "Aryanization" program. Although the intensity of such persecution eased a bit that summer, it reaccelerated in early October when the Nazis arrested Jews and wrecked many Jews' businesses.[39] From October 14 to 20, 1938, Nazi supporters conducted pogrom-like riots against synagogues and prayer houses, including setting on fire

---

36. Gerhard Botz, "The Dynamics of Persecution in Austria, 1938–1945," in *Austrians and Jews in the Twentieth Century: From Franz Josef to Waldheim*, ed. Robert Wistrich (New York: St. Martin's, 1992), 214.

37. Paul Schatzberg, as quoted in Ilana Offenberger, *The Jews of Nazi Vienna, 1938–1945: Rescue and Destruction* (New York: Palgrave Macmillan, 2017), 39.

38. Hans Safrian and Hans Witek, *Und keiner war dabei: Dokumente des alltäglichen Antisemitismus in Wien 1938* (Vienna: Picus Verlag, 1988), 267.

39. Pauley, *From Prejudice to Persecution*, 286.

Austrian Nazis and local residents watch as Jewish businessmen from the third district of Vienna are forced to their knees to scrub pro-Schuschnigg slogans off the pavement. (US Holocaust Memorial Museum)

the Leopoldstädter Tempel (Leopoldstadt synagogue). The fire department extinguished the blaze,[40] but less than a month later, antisemitic arsonists burned the synagogue to the ground. Historian and journalist Doron Rabinovici has explained the more brutal nature of the November Pogrom in Vienna, as compared with other cities in the Third Reich, as an outcome of these early episodes of violence and theft—by November, Viennese inhibitions had already been overcome.[41] Gentiles had witnessed Jewish colleagues' dismissal from jobs, "Aryanization" organized and regulated by the government, and the deportation of Jewish men to concentration camps in Germany. After the Anschluss and well before November 1938, the Nazis had accused Jews, rightly or wrongly, of supporting Schuschnigg

---

40. Angelika Shoshana Duizend-Jensen, *Jüdische Gemeinden, Vereine, Stiftungen und Fonds: "Arisierung" und Restitution* (Vienna: Historikerkommission, 2002), 43.

41. Doron Rabinovici, *Instanzen der Ohnmacht, Wien 1938–1945, der Weg zum Judenrat* (Frankfurt am Main: Jüdischer Verlag, 2000), 124.

and forced Jews to scrub from the city streets and sidewalks the political slogans in favor of Schuschnigg and the Vaterländische Front in acts of humiliation.[42] The many historical photographs of Jews scrubbing the Vienna streets on their hands and knees reflect this particular form of persecution and harassment.

The Nazis began to administer control in Vienna in the context of the particular frenzy of Austrian antisemitic violence and theft following the Anschluss. In 1938, Nazi policy against Jews involved the expropriation of their property, exclusion from professional and social circles, and forced emigration. The Nazi-defined body of Jewish Austrians included those who had converted to Catholicism and were considered "non-Aryan Christians." Regardless of personal religious identification, they too fell victim to Nazi racial laws, and thus Austrian Jews targeted for persecution totaled about 201,000.[43]

The IKG under the Nazis

Within days of the Anschluss, the thirty-two-year-old SS *Untersturmführer* (second lieutenant) of the Sicherheitsdienst (Sicherheitsdienst des Reichsführers-SS, the intelligence agency of the SS and the Nazi Party) Adolf Eichmann arrived in the city and began to coordinate the administrative machinery that targeted Austrian Jews. Nazi officials entered IKG headquarters on the Seitenstettengasse in Vienna's first district for the first time on March 16, 1938, to assess the organization and, while they were at it, plunder office supplies and other goods. They deemed the IKG "nonessential" two days later and raided and shuttered its offices.[44] They also arrested a number of Viennese Jewish community leaders, including Dr. Josef Löwenherz, a lawyer and the former vice president of the community.[45] Eichmann met with representatives of various Jewish organizations and conveyed that

---

42. This punishment interestingly originated with the Fatherland Front itself. It had punished illegal Nazis caught painting political slogans in this way. See Giles MacDonogh, *1938: Hitler's Gamble* (New York: Basic Books, 2009), 50.
43. Moser, *Demographie der jüdischen Bevölkerung Österreichs*, 18–19.
44. Rabinovici, *Instanzen der Ohnmacht*, 69.
45. Hans Safrian, *Eichmann's Men* (Cambridge: Cambridge University Press, 2010), 27.

the systematic expulsion of Austrian Jews stood as the Nazis' primary goal. The IKG would continue to exist but in a different form.[46]

By the end of April 1938, Eichmann was set up at Gestapo headquarters in the Hotel Metropol, made contact with imprisoned Jewish community leaders, and appointed Löwenherz to head that body. Löwenherz's first item of business, Eichmann told him, was to devise a plan for the emigration of twenty thousand destitute Jews from Austria within the year, and Löwenherz would remain in jail until he had done just that.[47] Eichmann freed Löwenherz on April 20, 1938,[48] and ordered the IKG offices to reopen on May 2, 1938. All Jewish organizations fell under its umbrella, each forced to contribute to the work of carrying out the devastating task of coordinating the mass emigration of Viennese Jews.[49] With Löwenherz at the helm, IKG staff cooperated, as they accepted this as their community's only chance for survival.

As historian Ilana Offenberger has explained, the IKG became the central lifeline for Vienna's Jews. Under its new orders, it assumed the management of all Jewish affairs in the city, both public and private. With an emphasis on emigration and a newly formed Auswanderungsabteilung (Emigration Department), IKG staff offered assistance with all aspects of the process, from recruitment and administration to providing advice and funding. The community cared for its members as they faced great hardship, providing food, shelter, clothing, work, education, medical care, and much-needed leadership. Offenberger argues that the IKG's support bolstered the Jewish community's strength and brought them together.[50]

Reichskommissar für die Wiedervereinigung Österreichs mit dem Reich (Reich's Commissioner for the Unification of Austria with Germany) Josef Bürckel announced the establishment of the Nazi Zentralstelle für jüdische Auswanderung (Central Office for Jewish Emigration, or Central Office) on

---

46. David Cesarani, *Becoming Eichmann: Rethinking the Life, Crimes, and Trial of a "Desk Murderer"* (Cambridge, MA: Da Capo, 2006), 64–65.
47. Ibid., 65.
48. Rabinovici, *Instanzen der Ohnmacht*, 82.
49. Ibid., 85.
50. Offenberger, *Jews of Nazi Vienna*, 78.

August 20, 1938, and named Dr. Franz Stahlecker, the head of the Sicherheitsdienst (SD) of the SS-Oberabschnitt Donau (Danube SS Region), as its director.[51] In practice, however, Adolf Eichmann ran the organization.[52] The Central Office oversaw all administrative processes of the forced emigration of Austrian Jews, including the supervision of Jewish political organizations and occupational retraining centers, and served as a model for methods used throughout Greater Germany.[53] In addition, the Nazi practice of commandeering Jewish community leadership to carry out the regime's intended dirty work evolved into the establishment of *Judenräte* (Jewish councils) in ghettos in the east.[54]

Forced Emigration

The main goals of the IKG were to move as many members of the community as possible to safety abroad, to provide support and instruction prior to their departure, and to care for the elderly and the ill who were unable to leave. On Eichmann's orders, the Kultusgemeinde created the Emigration Department to organize, finance, and manage the entire process of emigration, all under the control of the Central Office.[55] Registration for flight under the IKG's auspices began with a four-page questionnaire submitted to the Emigration Department to declare such intentions and to provide information that included biographical and financial details, the status of an applicant's and his or her dependents' identification documents, and any others necessary for departure, as well as potential locations for their emigration abroad. IKG staff researched and provided information about

---

51. Gerhard J. Teschner, "Saar Region," in *The Greater German Reich and the Jews: Nazi Persecution Policies in the Annexed Territories, 1935–1945*, ed. Wolf Gruner and Jörg Osterloh (New York: Berghahn Books, 2015), 27.
52. Safrian, *Eichmann's Men*, 31.
53. Ibid., 33.
54. Rabinovici, *Instanzen der Ohnmacht*, 82. For more about the Nazi development of Jewish administrations in communities and eventually in ghettos, see Dan Michman, *The Emergence of Jewish Ghettos during the Holocaust* (Cambridge: Cambridge University Press, 2011).
55. This department handled immigration needs to all countries except Palestine, for which the Pal-Amt (Palestine Office) had been established. See Offenberger, *Jews of Nazi Vienna*, 82.

possible destinations and educated hopeful émigrés on the Nazi demands placed on them before their departure from the Reich, as well as different countries' requirements for entry.

Many potential places of refuge sought to admit agricultural workers and qualified craftspeople, while the United Kingdom, for example, wanted young and middle-aged women to serve as domestic workers.[56] The Emigration Department coordinated and delivered relevant training programs and language classes to prepare eager émigrés. Kultusgemeinde leaders secured and managed funding from foreign Jewish aid groups for use in complying with Nazi decrees, financial and other, and provided social welfare to their members.[57] The IKG encouraged Jews to emigrate under the auspices of the Emigration Department and therefore in accordance with the regulations of the Central Office. It assured its members that leaving the country was their only option, urged the younger generation to leave elderly parents behind, and advised parents to send children to safer locations.[58]

Securing the clearance to leave Austria often proved more difficult than obtaining the permission to do so. Émigrés needed visas to enter a foreign country, but to get one, they typically had to provide an affidavit with the promise of support by a friend or relative at that destination, as well as proof of official approval to leave the Reich. The exit process instituted by the Nazis involved hefty fees and special tax requirements, the payment and the certification of which took time to secure. On top of the interminable lists of the Nazis' arbitrary and extensive requirements for documentation to depart legally and long waits at government offices, those seeking to emigrate endured lengthy queues at the embassies and consulates of countries to which they hoped to go.[59]

---

56. For more on these women, see Traude Bollauf, *Dienstmädchen—Emigration: Die Flucht jüdischer Frauen aus Österreich und Deutschland nach England 1938/39* (Vienna: LIT Verlag, 2011); and Tony Kushner, "An Alien Occupation—Jewish Refugees and Domestic Service in Britain, 1933–1948," in *Second Chance: Two Centuries of German-Speaking Jews in the United Kingdom*, ed. Werner E. Mosse (Tübingen: J. C. B. Mohr, 1991), 564.

57. Offenberger, *Jews of Nazi Vienna*, 76.

58. For example, see *Zionistische Rundschau*, May 27, 1938.

59. In *Flight from the Reich*, Debórah Dwork and Robert Jan van Pelt note an unanticipated result of the lengthy queues at offices in Vienna: an opportunity for young people to earn money

The Nazis also required Jews to register their property for official expropriation as yet another required step in the process of leaving Nazi Austria. "Wild Aryanization" in Vienna at the time of Anschluss and afterward had shown the regime the need to regulate the confiscation of Jews' assets. The Nazis counted on the appropriation of the Viennese Jewish community's and individual Jews' wealth, and Austrians had already plundered too much. The "Law on the Registration of Jewish Assets" of April 26, 1938, led to the establishment of the Vermögensverkehrstelle (Assets Transfer Agency), which served the needs of official "Aryanization" and expropriation policies through the registration of Jews' assets and their subsequent facilitation to "Aryan" ownership.[60] All those who were recognized as Jews under the Nuremberg racial laws and in possession of assets valued at more than five thousand Reichsmark had to file a *Vermögensanmeldung* (property registration form), a four-page questionnaire detailing the type and sum of the person's total assets, to be completed in triplicate. With this information and the work of the Assets Transfer Agency, the Nazi state obtained the precise records needed for the systematic expropriation of Austrian Jews' wealth.

The acquisition of a valid passport posed a particular set of difficulties. With the Anschluss, Austrians had become citizens of the Greater German Reich. Their passports suddenly invalid, they had to replace them with German documents. Many born outside the First Republic, in parts of the Habsburg Empire that had since become independent countries, had obtained neither formal citizenship nor a passport during the interwar years and were required to apply for the latter at the embassy of the country of their birth. To add a further layer of difficulty, the Nazis also required that Jews' passports be stamped with a red J for *Jude* (Jew).[61]

---

by standing in line for others to obtain necessary forms and papers for a fee. See Dwork and van Pelt, *Flight from the Reich: Refugee Jews, 1933–1946* (New York: Norton, 2009), 120–21.

60. Copies of these registrations are held in the IKG Archive and in microfilm copies of IKG files at the USHMM. See Offenberger, *Jews of Nazi Vienna*, 150.

61. Feeling deluged by Jewish refugees after the Anschluss, Swiss authorities sought to impose a visa obligation on all Germans. The Germans countered with the suggestion that they mark all Jews' passports with an identifier. For a detailed description of the negotiations between Swiss and Nazi officials on this matter, see Dwork and van Pelt, *Flight from the Reich*, 157–62.

Documents that certified the forfeiture of assets to the Nazi state and proved payment of taxes were valid for one year, as were the quota numbers granted to refugees, visas, passports, and the affidavits they had secured from friends or family in destination countries. If it took more than eleven months to acquire the many documents necessary, departure had to take place in weeks or even days, or the first received certificates would expire. This happened frequently and forced refugees to start their entire emigration process over again.

Immediately after the Anschluss, Austrian Jews sensed the need to escape. The violence and oppression that had escalated gradually over the course of five years in Germany seemingly erupted overnight in Austria, and Jews confronted a stark reality. As persecution intensified, as the Nazis arrested Jewish men, and because of the IKG's encouragement and direction, more families set their sights on emigration, and the Jewish community accelerated its work. By October 1938, the Central Office had received applications from 43,336 heads of households representing a total of 117,979 people seeking to leave Austria.[62] The following month's devastating November Pogrom brought home the unrelenting nature of Nazi persecution, plunder, and violence. The work of the IKG's Emigration Department intensified, and community leaders pressed parents to respond to the United Kingdom's willingness to accept Jewish children from Germany, Austria, and Czechoslovakia. News of Nazi violence and persecution during the November Pogrom had prompted public sympathy and governmental response in Great Britain. With the permission of the British, Dutch, and Swedish governments, aid organizations across Nazi Germany and Austria organized *Kindertransporte* to send unaccompanied children under the age of seventeen to the west on trains that crossed through Germany and into the Netherlands, where the children boarded boats to sail for England. The Anglo-Jewish community organized financial and human resources to

---

62. "Jewish Community of Vienna Archive, Jerusalem Component," reel 294, IKG-A/W 126, *Report of the Vienna Jewish Community. A Description of the Activity of the Israelitische Kultusgemeinde Wien in the Period from May 2nd 1938–December 31st 1939 (2 Exemplare)*, RG 17.017M, USHMM.

provide foster families, children's homes, and other hospitality for caring for the refugee children.

And indeed, from the start of May 1938 through December 31, 1939, the IKG helped 117,409 Jews to flee.[63] By November 11, 1941, a total of 146,816 (of the 206,000 Austrian Jews estimated to be living in Austria as of May 2, 1938) had emigrated to other countries.[64] The mass emigration of community members remained the IKG's main goal. When that proved challenging, it facilitated transmigration to locations to which people could more immediately travel and that were—or appeared to be—transit points to further destinations. The IKG helped support refugees in passage and provided financial assistance with the support of the American Jewish Joint Distribution Committee (the Joint or the JDC).[65] Major concerns for potential émigrés included not only funding but also factors such as climate, language, and employment opportunities in the desired destination. Men with professional contacts around the world tried to secure positions abroad, and many families contacted relatives in other countries.[66] Jews resorted to scouring telephone books from across the globe for anyone with the same family name in search of even a remote kinship connection. As the Nazi yoke tightened particularly on men and the traditionally male realms of professional life, women assumed new responsibilities in leading their families to safety.

New Gender Roles

The persecution and arrest of many male Jewish heads of household forced women into new positions of family responsibility. With their husbands in Dachau and Buchenwald, wives assumed control of their families' futures,

---

63. Ibid.

64. Wolfgang Muchitsch, *Österreicher im Exil: Großbritannien 1938–1945; Eine Dokumentation*, ed. Dokumentationsarchiv des österreichischen Widerstandes (Vienna: Österreicher Bundesverlag, 1992), 8. Jonny Moser finds the estimate of 206,000 Austrian Jews to be about 5,000 too high and comes to the total of 201,000. See his calculations and explanation in Moser, *Demographie der jüdischen Bevölkerung Österreichs*, 18–19.

65. Offenberger, *Jews of Nazi Vienna*, 132.

66. Dwork and van Pelt, *Flight from the Reich*, 122.

which included attempts to find safety outside Austria. In the book *Between Dignity and Despair*,[67] historian Marion Kaplan illuminates the experiences of Jewish women in Nazi Germany and the gender role reversal that occurred within their families under the Nazis. Austrian Jewish women reacted and responded similarly when the same persecution and oppression befell their communities and families.

As Kaplan has pointed out, women often saw the need to flee sooner and more clearly than men did. In Vienna, too, their interactions in the community brought them into contact with their gentile neighbors in everyday situations, and they felt the atmosphere of hostility and antisemitism more keenly than did men who mainly worked with other Jewish men and remained in largely Jewish social circles. Kaplan has argued that German men felt more at home with German culture and politics, and many Jewish veterans of World War I mistakenly reasoned that their military service would prompt protection from the state. Men were "more German" than women were in their sense of patriotism and in their specific training and education in Germany.[68] And just as German Jews believed that their Germanness would save them, Austrian Jews also thought of their Austrianness as protection.

When Austrian Jews encountered the onslaught of persecution immediately after the Anschluss, many wives saw with sober lucidity the reality that they confronted and the colossal task before them and worked to organize their families' emigration. They chose destinations, navigated the bureaucratic requirements involved with their families' departures, handled the sale of businesses and properties, and otherwise made decisions that they would not have taken previously. Many of them did all this with the urgent burden of the endless work needed to secure the release of husbands imprisoned in Nazi concentration camps. Charlotte Czuczka arranged and submitted all the paperwork involved in freeing her Viennese husband, Fritz, from Buchenwald, including providing the Gestapo and camp administration with

---

67. Marion Kaplan, *Between Dignity and Despair: Jewish Life in Nazi Germany* (New York: Oxford University Press, 1998).

68. Ibid., 65–66.

photographs of the tickets purchased for the family to sail to the United States. When she failed to hear from Fritz or from the camp authorities in the specified amount of time, she first telephoned the Gestapo in Vienna and then called the main Berlin Gestapo office to investigate. An officer assured Charlotte that he would settle the matter within forty-eight hours, and shortly thereafter she received a telegram from Fritz informing her that he was on his way home. He was released from Buchenwald on February 18, 1939,[69] and arrived at Vienna's Ostbahnhof (East Train Station) the following morning. Charlotte, Fritz, and their son, George, sailed for New York a month later.[70]

Kaplan has argued that female identity was more family oriented, and once women realized their position as the only person left to defend their traditional realm of home and family, they took on all that their husbands could not. Women reacted and responded in new ways, with new assertiveness, and with authority in traditionally male roles in order to preserve and maintain their *familial home*, the traditionally female sphere. For many, preserving home ultimately meant fleeing, which required moving to a new place of security. All that they organized and managed served to protect their traditionally female familial responsibilities but required the additional assumption of formerly male obligations to do so.

Lands of Exile

Austrian Jews fled around the globe to places as distant and diverse as Ecuador, the Dominican Republic, China, Syria, Lebanon, the United States, Turkey, Venezuela, the West Indies, and Cyprus.[71] Many others managed to escape to other European countries, the lucky ones to the United Kingdom or other places that were not later invaded and occupied by the Germans. Palestine stood as the destination for 14,093 Austrian Jews, 1,000

---

69. Fritz Czuczka Buchenwald prisoner file, 1.1.5.3/5715087/ITS Digital Archive, USHMM.
70. George Czuczka, interview by Phillip Rohrbach and Konstantin Wacker, New York, June 5, 2008, AHC 3994, Austrian Heritage Collection, Leo Baeck Institute, New York, NY.
71. Registration documents of returnees, A/VIE/IKG/III/BEV/Rück/1/2, Das Archiv der Israelitischen Kultusgemeinde Wien (IKG Archive), Vienna, Austria.

of whom transited through Slovakia and Hungary; nearly 12,000 arrived there.[72] A total of 37,710 Austrian Jews fled with hopes of reaching the United States, including 8,130 who traveled through a third transit country and 200 who finally settled in Mexico.[73] For many, Shanghai emerged as an unlikely last resort. Neither visa nor medical exam was required to travel there—one needed only to sign a waiver acknowledging an understanding of the medical risks of traveling to and living in the Far East.[74] The first Austrian Jews arrived in Shanghai in August 1938,[75] and a United Nations Relief and Rehabilitation Administration (UNRRA) document reveals that, of the 16,300 European Jews who found refuge in Shanghai, 4,298 of them were Austrians.[76]

Labor camps in Karaganda in Kazakhstan became another improbable place of survival. As historians Debórah Dwork and Robert Jan van Pelt note in *Flight from the Reich*, "internment camps proved a harsh blessing for those who escaped to the Soviet Union."[77] When the Red Army invaded the Baltic states in the summer of 1940, the Soviets refused to recognize as victims of the Nazis the Austrian and German Jewish refugees who had fled there. Rather, they saw them as German citizens in Soviet territory, and when Nazi Germany invaded the Soviet Union on June 22, 1941, the Russian Security Police arrested and deported all foreigners.[78] Thus, Social Democrats and Communists who had fled the Nazis, and some who earlier had fled the Austrofascist regime, found themselves interned in Siberia

---

72. Jonny Moser writes that 1,000 Austrian Jews who fled with hopes of reaching Palestine ended up in Mauritius and another 1,107 in Yugoslavia. Moser, *Demographie der jüdischen Bevölkerung Österreichs*, 76. As an illustration of the difficulties of establishing confirmed statistics on Austrian Jewish emigration, it should be noted that Hugo Gold reports that only 9,195 Austrian Jews emigrated to Palestine between March 13, 1938, and mid-November 1941. See Gold, *Geschichte der Juden in Wien: Ein Gedenkbuch* (Tel Aviv: Olamenu, 1966), 133.

73. Moser, *Demographie der jüdischen Bevölkerung Österreichs*, 79.

74. Offenberger, *Jews of Nazi Vienna*, 135.

75. Elisabeth Buxbaum, *Transit Shanghai: Ein Leben im Exil* (Vienna: Edition Steinbauer, 2008), 15.

76. Dwork and van Pelt, *Flight from the Reich*, 318.

77. Ibid., 244.

78. Joint correspondence about Karaganda internees, April 8, 1947, 3.1.1.3/78788142/ITS Digital Archive, USHMM.

and, later, in or near Karaganda. Refugees lived and worked in labor camps, where many remained until the possibility of remigration after the war.[79]

An estimated 28,250 Austrian Jews found refuge in the United Kingdom.[80] A number of politically affiliated Jews went with party comrades; others found their way to their respective parties once in exile. After the British government responded to the November Pogrom by opening its doors to Jewish children from Germany, Austria, and Czechoslovakia, many parents sent their children to live with foster families in the United Kingdom. Single women (and some married) secured positions as domestic servants, while others somehow got work via contacts in their fields. Once in Britain, young men joined the armed forces, as did many Jewish refugees in the United States, and thus later took an active part in liberating Europe and their former homes from Nazi oppression.

An IKG summary of 1940 reported that a total of 123,490 *Glaubensjuden* (those who identified as religious Jews) had emigrated by the end of that year.[81] After the outbreak of war on September 1, 1939, however, opportunities for emigration dwindled, but the Nazis continued to force IKG employees to provide lists and reports related to the status of the Jewish community and its members. By the spring of 1941, the purposes that required such data changed. Instead of information employed in the organization of Jews' flight from the Third Reich, the regime turned to utilize it in the facilitation of the deportation of Jews to the Nazi-occupied east. The first transports from Vienna forced 1,584 Jews to Nisko in October 1939, and deportations to the east continued through March 19, 1945. The Nazis expelled Austrian Jews to destinations such as Opole, Kielce, Modliborzyce, Lagow, Opatow, Lodz, Kovno, Minsk, Riga, Izbica, and Wlodawa, as well

---

79. See Edith Sekules, *Surviving the Nazis, Exile, and Siberia* (Portland, OR: Vallentine Mitchell, 2000).

80. According to Jonny Moser, of 31,250 Austrian Jews seeking to flee to the United Kingdom, 3,000 ended up in other countries in North and South America, as well as Australia. Of the total, 3,500 reportedly traveled through a third (European) transit country. Moser, *Demographie der jüdischen Bevölkerung Österreichs*, 74. Hugo Gold reports that a total of 128,500 Jews fled Vienna to other countries between March 13, 1938, and mid-November 1941, and 30,850 of them went to England. Gold, *Geschichte der Juden in Wien*, 133.

81. Moser, *Demographie der jüdischen Bevölkerung Österreichs*, 27n85.

as the death camps of Sobibor and Auschwitz. But the vast majority of Austrian Jewish deportees—more then 15,000—arrived in Terezín sometime between June 1942 and March 1945.[82]

Nonetheless, an additional 6,000 Austrian Jews managed to escape in 1941,[83] but only after extraordinary measures were taken to have them exempted from the transports that began in spring 1941, transports that historian Helga Embacher has argued marked the moment at which the IKG became a completely powerless tool of the Nazis.[84] As of June 30, 1941, 44,000 Jews remained in Vienna.[85] After the mass deportations in October 1942, the Nazis removed the IKG's legal status under public law and, as of November 1, 1942, renamed the remaining group of leaders the Ältestenrat der Juden in Wien (Jewish Council of Elders in Vienna), tasking them with the support of the fewer than 8,000 Jews remaining in Vienna,[86] as well as the oversight of organizations that served so-called non-Aryan Christians.

Jews who remained in Vienna lived in protected situations that included marriage to a gentile, being a so-called *Mischlinge* (literally, mongrels— those with a partially Jewish heritage) or a product of such a union, and employment with the Ältestenrat, while others survived the war in hiding. Of some 201,000 Jews in the capital city before the Anschluss, 146,816 had managed to emigrate, an estimated 135,000 of them to safety and out of reach of further Nazi domination. The Nazis had systematically expropriated their property and assets, forcing them to leave with little financial means and few personal belongings. In the end, the Nazis murdered some 65,000 Austrian Jews, but the great efforts of the IKG employees working under incredible pressure from their Nazi oppressors had led to the

---

82. Ibid., 80–83.
83. Rabinovici, *Instanzen der Ohnmacht*, 229.
84. Helga Embacher, *Neubeginn ohne Illusionen: Juden in Österreich nach 1945* (Vienna: Picus Verlag, 1995), 27.
85. Rabinovici, *Instanzen der Ohnmacht*, 297.
86. At the beginning of 1943, there were only 7,989 Jews left in Vienna, and by December, the number had dwindled to 6,259. Of these, 1,080 belonged to another confession, 85 were foreign, and 5,094 lived in mixed marriages. Statistics from the Ältestenrat der Juden in Wien, "Bericht über die Tätigkeit im Jahre 1943," as cited in Rabinovici, *Instanzen der Ohnmacht*, 116.

emigration and thus the possibility of survival for more than 65 percent of the Jewish community.[87]

In the opening section of *Wie wir gelebt haben*, illustrations of typical Jewish family life in the Habsburg Empire—which is to say, images of typical family life in the Habsburg Empire—continue chronologically to representations of Jewish families' experiences under the Nazis. The second section, "Holocaust," makes clear that in fact this volume does not constitute a collection of photos reflecting happy and fond memories but rather depicts aspects of the stark reality of what became of many Jews of the former empire who fell victim to Nazi oppression, persecution, and ultimately genocidal policy. The activities and struggles of refugees in points of exile across the globe are illuminated, along with the faces of murdered family members. A few photos even reveal the hard life of internees in the Opole ghetto.[88]

The closing chapter of *Wie wir gelebt habe*, however, returns to parallel the opening in that it again reveals the experiences of (now specifically) Viennese Jewish families and thus in many ways mirrors those of typical Viennese families. This final portion, "Das Leben nach dem Holocaust" (Life after the Holocaust), depicts lives reestablished in Vienna—for many, their hometown—and a resumption of life in postwar Austria, after the Holocaust and the destruction of European Jewry. Those pictured were among the few thousand Austrian Jews who reestablished lives, homes, and families in the capital.

---

87. After the war, Ältestenrat leaders (particularly Josef Löwenherz and Benjamin Murmelstein) came under intense criticism, and some people accused them of collaboration with the Nazis. Doron Rabinovici argues against such a judgment, and I agree with his assertion that Jewish community leaders were at the absolute mercy of their Nazi oppressors and were "authorities without power." See Rabinovici, *Instanzen der Ohnmacht*, 36.

88. The Nazis established a ghetto in Opole, Poland, in March 1941 and concentrated Jews from Poland, Austria, Slovakia, and France there under horrible conditions. The ghetto was liquidated and the residents deported in the spring of 1942, Lilli (Schischa) Tauber's parents among them. During their internment, her parents sent letters and photographs to relatives in Vienna. One aunt survived the war and afterward gave them to Lilli, who submitted them for inclusion in Centropa's publication. Lilli's parents were deported from Opole to either Sobibor or Belzec, where they were murdered. See Eckstein and Kaldori, *Wie wir gelebt haben*, 164–67.

Holocaust survivors living in Vienna today contributed the photos in this section and indeed in the entire book. They show everything from one young man's excited and smiling face just before departure from Palestine to return to his hometown to joyous occasions in postwar Vienna, including weddings and picnics. We see the proud owners of new cars, as well as entrepreneurs posed in front of businesses—new ones and, in a few cases, those restituted to them. By the time these photos were taken, the empire was a memory, as was the Third Reich and "Greater Germany." Austria had returned to its post–World War I form of a "rump state" of some eight million citizens and had regained its name, no longer the Nazi German province the Ostmark. Much like the pictures of the first section, these reveal a cross-section of Jewish family life in the former imperial capital and show that Jewish family life in the postwar era also closely reflected the lives of all Viennese residents.

Most of those who are pictured in *Wie wir gelebt haben* represent the subjects of this book—those who returned and reestablished lives in Vienna after the Red Army's conquest of the city and during Allied occupation. They were among the concentration camp survivors and exile returnees from abroad who resumed and reestablished lives in their hometown, along with some who had somehow survived in the city during the war and its aftermath. All had apprehensively awaited the war's end from various points around the globe, including those still in Vienna who listened as Soviet troops rolled in. And it is the context of some one thousand years of Jews living in this region, through all of Austria's incarnations, that frames the deep, although ambivalent, connection that many returnees felt toward the city as their *home*.

2

THE FIRST "RETURNEES," 1945

In the early hours of April 12, 1945, nine terrified Viennese Jews cowered in the cellar of the house at Förstergasse 7 in Vienna's second district. Until shortly before, all but one of them had lived openly in Nazi Vienna, safeguarded by positions as functionaries of the Ältestenrat. The ninth had been protected by his marriage to an "Aryan" woman. They sat helplessly, enduring the fear not only of their Nazi tormentors but also of Allied bombing raids. Waffen-SS (the armed wing of the SS that eventually developed into military combat units) and Wehrmacht (the regular Nazi army) troops entrenched in the surrounding streets no longer cared whether or not a Jew held protected status, and the nine suddenly found themselves forced to hide in a cold, dank basement, fearing for their lives.[1]

As they huddled together underground, they listened to the bedlam above. The Soviet Army had reached the southern and eastern outskirts of Vienna on April 6, 1945, but it took another five days to seize the capital. On the evening of April 11, fires blazed as remnants of recent battles on the grounds of Vienna's famous park, the Prater, and throughout the city. Looting citizens skirted rubble in the streets as they competed for scarce foodstuffs and plundered the stalls of the city's prized market, the Naschmarkt,

---

1. Erika Weinzierl, *Zu wenig Gerechte: Österreicher und Judenverfolgung in 1938–1945* (Graz: Verlag Styria, 1969), 93.

for the first time in the course of the war. The desperate ate meat from dead cavalry horses lying in the streets.

As evening fell, the narrow Danube Canal became the battlefront, with the Red Army poised on the first-district side and Nazi Panzers and infantry positioned throughout the second and twentieth districts on the opposite bank.[2] Waffen-SS officers retreating through the streets toward the Danube River still found time to conduct a hunt for hiding Jews when neighbors informed them of the group in the cellar at Förstergasse 7.[3] The group, aware they had been betrayed, debated whether to seek new hiding places. Martin Schaier encouraged them all to scatter into neighboring cellars.[4] The others considered his plan but decided that the women among them and the men in mixed marriages could safely stay put; only Schaier and other "full Jews" should disappear. Schaier fled to the shelter of a neighboring basement, leaving his wife, Genia, with eight others deemed secure. From his hiding place, he heard a shout: "We still have time to get us the Jews!" He listened as the SS officers gathered the five women and four men who had remained in their hiding place, robbed them of valuables, and marched them outside.[5] Only after kicking them into the street, beating them with rifle butts, and stabbing them with bayonets, did the officers finally shoot them and dump their bodies into a nearby bomb crater.[6] A few hours later, the Red Army crossed the Danube Canal, reached Förstergasse,

---

2. Ibid.

3. Wolfgang Neugebauer, *Widerstand und Verfolgung in Wien, 1934–1945: Eine Dokumentation*, vol. 3 (Vienna: Österreichischer Bundesverlag für Unterricht, Wissenschaft und Kunst, 1975), 310.

4. Martin Schaier lived in the building at Förstergasse 7 during the war. See List of Austrian Jews Residing in Vienna during the Occupation, November 30, 1945, 3.1.1.3/78804753/ITS Digital Archive, United States Holocaust Memorial Museum (USHMM), Washington, DC.

5. Elizabeth Welt Trahan, *Walking with Ghosts: A Jewish Childhood in Wartime Vienna* (New York: Peter Lang, 1998), 243–43.

6. The victims were Dr. Nelly Blum (fifty-four), Erna Klüger-Langer (eighty-two), Grete Klüger-Langer (forty-four), Marie Margolin (forty-four), Genia Schaier (forty-eight), Arthur Holzer (fifty-nine), Arthur Klein (fifty-six), Kurt Mezei (twenty-one), and Emil Pfeiffer (sixty-six); as listed on a memorial plaque at Förstergasse 7, 1020 Vienna. The IKG erected the current plaque on April 14, 1960. It replaced one installed there by the KZ-Verband on April 12, 1954. The same nine victims are also listed on the Vienna City Press and Information Service website, but spellings (i.e., Genia Schaier) and ages differ slightly from IKG figures.

and took total control of Vienna.⁷ As the Soviets secured the city, Vienna's remaining Jews reemerged. Schaier and a few others found that their first task upon "return" entailed the retrieval of the nine fresh corpses for proper burial.⁸

When interviewed after the war, Ältestenrat Director Dr. Josef Löwenherz could have provided hundreds of examples of Nazi brutality but chose the story of the Förstergasse massacre to convey the ruthlessness of the Nazis in Vienna.⁹ A matter of hours separated the last Jews murdered in the city from the first to reemerge and "return." Thrust from society but not from the city, some five thousand Jews had managed to survive in the capital under differing circumstances of protection and privilege and began to rebuild their lives in the immediate moments of the Red Army's victorious conquest.

WHO REMAINED IN VIENNA IN APRIL 1945?

Ältestenrat statistics from December 1944 reveal that 5,799 Nuremberg-defined Jews resided in Vienna, 1,053 of whom practiced Judaism. Nearly all of those alive in the city at that point lived to see the Nazis fall from power.¹⁰ Estimates of the total number of Jews who survived the war in Vienna range from a little more than 5,500 to 5,600.¹¹ Of them, just some 600 self-identified as Jews, a group that included 150 technical workers with the firm Wittke and Grimm, 35 Ältestenrat clerks and officials, 35 World War I veterans whom the Nazis had somehow overlooked, 60 prisoners in

---

7. Weinzierl, *Zu wenig Gerechte*, 93.
8. Trahan, *Walking with Ghosts*, 242–43.
9. "President of Jewish Community in Vienna under Nazi Regime Found in Prague Hospital," Jewish Telegraphic Agency, August 28, 1945.
10. Doron Rabinovici, *Instanzen der Ohnmacht: Wien 1938–1945, der Weg zum Judenrat* (Frankfurt am Main: Jüdischer Verlag, 2000), 241.
11. Jonny Moser, *Demographie der jüdischen Bevölkerung Österreichs, 1938–1945* (Vienna: Dokumentationsarchiv des österreichischen Widerstandes, 1999), 55 (5,500); Gertrude Schneider, *Exile and Destruction: The Fate of Austrian Jews, 1938–1945* (Westport, CT: Praeger, 1995), 157 (5,600).

different jails, over 100 foreign Jews never picked up for deportation, and 150–200 Jews who physically hid from their persecutors.[12] The other nearly 5,000 persons who were targeted by the Nazis but who did not identify as Jews included those who had intermarried with non-Jews, the offspring of such mixed marriages, and the relatives of some Ältestenrat employees. Living in the city under differing degrees of hardship and concealment throughout the war, most of these survivors did not question whether to "return," as they had never actually left. They reemerged into society in Vienna, the only home they had ever known. From one moment to the next, they found themselves free to move about their partially destroyed and shocked city, immediately engaging in what social and economic life existed or had just begun. Who were these survivors? How had they endured, and what did they face upon regaining their freedom?

U-Boote

U-Boote, the smallest subgroup of Jews to survive in Vienna, endured the Nazi regime in hiding or by concealing their identity with forged or falsified documents. Assimilation proved the critical factor for securing a safe refuge or the necessary papers, as close contact and good relationships with non-Jews better ensured their assistance.[13] Some lived for years in concealment, protected by friends and relatives. Lucia (Kraus) Heilman was twelve years old in 1941, when she and her mother went into hiding in Reinhold Duschka's metal workshop at Mollardgasse 85a in the sixth district.[14] Heilman's father had fled to Tehran when the political situation became dangerous in Vienna, but his attempts to bring his wife and daughter to join him failed. His close friend and fellow Alpinist Duschka assumed their care and saved their lives.[15] Many others had felt secure in mixed marriages

---

12. Schneider, *Exile and Destruction*, 157.

13. C. Gwyn Moser, "Jewish *U-Boote* in Austria, 1938–1945," *Simon Wiesenthal Center Annual* 2 (1985): 58.

14. Dieter J. Hecht, Eleonore Lappin-Eppel, and Michaela Raggam-Blesch, *Topographie der Shoah: Gedächnisorte das zerstörten jüdischen Wien* (Vienna: Mandelbaum Verlag, 2015), 535.

15. National Fund of the Republic of Austria for Victims of National Socialism, "Hidden in Vienna, Luzia Treister," accessed May 4, 2012, http://www.en.nationalfonds.org/sites/dynamicae6d.html?id=news20080207115228049. In 1990, the State of Israel and Yad Vashem

or because of mixed heritage for much of the Nazi period, but they too took to hiding in the final chaotic days. Many Jewish *U-Boote* considered themselves Catholics because of their own conversion or those in earlier generations of their family, but they nonetheless fell victim to Nazi racial definitions of Jews outlined in the 1935 Nuremberg Laws.

Hidden Jews came from all strata of Viennese society, but their rescuers stemmed largely from *kleinbürgerlichen* (lower-middle-class) backgrounds. Most helped their Jewish beneficiaries out of compassion, receiving no monetary compensation.[16] As in the case of the Heilmans, many had close relationships with those whom they saved, and some *U-Boote* stayed on with their protectors after the end of the war. Historian Brigitte Ungar-Klein counts more than fifty marriages between survivors and their rescuers and attributes this largely to close pre-Anschluss relations rather than wartime situations.[17]

As many as 800 Jews may have lived to the war's end in hiding in Vienna,[18] but estimating the number of *U-Boote* in the city and accurately counting those who survived proves difficult, as scholars rely on inherently flawed sources.[19] Historian Gwyn Moser took these problems into account when she analyzed 619 *U-Boote* survivors' files, including questionnaires from the KZ-Verband (an association of concentration camp survivors), files from the Bestände der Zentrallen Registrierstelle für die Opfer des NS-Terrors (Office for the Central Registration of Victims of Nazi Terror), and Opferfürsorge (Victims' Welfare) applications.[20] Registration

---

recognized Duschka as one of the "Righteous Among the Nations," the honor awarded to gentile rescuers of Jews during the Holocaust. In addition to Duschka's morality and sense of goodness, Lucia Heilman also specified that Duschka and her father were Alpinists and stated that the deep commitment among this group to preserve one another's lives grounded Duschka as he risked his life to rescue his best friend's wife and child.

16. Brigitte Ungar-Klein, "Überleben im Versteck—Rückkehr in die Normalität?," in *Überleben der Shoah—und danach*, ed. Alexander Friedmann, Elvira Glück, and David Vyssoki (Vienna: Picus Verlag, 1999), 36.

17. Ibid., 38.

18. Ibid., 35.

19. Brigitte Ungar-Klein, "Bei Freunden untergetaucht—U-Boot in Wien," in *Der Pogrom 1938: Judenverfolgung in Österreich und Deutschland; Dokumentation eines Symposiums der Volkshochschule Brigittenau*, ed. Kurt Schmid and Robert Streibel (Vienna: Picus Verlag, 1990), 87.

20. Moser, "Jewish *U-Boote* in Austria," 54.

with these organizations took place on a voluntary basis, and some people refused to list their names as survivors or to apply for state-supported assistance. In addition, work on Opferfürsorge did not take place until the 1960s and required embarrassing verifications that deterred application. For these reasons, many *U-Boote* survivors left no formal record of their experience or died without opportunity to register. Then, too, the definition of *U-Boote* varied from organization to organization. Consequently, such official documentation provides an incomplete count. In addition, it is thought that for every *U-Boote* survivor, at least two were caught, arrested, and deported. Thus, the tenuous nature of life in hiding in Nazi Vienna furthered the impossibility of including an accurate estimate of the number of *U-Boote* among those who were caught and murdered by the Nazis.[21]

Ältestenrat Officials and Their Families

Both in Germany and in Austria, the Nazis pressed the leaders and employees of the formal Jewish communities into roles laboring to serve any remaining Jews, those of mixed ancestry, and those who were baptized but had a Jewish family heritage, the so-called non-Aryan Christians. Composed of the remaining few employees of the Israelitische Kultusgemeinde Wien (Vienna's formal Jewish community, also referred to as the IKG or the Kultusgemeinde), the Ältestenrat was formed by the Nazis in November 1942, following mass deportations of Viennese Jews in October.[22] In Germany, the Reichsvereinigung der Juden in Deutschland (Reich Association of Jews in Germany) had a similar function but was officially dissolved in the summer of 1943. It continued to exist de facto to carry out some services to Germany's remaining Jews who were married to non-Jewish partners.[23] In Vienna, however, the Ältestenrat functioned throughout

---

21. Ibid., 61. To add to the difficulty with such counts, Gestapo files report the arrests of hidden Jews and their rescuers that do not appear in other places. With the establishment of Israel and Yad Vashem's "Righteous Among the Nations" honors, more *U-Boote* survivors were discovered as they came forward to honor their rescuers.

22. Rabinovici, *Instanzen der Ohnmacht*, 241.

23. Beate Meyer, "Between Self-Assertion and Forced Collaboration: The Reich Association of Jews in Germany, 1939–1945," in *Jewish Life in Nazi Germany: Dilemmas and Responses*, ed. Francis R. Nicosia and David Scrase (New York: Berghahn Books, 2012), 149–69.

the war. Its employees and some of their family members lived in Nazi Vienna under special protected status. As of January 17, 1943, 248 paid employees and 70 volunteers of the Jewish community remained in Vienna, 221 of whom were subject to persecution as "full Jews" by Nazi law. The Nazis permitted each of these to protect one person, and in this way another 170 relatives were saved.[24] A few employees of the Jewish hospital and the Jewish nursing home also enjoyed such relative security and safety.[25] Franzi Danneberg-Löw served throughout the war as a social worker with the IKG and the Ältestenrat,[26] and her status enabled her to protect her mother. Danneberg-Löw's employment and marriage to a non-Jew gave her the extraordinary possibility of moving back and forth to and from labor camps in Hungary, where she helped provide food and clothing to prisoners, as well as information to family members in the camps and in Vienna.[27]

The formation of the Ältestenrat was in part a Nazi strategy for eliminating Vienna's Jewish population without frightening or harming the *Volksgenossen*, a National Socialist term referring to the community of "Aryan" German citizens.[28] The Nazis recognized that caring for the remaining Jewish population actually served the whole population, as non-Jewish Austrians claimed Nazi-defined Jews as family members. Thus, a Jewish cemetery hosted burials, and a Jewish hospital served patients. Jews warranted medical care, even if only to save the non-Jewish population from disease, and therefore required separate Jewish medical facilities.

Mixed Marriages

Marriage to "Aryan" spouses afforded many Viennese Jews protected status for the duration of the war. As they helplessly watched the deportation of relatives and friends, they endured a terrified and insecure existence,

---

24. Rabinovici, *Instanzen der Ohnmacht*, 345.
25. Helga Embacher, *Neubeginn ohne Illusionen: Juden in Österreich nach 1945* (Vienna: Picus Verlag, 1995), 27.
26. Mitarbeiter des Ältestenrates der Juden in der Seitenstettengasse 2–4, July 24, 1945, 3.1.1.3/78804912/ITS Digital Archive, USHMM.
27. Franzi Danneberg-Löw, interview, 515, Dokumentationsarchiv des österreichischen Widerstandes (DÖW), Vienna, Austria. Danneberg-Löw's father died of natural causes in 1938.
28. Rabinovici, *Instanzen der Ohnmacht*, 317.

recognizing the ever-present threat of the revocation of their shielded position. In addition to potential Nazi whims of policy, the death of or divorce from a non-Jewish spouse could mean deportation. During the war, some of these Jews enjoyed a level of tolerance in their social surroundings, but many suffered discrimination and outright persecution. Their non-Jewish spouses also experienced penalties, including the loss of civil-service positions, the inability to secure certain kinds of government-regulated loans, and the requirement to pay additional taxes. Teachers and students harassed schoolchildren from mixed families, while the regime obstructed custody disputes and pressured "Aryan" partners to divorce their Jewish spouses.[29]

Most Jews in mixed marriages kept a low profile and used discretion when moving about in public. A law passed on September 1, 1941 stipulated that, as of September 15, all Jews residing in the German Reich must wear a so-called *Judenstern* (Jewish star) in public.[30] Bertha Koppe did not leave her family's second-district apartment for more than two years during the Nazi regime. Although her marriage to an "Aryan" protected her existence, to venture into the streets with the yellow Star of David invited the possibility of harassment, humiliation, and even arrest.[31] Gender did indeed prove an important component to survival for Jews in mixed marriages. Under Nazi law and administration, intermarried Jewish men were in greater danger than were intermarried Jewish women.[32] In male-dominated Nazi society, gentile men had more influence than women did with Nazi officials and thus were of more protection to their Jewish spouses.[33] Nazi policy toward intermarriage was "neither race-neutral nor gender-neutral," as historian Matthew Stibbe has noted. Rather, "it favoured the 'Aryan' over the

---

29. Evan Burr Bukey, *Jews and Intermarriage in Nazi Austria* (New York: Cambridge University Press, 2011), 3.

30. Polizeiverordnung über die Kennzeichnung der Juden, in *Deutsches Reichsgesetzblatt*, part 1, zweites Halbjahr 1941, September 1, 1941, 547.

31. Dr. Fritz Koppe (son of Bertha Koppe), conversation with author, Vienna, Austria, November 22, 2011.

32. Bukey, *Jews and Intermarriage in Nazi Austria*, 157.

33. Claudia Koonz, *Mothers in the Fatherland: Women, the Family, and Nazi Politics* (New York: St. Martin's, 1987), 379.

Jew, the wife over the husband and the mother over the childless woman."[34] In the case of Bertha Koppe, her son, Fritz, also believed that his non-Jewish father had held additional leverage as a Berliner who spoke with a German accent.[35]

Most intermarried couples, as well as many of mixed ancestry, were left to fend for themselves in Nazi Vienna. The IKG and its successor institution, the Ältestenrat, proved of little assistance, as they either shunned the Jewish spouses in mixed marriages as nonreligious or were unable to stretch their sparse resources to include nonmembers. Despite the challenges facing intermarried couples, 85–87 percent of Vienna's intermarried Jews survived the Holocaust.[36]

"Mischlinge"

Many children resulting from marriages between Jews and non-Jews managed to outlast the war in Vienna. They owed their survival to the fact that the racial specifications and qualifications of the Reichsbürgergesetz (Reich's Citizenship Law, one of the Nuremberg Laws) and the Gesetz zum Schutze des deutschen Blutes und der deutschen Ehre (Law for the Protection of German Blood and Honor) did not deem them *voll Juden*, or "full Jews." Both laws were passed on September 15, 1935, and went into effect on November 14, 1935, and were used to officially define "Jews" as a legal basis for their persecution and exclusion from society. Those who received the designation of "full Jew" counted three or four Jewish grandparents in their lineage and as a result lost all rights of citizenship in the German Reich.[37] As "partial Jews," so-called "Mischlinge," who had only one or two Jewish grandparents, retained citizenship, and the Nazis permitted them to stay in the city, although the threat of future deportation loomed constantly.

---

34. Matthew Stibbe, *Women in the Third Reich* (London: Arnold, 2003), 70.
35. Dr. Fritz Koppe (son of Bertha Koppe), conversation with author, Vienna, Austria, November 22, 2011.
36. Bukey, *Jews and Intermarriage in Nazi Austria*, 191.
37. Nationalsozialistische Deutsche Arbeiter-Partei and Robert Ley, *Organisationsbuch der NSDAP* (Munich: Zentralverlag der NSDAP, 1940), 569–75.

Anticipating a potential backlash to the persecution of "partial Jews," Nazi leadership sought to minimize alienating the sizable portion of the population with relatives falling into such a categorization by classifying "Mischlinge" in degrees based on the number of Jewish grandparents. A *Mischling ersten Grades* ("Mischling" of the First Degree) descended from two Jewish grandparents, while *Mischling zweiten Grades* ("Mischling" of the Second Degree) traced their lineage back to only one.[38] As long as a "Mischling" was not a member of the IKG, he or she might have the possibility to remain alive in Nazi Vienna. If one held membership in the Jewish community, however, the Nazis termed one a *Geltungsjude* (meaning that he or she counted as a "full Jew") and doomed one to suffer the full brunt of Nazi racial policy. Other "Mischlinge" deemed *Geltungsjuden* included those who were married to full Jews, children born from mixed marriages that took place after September 17, 1935, and the illegitimate children resulting from "Aryans'" forbidden extramarital relations with Jews after July 31, 1936.[39]

Fritz Koppe, the son of the intermarried Bertha and Max Koppe, received the most protected qualification of *Mischling ersten Grades*. Nevertheless, despite good marks in school, Nazi law prohibited him from attending *Gymnasium* (academically oriented high school), and his father arranged an apprenticeship to train with a pharmacist.[40] Although Fritz was able to move about the city, he and his parents nonetheless decided that he should not leave the house except for his training, lest he encounter trouble or violence in the streets.[41]

"Mischlinge" of both degrees served in the Wehrmacht and in the Reich Labor Service. However, the Nazis did not permit them to hold positions of authority in either organization, to become public officials, or to own an entailed farm estate.[42] Thus, with the ability to retain German citizenship and a differentiation between "full Jews," "half Jews," and even "quarter

---

38. Ibid.
39. Ibid., 573.
40. Dr. Fritz Koppe, interview with Barbara Kintaert, April 11, 2012, private collection, Vienna, Austria.
41. Dr. Fritz Koppe, conversation with author, Vienna, Austria, November 15, 2011.
42. Bukey, *Jews and Intermarriage in Nazi Austria*, 15.

Jews," some so-called Mischlinge lived precariously in Nazi Vienna, so long as they observed all regulations and policies governing their acceptance in society and as long as their "Aryan" parent remained alive.

SURVIVORS RESURFACE

The final days of World War II proved some of the most dangerous and terrifying for Jews in Vienna. The end of the war brought chaos, uncertainty, and increased antisemitic hostility. In addition to harassment, violence, and risk of arrest by the Nazi authorities, bloody fighting between the Red Army and the Wehrmacht and SS raged in the streets, and Allied bombers threatened the city's residents from above. Vienna's Jews, from their positions of cover, experienced their city's partial destruction and finally emerged to welcome the arrival of Soviet troops and the end of the war.

The Final Moments

Jewish and non-Jewish residents of Vienna took cover in air-raid shelters and basements around the city in the final moments of the war, seeking protection from battles between Nazi and Soviet troops, as well as from Allied bombs. In some cases, antisemitism placed Jews in additional danger. Non-Jewish neighbors denied Trude Berger's father access to the basement of their apartment building in the second district, just meters from the war front. Berger and her non-Jewish mother, both permitted to take shelter there, sat wracked with fear each time they endured a bombing, thinking of their father and husband fending for himself above.[43]

Loud explosions shook Viennese residents on the evening of April 12, 1945, as retreating Nazi troops blew up all but one bridge spanning the Danube Canal. The following day, the Red Army took total control of

---

43. Trude Berger, interview 47865, Visual History Archive (VHA), USC Shoah Foundation, Los Angeles, CA, accessed at the Strassler Center, Clark University, May 2, 2010. Trude Berger also recalled the massacre on Förstergasse and heard the shots that killed the last nine Jewish victims in Vienna.

Destroyed bridge in Vienna, 1945. (US Holocaust Memorial Museum, courtesy of Ilana Offenberger)

Vienna. Hiding in a family friend's cellar apartment not far from the canal, "Mischling" Ruth Mirecki heard the blasts and remembers the following day's silence. She cautiously peeked from a window to assess the activity outside and for the first time saw Soviet officers patrolling the streets. She saw no sign of either the SS or Wehrmacht men.[44] These early moments of peacetime provided Viennese residents the first glimpse of the occupation forces that would shape so much of their lives for the next decade.

Survivors' initial reactions were mixed. Those who spoke Slavic languages tried to communicate with their occupiers. Many were surprised by the presence of Jews in Red Army units. Lucia Heilman's mother was shocked when she questioned a soldier in Polish and he replied in Yiddish. He then explained that he too was amazed; he and his comrades never expected to find Jews left alive in Vienna.[45]

---

44. Ruth Merecki, interview 38836, VHA, accessed at USHMM, August 1, 2011.
45. Lucia Heilman, interview 30402, VHA.

Searching for Family

Once the fighting stopped and when all residents, Jews and gentiles, realized that the Soviets had taken over the city, they ventured out to survey the destruction, to find food and water, and to search for surviving friends and family members. Berger and her mother emerged from the basement to discover the second district—and especially their street, Glockengasse—severely damaged. Despite an unexploded bomb that had dropped through the roof into their top-floor apartment, they found Berger's father there, alive. The family cleaned and settled back into their partially destroyed home, where the roof remained unrepaired for many weeks and rain poured in.[46]

Once survivors had accounted for immediate family members in their vicinity, they sought to locate relatives in other parts of the city. With no public transportation in working order, residents moved about on foot, confronting massive destruction and the remnants of battlefields. The fifty-three Allied air raids that the city had endured had damaged 28 percent of buildings in the once-grand capital of the Habsburg Empire and killed 8,769 Viennese civilians.[47]

Berger, hoping to find her maternal grandmother, walked with her mother from the second to the seventh district. They started off across a temporary makeshift bridge erected by the Soviets, which spanned the Danube Canal. In doing so, they traversed the former front lines. In the first few moments of their trek, they passed a corpse and a decapitated head. They walked among dead cavalry horses and took in the appalling devastation that surrounded them. They were relieved to reach the grandmother's apartment and find her at home. Moreover, neighbors had looted a nearby shop and shared their booty, including copious amounts of wine. Berger and her mother also savored the opportunity to wash for the first time in two weeks.[48]

---

46. Berger interview.
47. Walter Kleindel, *Die Chronik Österreichs* (Dortmund: Chronik Verlag, 1984), 537.
48. Berger interview.

Securing Basic Needs

Jews and gentiles alike emerged from shelter taken in the last moments of war to discover a changed and partially destroyed Vienna. Citizens navigated the rubble to begin the process of starting lives anew, struggling simply to secure basic needs. The city lacked infrastructure, resources, a skilled labor force, and energy sources. Perhaps most immediately significant was the scarcity of food. In spring and summer 1945, the urban population subsisted on a near-starvation diet of 250–800 calories per person. In the first weeks, the Red Army provided dried peas in bulk, which staved off actual starvation.[49] Survivors often recall those worm-ridden peas and how tired they became of eating them, day after day.

City residents waited in long lines to secure food. This situation presented a quirky benefit for some Jewish survivors, as their identity papers marked with a *J* sometimes helped them to the front of the queue with sympathetic shopkeepers. That which had represented doom only days before suddenly offered potential benefit. This turn of status prompted a former-Nazi neighbor to glibly ask Trude Berger how she too might obtain a "J-Ausweis"; Berger admitted that she had flaunted her sudden privilege by showing her neighbor bread she had gotten in such a way.[50] This short supply of basic food goods, as well as other necessities, also provided fertile ground for a flourishing black market that both Jews and non-Jews alike utilized.

Not all emerging survivors could reclaim or return to their apartments. For the homeless, securing a place to live became a top priority. Somewhat surprisingly, a number of Jews found new apartments quite easily in the first chaotic weeks of peacetime, well before laws about restitution went into effect. Many homes stood completely furnished but empty, after their Nazi residents fled the approaching Soviet Army just days before. On May 8, 1945, Elizabeth Welt Trahan and her father returned

---

49. Jill Lewis, "Dancing on a Tight Rope: The Beginning of the Marshall Plan," in *The Marshall Plan in Austria*, ed. Günter Bischof, Anton Pelinka, and Dieter Stiefel (New Brunswick, NJ: Transaction, 2000), 142.

50. Berger interview.

to their former apartment on the Strudlhofgasse and found it occupied.[51] The Nazi tenants who had lived one floor below had left, however, and Trahan and her father assumed residence there. While setting up house, Trahan found the previous inhabitants' copy of *Mein Kampf* in a drawer and threw it away immediately. She feared that somehow the Soviet occupiers might find it among their possessions and mistake them for Nazi sympathizers.[52] The Soviets also assigned such recently vacated homes to others. Occupation authorities gave Lucia Heilman and her mother a former Nazi's apartment. Heilman recalled that, at first, she simply sat and looked around her. She had forgotten how an apartment looked after more than four years of hiding in a metal workshop. "There was a table and a chair and an armoire. It was an apartment, with curtains. It was amazing to me!"[53]

By August 1945, however, the provisional Austrian government had taken responsibility for the assignment of property, and problems and uncertainties arose. The central office created to handle such claims annulled the decisions the local council had reached under Soviet supervision and declared them "not yet legal," thus protecting those who had exploited the benefits of Nazi "Aryanization" policies. Thus, Jews who had regained their former businesses feared losing them again.[54] Jews and gentiles alike sought assistance with housing arrangements at the municipal *Wohnungsamt* (housing office). As officials matched the homeless with vacant apartments, they too provided Jews with the unoccupied homes of Nazis who had fled, but always with the stipulation that they agree to relinquish the property to the "rightful" owners, should they return. Historian and Jewish survivor Jonny Moser recalled that his family agreed to this condition, and without a second thought. They simply needed a place to live. The Mosers were lucky;

---

51. In 1946, Elisabeth Welt and her father were registered as living at Strudlhofgasse 12/14 in Vienna's ninth district. See Liste der in Wien lebenden Glaubensjuden, 1946, 3.1.1.3/78805460/ ITS Digital Archive, USHMM.
52. Trahan, *Walking with Ghosts*, 214.
53. Heilman interview.
54. "Confusion in Austria Makes It Difficult for Jews to Regain Their Former Dwellings," Jewish Telegraphic Agency, August 30, 1945.

the previous occupants never returned, and the family could remain in their new home.[55]

Arrangements for furnishings presented a problem for many survivors, and the municipality tasked an office with providing those in need with basic home goods, if only temporarily. The city of Vienna gave Gertrude Putschin's family a Nazi's abandoned furniture "on loan" and with the same requirement that they give it back in the event of his or her return. In Putschin's case, that person did come back and claimed the furniture. "I don't know exactly how he got it back," she said, "but in any case, we had to return it."[56] Many survivors speak of the obligation imposed on them by city authorities to return Nazi property they used after the war. The irony of the situation escaped no one; much of this "loaned" furniture had originally been stolen from Jews after the Anschluss.

Beginning to Reestablish Lives

Reemerging survivors confronted the challenge of habituating to the activities and tasks of daily life that were foreign to them under Nazi oppression. Suddenly they were to interact with the same people they had avoided or from whom they had hidden. Those coming out of concealment relearned the use of regular speaking voices after years of whispering. Children encountered others their own age, some for the first time. Trude Berger felt a deep sense of freedom after seven years of secrecy and distrust. Berger and her father reveled in speaking their minds without the need to guard their words, with no worry as to who might overhear, although Berger's mother scolded them for doing so.[57] Berger's mother remained cautious, conditioned by her experiences and with fear and distrust for the gentiles

---

55. Jonny Moser, interview with author, Vienna, Austria, February 9, 2011. Also see Jonny Moser, *Wallenbergs Laufbursche: Jugenderinnerungen, 1938–1945* (Vienna: Picus Verlag, 2006), 349–50.

56. Brigitte Bailer, Florian Freund, Elisabeth Klamper, Wolfgang Neugebauer, Gerhard Ungar, and Brigitte Ungar-Klein, *Erzählte Geschichte: Berichte von Widerstandskämpfern und Verfolgten*, vol. 3, *Jüdische Schicksale* (Vienna: Österreichischer Bundesverlag, 1992), 687–88.

57. Berger interview.

among whom they lived and who so shortly before had participated in their persecution.

Above all, survivors confronted the insecurities and skepticism they had developed toward their neighbors over the course of the Nazi regime. After Lucia Heilman and her mother left their hiding place in Mr. Duschka's workshop, the older woman trusted no one and asserted her belief that "99 percent of all Austrians [were] Nazis." Lucia claimed not to have encountered much antisemitism after the war but added, "at least none to my face."[58] Survivors knew that, blatant or not, Austrian antisemitism had existed for centuries, paving the way for their neighbors' enthusiastic and thorough participation in the Nazi expropriation of Jews' property, followed by their expulsion and mass murder. Surely, this did not disappear from one day to the next. This awareness coupled with caution after the violence and murder of the previous years guided Viennese Jews' careful maneuvering to return to life in their hometown.

REBUILDING IN THE CONTEXT OF POSTWAR OCCUPATION

The first phase of Vienna's occupation began upon the Soviet conquest of the city in April 1945. Surviving Jews reemerged into a partially destroyed city that lacked most basic supplies. The Red Army worked to reconstruct an infrastructure and to provide for residents, but soldiers' feelings of anger and revenge after a traumatic, brutal, and costly war sometimes took the form of aggression and violence.

As everyone in Vienna awaited the arrival of the Western Allies and the assumption of their occupation duties, Austrian politicians filled leadership roles to shape a new government and at the same time set in motion the formation of a postwar Austrian identity as the Nazis' first victim, a myth that would endure for decades. Founded in the wording of the Allies' 1943 Moscow Declaration and augmented and sustained by all four occupation

---

58. Heilman interview.

powers' eventual endorsement and acceptance, this "victim myth" guided Austrian foreign and domestic policy.[59] Throughout the tumult of postwar reconstruction and international public knowledge of the extent and ruthlessness of the Nazi genocidal campaign, Austria saw little reduction in antisemitism among its citizens or leaders. On the contrary, new ways of discrimination and persecution emerged with the new role of Austria and Austrians as "victim."

Soviet Occupiers

The first Red Army troops arrived after advancing from the east through Hungary, along the way witnessing Wehrmacht and SS crimes firsthand. Compounded with the knowledge of atrocity and mass murder that the Germans and their allies committed against these soldiers' families and communities at home, the Soviets found civility and compassion difficult in their roles as occupation troops and frequently turned to revenge.

Many Austrian women suffered rape by Red Army soldiers, and even more recall the persistent fear of such assault. Although no confirmed statistics exist regarding the number and rate of occurrence of sexual assault,[60] it is estimated that as many as 270,000 rapes were reported under the Soviet occupation in Austria, 240,000 of them in Vienna and Lower Austria, 10,000 in the province of Styria, and 20,000 in Burgenland. Many women suffered not one but between two and four rapes, and many of the rapists were repeat offenders.[61] Soviet soldiers' knowledge of Nazi policy and practice inflicted on their families, communities, and compatriots fueled their anger and desire for revenge, and Austrian women often became their targets.

---

59. See US Congress, Senate Committee on Foreign Relations, and US Department of State, *A Decade of American Foreign Policy: Basic Documents, 1941–49* (Washington, DC: Government Printing Office, 1950).

60. Irene Bandhauer-Schöffmann and Ela Hornung, "War and Gender Identity: The Experience of Austrian Women, 1945–1950," in *Austrian Women in the Nineteenth and Twentieth Centuries: Cross-Disciplinary Perspectives*, ed. David F. Good, Margarete Grandner, and Mary Jo Maynes (Providence, RI: Berghahn Books, 1996), 219.

61. Marianne Enigl and Christa Zöchling, "Die ungeliebten Befreier," *Profil*, May 7, 2012, 33.

The Red Army pillaged Austrian industry and equipment systematically, as it did in its occupation zones in Germany. The Allies had decided on the issue of reparations at the July 1945 Potsdam Conference, where they determined that the Soviets would seize German industrial machinery and equipment from their occupation zones, as well as 15 percent of what the Western Allies' confiscated and another 10 percent of all such industrial equipment. The Western Allies were to take reparations from German assets abroad and from gold reserves in Germany.[62] Historian Vladislav M. Zubok writes that Germany and Austria ended up constituting "a giant shopping mall," where the Soviets did not pay for a thing. Some 100,000 railcars reached the Soviet Union in the first few months of the occupation packed full of "construction materials" and "household goods," including some 60,000 pianos, 459,000 radios, 188,000 carpets, almost a million "pieces of furniture," 3.3 million pairs of shoes, and 1.2 million coats.[63]

At the same time, during the first few months of the Soviets' solo occupation of Austria, they worked to reestablish municipal services, to restore gas and electricity, and to feed the population suffering from food shortages. Such efforts sometimes seemed to be at the expense of the occupation troops, and soldiers raised complaints that civilians received better rations. In Burgenland, the easternmost province of Austria and located in the Soviet occupation zone, for example, Red Army soldiers received six hundred calories per day less than the civilians at the beginning of 1946.[64] With necessities scarce, a black market flourished, and Soviet officers and soldiers took part along with Austrians.

Seeking to assemble a governmental structure and support for Soviet interests, Stalin's generals and representatives in Vienna acted on the head start gained by being the first to arrive in the capital. Days after their conquest of Vienna and before the official end of the war in Europe, they set in motion the assembly of Austrian leadership most favorable for the Soviet

---

62. Nana Sagi, *German Reparations: A History of Negotiations* (Jerusalem: Magnes Press, Hebrew University, 1986), 10–13.
63. Vladislav M. Zubok, *Failed Empire: The Soviet Union in the Cold War from Stalin to Gorbachev* (Chapel Hill: University of North Carolina Press, 2009), 9.
64. Enigl and Zöchling, "Die ungeliebten Befreier," 35.

Union. This group of Austrian politicians went on to organize a provisional government that laid the footings of postwar Austrian identity formation with regard to both foreign and domestic policy.

The Renner Government

Austrian politicians of the postwar provisional government worked diligently to sidestep culpability for Nazi war crimes by immediately placing total blame on the Germans. They ultimately took advantage of evolving Cold War politics to pit Western powers against the Soviets for financial gain and to secure all four Allies' acceptance of the narrative of Austria as the Nazis' first victim. Ignoring both the voluntary and thoroughly nonviolent nature of the union of Austria with Germany and the frenzied, joyful welcome that Nazi troops received upon entering the country, Dr. Karl Renner and his government rewrote the Anschluss as an aggressive military invasion and occupation of a foreign power. They maintained that from 1938 to 1945 Austria had ceased to exist and therefore was not responsible for Nazi crimes. Further, the German occupiers had forced Austria into an unwanted war. With this logic, Austria as a country and all Austrians as individuals were victims. The "victim myth" became official Austrian foreign policy, putting in place a decades-long discourse that also involved antisemitism, as in this narrative all Austrians were victims and no subgroup was to be singled out as special or different. With this argument, politicians also made great efforts to avoid providing aid to surviving Jews, particularly those living abroad.

Within days of taking Vienna in April 1945, the Soviets unilaterally appointed Renner as interim chancellor of Austria and tasked him with assembling a provisional government. Renner had been the chancellor of the First Austrian Republic immediately after World War I and the last president of Parliament before the Austrofascist period. In the final days of the war, he had initiated contact with the Soviet Army to negotiate protection for Austrian citizens and to offer his assistance in establishing a postwar government.[65] British and US leaders were infuriated by their exclusion

---

65. Kleindel, *Die Chronik Österreichs*, 539.

from this decision,⁶⁶ and the Western Allies' official recognition of the Renner government came slowly, as they perceived Austria as a potential Soviet puppet, in the fashion of Romania, Bulgaria, and Poland.⁶⁷

Renner's first official statement on April 27, 1945, proclaimed Austrian independence and autonomy and declared the Anschluss null and void. The pronouncement listed the ways Nazi Germany had victimized Austria, including an "occupation" forced on the "helpless" Austrian people, the degradation of Vienna to a provincial city, and the economic and cultural plunder of Austria's priceless art objects and natural resources. The provisional government stated in no uncertain terms that Germany had forced Austria into a war that "no Austrian ever wanted,"⁶⁸ although Renner himself had loudly supported Anschluss with Germany until 1938.⁶⁹ His concerns about the nation's pain, suffering, and damages never included the loss of nearly two hundred thousand Austrian Jews to forced emigration and murder.

Exploiting the Allies' wording of the 1943 Moscow Declaration, the provisional government assigned blame and responsibility to the Germans as invaders and occupiers, characterizing the end of the Nazi regime in Austria as "liberation" by Austrian resistance fighters and the Red Army.⁷⁰ An August 1945 memo from the chancellery about foreign policy and international legal aspects regarding the claims of Jewish victims held Germany solely responsible for Nazi crimes. It rationalized that Austria had not existed as a state from 1938 to 1945 and that the "occupied Ostmark" (as the

---

66. Günter Bischof, "Allied Plans and Policies for the Occupation of Austria, 1938–1955," in *Austria in the Twentieth Century*, ed. Rolf Steininger, Günter Bischof, and Michael Gehler (New Brunswick, NJ: Transaction, 2009), 174.

67. Günter Bischof, "Between East and West: The Origins of Post–World War II Austrian Diplomacy during the Early Occupation Period," in *Austrian Foreign Policy in Historical Context*, ed. Günter Bischof, Anton Pelinka, and Michael Gehler (New Brunswick, NJ: Transaction, 2006), 114.

68. Bundesministerium für Unterricht, *Freiheit für Österreich: Dokumente* (Vienna: Österreichischer Bundesverlag, 1955), 11–14.

69. David Wilsford, *Political Leaders of Contemporary Western Europe: A Biographical Dictionary* (Westport, CT: Greenwood, 1995), 385–86.

70. Heidemarie Uhl, "From Victim Myth to Co-responsibility Thesis: Nazi Rule, World War II, and the Holocaust in Austrian Memory," in *The Politics of Memory in Postwar Europe*, ed. Richard Ned Lebow, Wulf Kansteiner, and Claudio Fogu (Durham, NC: Duke University Press, 2006), 66.

Third Reich province composed of Austrian territory was known) had been powerless to prevent German actions. Therefore, the newly reconstituted Austria was not accountable for Nazi offenses and not responsible for fulfilling Jews' claims for restitution.[71]

The Renner government did pass an Opferfürsorgegesetz (Victims' Welfare Act) in July 1945 for "victims of fascism," which included assistance to those who were persecuted on political grounds and for resistance fighters. It made no provision, however, for those who were oppressed on the basis of race, religion, and nationality.[72] This de facto exclusion of the vast majority of Austrian Jews from qualifying for welfare benefits represents a particularly shameful episode in Austrian history. The nation and its citizens profited immensely from the vast wealth commandeered from Austrian Jews under the Nazi regime. After the war, impoverished, physically abused, and mentally traumatized Jews constituted the most vulnerable and devastated victim group. As part of the postwar quest to cast the nation as the innocent victim of the Germans, however, Austrian law delineated victim groups in a way that comprised most all citizens *except* Jews but included returning Wehrmacht soldiers, lesser implicated Nazis, and bystanders.[73] Governmental victim benefits provided housing, clothing, and food to concentration camp survivors who had been persecuted on political grounds; those who had been mistreated "on racial grounds only" were specifically excluded.[74] The nongovernmental KZ-Verband (concentration camp survivor association) established in 1945 also refused membership to Jews, as well as to Roma and Sinti, homosexuals, and those who had been punished for helping slave laborers.[75] Jewish survivors could turn only to the devastated IKG and foreign Jewish organizations conducting relief work in the city.

---

71. Robert Knight, *"Ich bin dafür, die Sache in die Länge zu ziehen"*: *Wortprotokolle der österreichischen Bundesregierung von 1945–52 über die Entschädigung der Juden* (Frankfurt am Main: Athenäum Verlag, 1988), 105.

72. Bailer et al., *Erzählte Geschichte*, 672.

73. Günter Bischof, "Founding Myths and Compartmentalized Past: New Literature on the Construction, Hibernation, and Deconstruction of World War II Memory in Postwar Austria," in *Austrian Historical Memory and National Identity*, ed. Günter Bischof and Anton Pelinka, Contemporary Austrian Studies 5 (New Brunswick, NJ: Transaction, 1997), 307.

74. Bailer et al., *Erzählte Geschichte*, 672.

75. Embacher, *Neubeginn ohne Illusionen*, 196–98.

The KZ-Verband finally did take on a representative from the IKG and made *Opferausweise* (victim identification papers) available to Jewish victims in 1946.[76] But surviving Jews in Austria were denied the status provided by the government to their non-Jewish compatriots and received neither significant monetary support nor tax relief until 1949. The government fleeced them of what should have been their entitlement as Austrian citizens during the desperate postwar years. For the second time within a decade, the Austrian government robbed the Jews.

Even after victim welfare laws began to accommodate Jews in 1949, specifically complicated language excluded the majority of prewar Austrian Jewry because of a requirement that one hold Austrian citizenship at the time of application for benefits. The Nazi regime had stripped Jews of their nationality before their expulsion or deportation, and to apply to regain it, the postwar Austrian government required that one reside permanently in Austria. Thus, the law rendered ineligible for victims' benefits the more than one hundred thousand Austrian Jews who were living abroad after fleeing the Nazi regime, together with any camp survivors who had declined to return, and they only obtained the possibility of recovery of citizenship much later, in 1952. Legislators also clearly conveyed that any monies provided to Jewish victims were intended to support and assist them as *Austrians*, as it did for other Austrian "victims," and did not constitute a form of *Wiedergutmachung* (compensation).[77]

As the government excluded Jewish Austrians, it at the same time accommodated needy "Austrian war victims," including political persecutees, resistance fighters, and ultimately, veterans of the Wehrmacht. By denying Austrian Jews their rightful citizenship, the postwar government validated the underlying sentiment that their prewar standing as unofficial second-class citizens had been strengthened by seven years of Nazi ideology. Rather than an attitude shift accompanying what seemed a radical change in leadership and the end of persecution and genocide, Nazi racial thought remained embedded in the Austrian national mind-set and in official policy, although the Nuremberg Laws were formally annulled early in

---

76. Bailer et al., *Erzählte Geschichte*, 672.
77. Ibid., 673.

the Second Republic. In the Renner government's fervent effort to portray Austria internationally as distinctly *not* German and to evade blame for misdeeds in which the nation and its citizens actively took part, it revealed its understanding of the massive crimes committed. By erasing details, it defined both the distinctly *German* Nazi crimes and Austria's innocence. The government positioned itself solidly with the Allied endorsement of its "first victim" status and began a decades-long shirking of responsibility and financial obligation to its former citizens, while also framing the development of postwar Austrian national identity.

Western Occupation Powers in Vienna

The Allies officially delineated the four occupation zones of Austria on July 4, 1945, and at the same time established the Allied Council to govern the occupation regime. However, the Soviets worked alone in Vienna until the end of July 1945, when US advance teams arrived to commence preparations for the Allied Council and to set the groundwork for quadripartite control. Upon the urging of US General Mark W. Clark, the other Western powers joined the United States in Vienna in early fall 1945, and the first Allied Council meeting took place on September 12, 1945.[78] By early 1946, the Allies had approximately 260,000 troops in Austria, a number that included 150,000 Soviet, 55,000 British, 40,000 US, and 15,000 French soldiers.[79]

Even before the end of the war, seeds of coming Cold War tensions had spurred the British and Americans to worry about the spread of communism. Their planning for postwar Austria included the intention of handling the country to weaken both German and Soviet domination in eastern Europe. The British, the French, and the Americans set their sights on securing a neutral, autonomous Austria that would work toward the containment of Soviet expansion.[80]

---

78. Bischof, "Allied Plans and Policies," 175.
79. Enigl and Zöchling, "Die ungeliebten Befreier," 38.
80. Bischof, "Allied Plans and Policies," 167–68.

The Western powers finally recognized the Renner government on October 20, 1945,[81] and the start of the official four-power occupation helped launch it into a position of ruling the entire country. The Allies ultimately endorsed the "first victim" version of Austrian World War II history. All four accepted the fabrication, placing a higher priority on the political and economic integration of Austria in the context of increasing Cold War politics. The Western Allies' embrace of this view of Austria under the Nazis entailed dropping interest in denazification, demilitarization, and disarmament, all to quell the perceived threat of Austrian Communist leaders and a potential Soviet takeover.[82] At the same time, the Soviets felt wary of Austria becoming an "American colony," and they too supported Austrian neutrality. Cunning Austrian politicians exploited the Western Allies' fears of Soviet expansion to gain further investment, ultimately finding form in the funds of the US Marshall Plan, which also served to ease the economic burden created by the Red Army's exploitation of its occupation zone for de facto war reparations.[83] Austria secured its desired postwar identity as victim of the Nazis and in doing so dodged moral and financial responsibility for the many Austrian hands in Nazi crimes.

The First Austrian Elections

Throughout the initial power struggles, antisemitism in government remained constant. In October 1945, Aaron Ehrlich, the president of the Jewish Merchants' Association of Vienna, publicly cited the antisemitic speeches of Leopold Kunschak, prominent member of the Austrian People's Party and then deputy mayor of Vienna, and complained that Nazis still held governmental positions and that their anti-Jewish sentiments influenced the granting of licenses, the reinstatement of citizenship, and the allocation of housing. Gaining no support from the Austrian government,

---

81. Bischof, "Between East and West," 127.
82. Günter Bischof, *Austria in the First Cold War, 1945–55: The Leverage of the Weak* (New York: St. Martin's, 1999), 3.
83. Bischof, "Allied Plans and Policies," 178.

Ehrlich specified that the Jewish community waited and hoped for the Allied occupation officials' intervention.[84]

The first federal elections (November 25, 1945) ushered in a coalition government of the conservative People's Party and the Socialist Party, which lasted for more than twenty years.[85] Chancellor Leopold Figl continued Renner's foreign and domestic policies, including selling Austria as the Nazis' "first victim" to the international community to reestablish Austrian national identity as particularly anti-German.[86]

Election results proved disappointing for the Jewish community. Jewish leaders expressed dismay that not one Jew gained elected office, although the provisional Renner government had included three.[87] To make matters worse, well-known antisemites including Kunschak and Julius Raab in newly attained official positions reflected the preferences of the electorate. Kunschak had spent seven years in a Nazi concentration camp, convicted as a Catholic anti-Nazi, which lent him antifascist credibility. But he was also well known as a Catholic populist and militant antisemite from 1918, if not earlier. A speech he gave on April 16, 1946, offered examples of his views: "The Polish Jews should not come to Austria; we Austrians don't need the others either! . . . Austrian industry should not fall into Jewish hands."[88] Raab had been the leader of the Lower Austrian Heimwehr and was an active leader in the Austrofascist regime. Despite his political activity and although he held the position of minister of commerce under Schuschnigg at the time of the Anschluss (he was appointed just four weeks before), he

---

84. "Anti-semitism in Austria Is Now as Strong as Under the Nazis, Jewish Leader Charges," *Jewish Telegraphic Agency*, October 3, 1945.

85. The present-day Sozialdemokratische Partei Österreichs (the SPÖ, or Austrian Social Democratic Party) was founded on January 1, 1889, as the Sozialdemokratische Arbeiterpartei Österreichs (SDAPÖ, or Austrian Social Democratic Workers' Party). It retained the name through the end of World War II, when members adopted the title Sozialistischepartei Österreichs (the SPÖ, or Austrian Socialist Party). In 1991, it assumed the current title, Sozialdemokratische Partei Österreichs. "Geschichte der österreichischen Sozialdemokratie," Rot Bewegt (the website of the history of the SPÖ), accessed June 25, 2013, http://www.rotbewegt.at.

86. Bischof, "Between East and West," 127.

87. "Austrian Provisional Government Includes Three Jews: Largest Number Ever Named to Cabinet," *Jewish Telegraphic Agency*, May 3, 1945.

88. Robert S. Wistrich, *A Lethal Obsession: Antisemitism from Antiquity to the Global Jihad* (New York: Random House, 2010), 217.

was able to escape Nazi persecution with the help of the Lower Austrian Nazi gauleiter Hugo Jury. Raab was well known as an antisemite; among other public evidence, he referred to Social Democrat Otto Bauer as "ein Saujud" (dirty Jew).[89] Chancellor Figl's response in defense of Raab's and Kunschak's appointments was telling. He explained, for example, that Kunschak "is not antisemitic on racial grounds, but economic grounds."[90] The Allied Control Commission actually vetoed Raab's appointment but permitted him to remain a member of Parliament; he later became Austrian chancellor (1953–61). Kunschak, however, retained his position.[91]

The IKG feared that the results would deter the repatriation of Austrian Jews who were still abroad and that those in Austria would become more determined to emigrate.[92] The Austrian Communist Party had also expected to earn a greater representation in the government but gained only 5 percent of the votes. After years of Nazi anti-Bolshevik propaganda, the anticommunist sentiment that existed before the Anschluss, and the more recent experience with the Soviet occupiers, Austrian voters felt no warmth for or interest in voting for Communist Party candidates.

RESTORING THE JEWISH COMMUNITY

In a September 1983 interview in *Gemeinde*, the Viennese Jewish community's monthly magazine, the IKG president at the time, Iwan Hacker, reflected on the immediate postwar months. No one believed in a future for the Kultusgemeinde at the time, he stated. On the contrary, he explained, most Viennese Jews thought that any formal Jewish institution in the capital

---

89. John Warren, "'Weiße Strümpfe oder neue Kutten': Cultural Decline in Vienna in the 1930s," in *Interwar Vienna: Culture between Tradition and Modernity*, ed. Deborah Holmes and Lisa Silverman (Rochester, NY: Camden House, 2009), 41.

90. "Anti-semites Named to Austrian Cabinet: Allied Council Must Approve Choices," Jewish Telegraphic Agency, December 10, 1945.

91. "Austrian Government Drops One Anti-semite after Allied Protest, but Retains Another," Jewish Telegraphic Agency, December 18, 1945.

92. "Anti-semites Win Seats in Austrian National Council: Jewish Leaders Fearful," Jewish Telegraphic Agency, December 3, 1945.

would simply serve as a cemetery office.[93] Indeed, Jewish leaders, who nonetheless planned to stay in Vienna themselves, considered their community temporary (*Liquidationsgemeinde*) and believed that sooner or later it would cease to exist.[94] The numbers were undeniably bleak. The Jewish community, once more than 185,000 official members strong, counted fewer than 5,000 by the end of 1945. The Nazis had forced the emigration of some 130,000 Austrian Jews and murdered 65,459.[95]

Reconstituting the IKG

As returning émigrés and camp survivors slowly started to join Vienna's remaining Jews, the reviving IKG encountered numerous obstacles in restoring its community and institutions. Allied bombs had damaged the IKG headquarters on the Seitenstettengasse and destroyed most of its official records. After the Soviet occupation, the IKG gathered the surviving property and papers and moved them by horse and cart to the community-owned building at Schottenring 25, where it reestablished a central office.[96] The Nazi-appointed Ältestenrat continued its leadership of the IKG in the immediate postwar days,[97] but ultimately many wartime officials were relieved of their duties. In June 1945, the provisional government's representative responsible for matters that included Jewish affairs named Professor Heinrich Schur as interim director of the IKG.[98] Schur had survived the war in the capital protected by his non-Jewish wife and had headed the department of internal medicine at the Jewish hospital on the Malzgasse. For no apparent reason, Schur resigned shortly thereafter.

---

93. Embacher, *Neubeginn ohne Illusionen*, 21.
94. Susanne Cohen-Weisz, *Jewish Life in Austria and Germany since 1945: Identity and Communal Reconstruction* (Budapest: Central European University Press, 2016), 88.
95. Embacher, *Neubeginn ohne Illusionen*, 19–21 (130,000); Jonny Moser, "Der Verfolgung der Juden," in Neugebauer, *Widerstand und Verfolgung in Wien*, 202 (65,459).
96. Evelyn Adunka, *Die Vierte Gemeinde: die Geschichte der Wiener Juden von 1945 bis heute* (Berlin: Philo Fine Arts, 2000), 18.
97. *Bericht des Präsidiums der Israelitischen Kultusgemeinde Wien über die Tätigkeit in den Jahren 1945 bis 1948* (Vienna: Israelitische Kultusgemeinde Wien, 1948), 3.
98. Adunka, *Die Vierte Gemeinde*, 20.

Front door of the Seitenstettengasse synagogue, 1945–46. It was the only synagogue in Vienna that was not destroyed during the November Pogrom. The sign on the door indicates the times of religious services. (US Holocaust Memorial Museum; courtesy of Paul Grisso)

The provisional government designated David Brill the acting director of the IKG on September 24, 1945, and the leadership and atmosphere finally began to stabilize.[99]

By the end of summer 1945, returning survivors of concentration camps made up a significant portion of the IKG's constituency. Pulling together a professional staff from this physically and psychologically traumatized pool proved challenging, and determining the best ways to serve this impoverished, malnourished, and emotionally distraught group represented the community's greatest problem. The needs of their members were previously unimaginable and unprecedented.

---

99. *Bericht des Präsidiums*, 3–5.

Meeting the Needs of a Traumatized Community

Before 1938, looking after the community's religious affairs and a few associated charitable activities had occupied the IKG leaders and staff. After the Holocaust, the priorities and tasks shifted dramatically. In 1945, no Jewish cultural or communal life remained, and the IKG had not yet resumed offering religious education. Youth-group efforts, such as the reestablishment of the Jewish community's athletic association in Vienna, Hakoah, represented the only Zionist life in the city.[100] As survivor and postwar resident of Vienna Leon Zelman has written, "[The IKG was] confronted with tasks we can't imagine today . . . just to make basic life possible."[101]

Over the course of the first postwar year, the IKG created new departments to meet the particular needs of returnees. In May 1945, the IKG's newly founded Fürsorgeabteilung (Welfare Department) reported that it had already provided financial support, clothing, and furniture to 450 Jews returning from concentration camps or emerging from hiding in Vienna. The IKG regained its 120-bed hospital on Malzgasse and assumed care for the 150 residents in its nursing home, as it did for the 20 children living in the *Kinderheim* at the community's recovered pediatric hospital. A lending library, an emergency soup kitchen, and a variety of workshops providing for the Kultusgemeinde's needs began or resumed work to support the community.[102]

A December 21, 1945, article in the New York–based German-language Jewish refugee (and anti-Nazi) publication *Aufbau* depicted the US High Commissioner for Austria General Clark and the forces under his command as particularly helpful to Vienna's Jews and their negotiations with the Allies to recoup property and institutions in their different zones of occupation. According to the report, by the last week of 1945, the IKG had regained and was running a hospital with 81 patients at Malzgasse 16; a nursing home with a special section for concentration camp returnees with

---

100. Kurt Lubinski, "Mission nach Wien," *Aufbau*, October 18, 1946, 2.
101. Leon Zelman, "Wiener jüdische Gemeinde nach 1945," *Mitteilungsblatt der Aktion gegen den Antisemitismus* 120 (November 1990), quoted in Embacher, *Neubeginn ohne Illusionen*, 29.
102. Adunka, *Die Vierte Gemeinde*, 18.

109 residents (82 in the home's hospital section) at Malzgasse 7; a home for concentration camp survivors with 30 residents at Tempelgasse 3; a home for concentration camp survivors with 52 residents at Unteren Augartenstraße 35; a home for concentration camp survivors with 306 residents at Seegasse 9; a former Jewish community bathing facility at Flossgasse 14 (to be converted for new use after repairing bomb damage); a lending library with 115 registered members at Seitenstettengasse 4, as well as a clothing-distribution and shoe-repair workshop at the same address; and the community's ceremonial halls at gates 1 and 4 at the Zentralfriedhof, Vienna's main cemetery (both had been destroyed by the Nazis during the November Pogrom and were unusable at the time of the IKG's recovery in 1945).[103]

In addition to the dramatically altered needs of the community, the postwar IKG also attracted new segments of the population to its membership. Many of those who took active roles in rebuilding the IKG had had marginal to no contact with a Jewish identity or with the Jewish community before 1938. In addition, many were politically affiliated with the Austrian Communist and Socialist Parties, and Communists dominated community leadership from 1945 to 1948.[104]

Support of Foreign Organizations

The postwar IKG depended on the financial support of foreign (primarily American) Jewish organizations. In particular, the American Jewish Joint Distribution Committee (Joint or JDC) played a crucial role in providing for survivors' urgent needs. Helga Embacher posited that the rebuilding of the IKG depended entirely on American Jewish organizations.[105] In the IKG's 1945–48 report of activities, the leadership specifically thanked the American Jewish community and American Jewish organizations for their assistance.[106]

---

103. "Vom Leben der Juden in Wien," *Aufbau*, December 21, 1945, 24.
104. Embacher, *Neubeginn ohne Illusionen*, 21.
105. Ibid., 28.
106. *Bericht des Präsidiums der Israelitischen Kultusgemeinde Wien*, 8.

The IKG and the Joint took the firm position of utilizing their limited resources to support Jewish community members only. The pre-Anschluss IKG, like other religious communities in Austria, had received monies from the state collected through a government-regulated tax on official members. These funds supported IKG services and institutions in the city, and contributors to the system were entitled to its benefits. Those who had left the formal community for whatever reason—most did so in order to marry non-Jews—had officially relinquished their membership and were no longer considered part of the community and thus held no claim to its support or services.

Before March 1938, the logic of this policy went unquestioned. The postwar IKG, however, encountered challenges when surviving "Mischlinge" and spouses in mixed marriages sought assistance as Jews. Persecuted on the basis of Nazi race laws for more than seven years, many felt entitled to assistance, although they had not been members of the IKG nor did they seek to be.[107] Others sought membership for the first time, some of them intent on showing solidarity. IKG members and leadership treated such new affiliates with suspicion, concerned that they officially joined the community to ensure the receipt of material benefits, such as Joint care packages.[108] Similar issues occurred in German Jewish communities. Rabbi Nathan Peter Levinson fled Nazi Germany to the United States in 1941 and returned to Germany in 1950 at the urging of Dr. Leo Baeck. According to Levinson's testimony, many people sought conversion to Judaism in the first postwar years. Among the reasons he lists included protest against the Nazis to identify as victims as well as, on the other end of the spectrum, opportunism—to get care packages.[109]

The Jewish community held that only those who identified as Jews— that is, members—had the right to assistance from the IKG with its

---

107. Melvin S. Goldstein, AJDC Paris, to AJDC New York, May 11, 1946, general letter #363, frame 0943, file 119, Collection AR45/54, Archives of the American Jewish Joint Distribution Committee (JDC Archives), New York, NY.

108. Embacher, *Neubeginn ohne Illusionen*, 48–49.

109. Michael Brenner, *After the Holocaust: Rebuilding Jewish Lives in Postwar Germany* (Princeton, NJ: Princeton University Press, 1997), 109.

limited funds. Dr. J. Benson Saks, the Joint's chief of Austrian operations, outlined the IKG's and his own organization's rationale for their policies in a letter to General Clark dated January 8, 1946. "From the point of view of [the] Jewish Community of Vienna," he explained, "and from that of traditional Judaism throughout the world, a person who has forsaken the faith and whose children are raised in another faith, or in no faith at all, are not viewed as Jews within terms of primary responsibility for their care and maintenance."[110]

In fact, JDC leadership had anticipated the dilemma of responsibility for and care of unaffiliated or Nazi-identified Jews, even before the end of the war, and stood fast in its endorsement of IKG policy.[111] Both the IKG and the JDC took the position that resources would be distributed based on the persecution suffered by the recipient. For example, they reasoned that "Mischlinge" and spouses in mixed marriages who had survived in Vienna under the Nazis had had access to food rations and other supplies, which justified their place at the bottom of that hierarchy. Joint representatives made it clear that if they possessed the means to help all those in need, they would do so. Given the situation and lack of resources, however, they maintained that only formal community members received benefits.[112]

In *Jews, Germans, and Allies: Close Encounters in Occupied Germany*, historian Atina Grossmann provides a description of a similar situation in postwar German Jewish communities. "In bizarre counterpoint to Nazi efforts to categorize Jews and 'Aryans,' an extraordinary amount of pained energy was now devoted to determining who was Jewish and who was not, whose defection had occurred under sufficient duress to be forgiven, and who was judged underserving of the modest but all-important relief services and packets offered by the Magistrat, the Jewish community, and Jewish aid organizations." Grossmann also points out that the Joint pressured

---

110. Dr. J. Benson Saks, Chief, Austrian Operations, American Joint Distribution Committee, to General Mark W. Clark, General in Command, US Forces Austria, January 8, 1946, frame 0945, file 119, Collection AR45/54, JDC Archive.

111. Embacher, *Neubeginn ohne Illusionen*, 50.

112. Saks to Clark, January 8, 1946, frame 0947.

the community into making such distinctions and that the community in turn credited the JDC for this uncomfortable restriction.[113]

Postwar issues of *Aufbau* illustrate the active interest and role of support taken by American Jewish organizations and individuals. This publication of the German-Jewish Club (later the New World Club) served as the mouthpiece for German-Jewish immigrants in the United States and evolved into a weekly anti-Nazi publication of the German press in exile under the leadership of Manfred George in the 1930s. It also provided readers news and information about the remnants of Europe's devastated Jewish communities and lists of survivors. Advertisements for organizations offering to ship packages of food and supplies to Jews in Europe filled its pages, and many specified their service to Vienna's Jews. *Aufbau* also publicized charity events held to raise money to help recovering Jews in Europe. An article on December 21, 1945, for example, described a benefit held earlier that month in Los Angeles. Organized by former Hakoah athletes to raise money to assist their fellow members and needy Jews in Vienna, the event raised the funds for the shipment of one hundred food parcels.[114]

The "Denazification" of the IKG

As the IKG reconstructed itself, controversy arose about the continuity of leadership. In 1945, the Allies brought to trial former Ältestenrat leaders, Jewish community employees, and Jewish doctors from the Jewish hospital to answer for their functions during the Nazi regime. The IKG naturally found this task most difficult and awkward. Nazi policies of robbery, forced emigration, and genocide had forced community leaders to cooperate with orders and regulations surrounding the deportation of the Jewish

---

113. Atina Grossmann, *Jews, Germans, and Allies: Close Encounters in Occupied Germany* (Princeton, NJ: Princeton University Press, 2007), 96–97. Historian Jay Howard Geller further points out that the Arbeitsgemeinschaft jüdischer Gemeinden in Deutschland (Working Alliance of Jewish Communities in Germany) forbade Jews married to non-Jews to serve on community boards. See Geller, *Jews in Post-Holocaust Germany, 1945–1953* (Cambridge: Cambridge University Press, 2005), 65.

114. "Gemütlicher Wiener Abend in Los Angeles," *Aufbau*, December 21, 1945, 15.

community. As Embacher points out, they did not have much room to maneuver under their Nazi oppressors. Jewish leaders had held little influence over the transports or the number of deportees the Nazis required, and they did not compile the deportation lists themselves. Nonetheless, the larger Jewish community credited them with more power than they actually had. The Jewish community had observed that some functionaries did have a modicum of leeway to negotiate in favor of special groups, like Jewish veterans, the ill, and IKG employees and their immediate family members. As a result, many community members viewed them as collaborators with the Nazi oppressors.[115]

In May 1945, the Soviets arrested and imprisoned Dr. Josef Löwenherz, the director of the IKG and Ältestenrat under the Nazis, and conducted a three-month investigation of his activities. Löwenherz had been executive director at the time of the Anschluss, and Adolf Eichmann himself pressed him into continuing his leadership role and consequently into assuming ultimate responsibility and oversight for the heartbreaking work with which Eichmann's men tasked IKG staff. Löwenherz's deputy Dr. Benjamin Murmelstein, the former rabbi at the Kluckygasse synagogue in Vienna's twentieth district and a Kultusgemeinde religion teacher, functioned as head of the IKG's Emigration Department and later, after his deportation, as a *Judenrat* (Jewish council) leader in Terezín.[116] There, in addition to his ambiguous role, Murmelstein's disposition and temper were well known, and inmates detested him. As news of his work assembling deportation lists for the Nazis spread, some Jews called him "Murmelschwein" (Murmel-pig).[117]

Controversy surrounded the work of the IKG under the Nazis and that of Löwenherz and Murmelstein in particular. They had headed the group responsible first for the successful emigration of more than 130,000 Austrian

---

115. Helga Embacher, "Viennese Jewish Functionaries on Trial: Accusations, Defense Strategies and Hidden Agendas," in *Jewish Honor Courts: Revenge, Retribution, and Reconciliation in Europe and Israel after the Holocaust*, ed. Laura Jockusch and Gabriel N. Finder (Detroit: Wayne State University Press, 2015), 182.
116. Rabinovici, *Instanzen der Ohnmacht*, 158.
117. Carla Cohn, *My Nine Lives* (Buckinghamshire, UK: Shield Crest, 2010), 63.

Jews and then the deportations that sent more than 65,000 persons to their deaths. After the war, some Jews claimed that they owed Löwenherz and Murmelstein their lives. Others accused the director and his deputy of collaborating with the Nazis and taking part in the genocide of their own people. Towiah Friedman, a Holocaust survivor and postwar Nazi hunter, compiled documents to build a criminal case against Löwenherz as Eichmann's "Schützling" (protégé).[118] In the book *Justice in Jerusalem*, Israeli legal expert and politician Gideon Hausner claimed that Murmelstein had served as a "submissive [tool] in the German extermination machinery."[119]

Both men argued that their actions had actually prevented death and loss. Murmelstein claimed that by giving the Nazis one thousand Jews for deportation, they saved another two thousand.[120] In an interview in the 1970s with the renowned filmmaker Claude Lanzmann, Murmelstein also gave examples of ways he felt his work had benefited Jews.[121] He stated that he had striven to protect older Jews (over the age of fifty-five), that he personally prevented a death march from Terezín ordered by Hitler, and that he negotiated to end a practice of replacing those who were exempted from transport lists with the names of other Jews.[122]

Soviet authorities arrested Löwenherz on April 21, 1945.[123] An investigation of his wartime activities took place in Prague, but allegations against him were cleared. About one year later, he was called to and appeared before an *Ehrengericht* (honor court convened by Jewish communities in the

---

118. Towiah Friedman, *Dr. Josef Löwenherz, Direktor der Kultusgemeinde Wien war Schützling Adolf Eichmanns und Brunners, 1938–45: Somit überlebte er den Krieg und das Nazi-Regimes* (Haifa: Institute of Documentation, 1995).

119. Gideon Hausner, *Justice in Jerusalem* (New York: Schocken Books, 1968), 204.

120. Embacher, *Neubeginn ohne Illusionen*, 31.

121. Dr. Benjamin Murmelstein, interview by Claude Lanzmann, videotape recording, 1975, Claude Lanzmann Shoah Collection, Steven Spielberg Film and Video Archive, USHMM. Lanzmann interviewed Murmelstein for his epic documentary *Shoah* but did not use any of the more than eleven hours of video in the final film. The interview can be accessed in full at the USHMM, while some clips are available on the museum's website, along with complete German- and English-language transcripts. Lanzmann used these interviews in his 2013 documentary, *The Last of the Unjust*, which focuses on Murmelstein specifically.

122. Murmelstein interview, tape 3171, camera rolls 50–52, 61–62.

123. Embacher, "Viennese Jewish Functionaries on Trial," 170.

postwar period) organized by Austrian Jewish exile groups in London in 1946. There Löwenherz defended himself and upheld that with the IKG's emigration program, he had saved many Viennese Jews. He also maintained that Eichmann's office had compiled the lists for and arranged the deportations of Jews from Vienna. He was again acquitted of all charges.[124] He and his wife left London immediately after the trial and went to the United States.

Murmelstein was arrested in July 1945 by the Czech government and was detained in Prague for the duration of an eighteen-month investigation. He was accused of collaboration, but the public prosecutor withdrew charges against him from the People's Court of Litoměřice because of insufficient evidence. He was set free once he officially declined to claim compensation for his detention.[125] Although both Löwenherz and his deputy were acquitted, neither returned to live in Vienna. Murmelstein took up postwar residence in Rome, and Löwenherz immigrated to the United States. Each remained in his adopted home for the remainder of his life. Löwenherz died in 1960 and Murmelstein in 1989.[126]

Löwenherz and Murmelstein have always been among the debated characters of this era. The profound complexity of their extraordinary positions as victims forced to serve as functionaries under the Nazis meant that they worked under pressures inconceivable to anyone not in their place or at that time. And, controversial leadership notwithstanding, the efforts of the IKG contributed to the flight of some two-thirds of the Viennese Jewish community through emigration. Passing definitive, measured judgment on them has always proven difficult, to say the least.

Lesser but still powerful figures of the Nazi-era IKG and Ältestenrat also came under scrutiny after 1945. Dr. Emil Tuchman survived in Vienna due to his privileged position as the head of the Jewish community's health service.[127] In April 1945, the Soviet authorities detained him

---

124. Rabinovici, *Instanzen der Ohnmacht*, 407–10.
125. Ibid., 374–75.
126. Adunka, *Die Vierte Gemeinde*, 19.
127. Mitarbeiter des Ältestenrates der Juden in der Seitenstettengasse 2–4, July 24, 1945, 3.1.1.3/78804912/ITS Digital Archive, USHMM.

briefly, but then on September 11, 1945, the Vienna State Police arrested him for criminal charges brought by former Jewish hospital employees.[128] He was described as a feared disciplinarian, even a "Jewish Hitler."[129] Others claimed that he took advantage of his position to protect friends and relatives, took bribes in return for keeping names off deportation lists, and sent individuals whom he did not like or who were otherwise unpopular to concentration camps.[130] But he also received praise for life-saving actions. Josef Rubin-Bittmann said he owed Tuchman his life, as the doctor had held him in the hospital when he found no accommodation as a *U-Boot*. Tuchman also delivered Rubin-Bittmann's son, an act that endangered the physician's life. Tuchman prevailed over the accusations, and although he declined the appointment, his wartime contact with the Red Cross and the Joint resulted in his nomination to the head of the Wiener Joint Komitees.[131]

Tuchmann's arrest by the Vienna State Police was one of a number of criminal proceedings brought against Jewish functionaries. Such proceedings were based on the June 1945 Austrian War Criminal Law (Kriegsverbrechergesetz), which aimed to punish a range of crimes that included offenses surrounding the November Pogrom in 1938, involvement in the deportation of Vienna's Jews, violence and murder in concentration camps and "euthanasia" institutions, and profiteering through so-called Aryanization.[132] That is to say that the Vienna State Police equated the forced cooperation of Jewish functionaries under the Nazis to actual collaboration. Factors including this role taken by the Vienna State Police and many Jews' view of the wartime Jewish community leadership as collaborators contributed to the fact that no actual "honor court" took place in Vienna.[133] The state had taken the role of trying Jewish functionaries along with Austrian Nazi criminals.

---

128. Embacher, "Viennese Jewish Functionaries on Trial," 180.
129. Ibid., 182.
130. Ralph Segalman, "Letters to My Grandchildren" (unpublished memoir of a social worker with the JDC in postwar Vienna, Northridge, CA, 2001), 77.
131. Embacher, *Neubeginn ohne Illusionen*, 36.
132. Embacher, "Viennese Jewish Functionaries on Trial," 166.
133. Ibid., 184.

Jewish leaders who served under Nazi domination would be questioned about their activities for decades to come. The Vienna-based Holocaust survivor and well-known Nazi hunter Simon Wiesenthal, for example, judged any and all of them guilty of collaboration with the Nazis. In 1966, he officially called for the IKG to bar all former *Kapos* (concentration camp prisoners elevated to positions of authority over other prisoners) and *Jüdenrate* (Jewish ghetto leadership) members from Jewish community functions.[134] Despite other survivors' supportive arguments on behalf of some former IKG employees and Jewish prisoner functionaries, and the official exoneration of many, several remained haunted and some committed suicide. Dr. Paul Klaar served as an IKG physician at a collection point in Nazi Vienna. He attempted to take his own life three times after the war and finally died after being run over by a tram on the Ringstraße. In *Last Waltz in Vienna: The Rise and Destruction of a Family, 1842–1942*, Klaar's nephew George Clare insinuated that he believed this too to have been an act of suicide.[135] Memories and conscience also haunted Wilhelm Reisz, a former Jewish *Ausheber* (a marshal who had assisted in finding Jews for deportation) who hanged himself in his jail cell after receiving a sentence of fifteen years in the Austrian people's court for his crimes of collaboration.[136] In describing the position of the leaders of the Viennese Jewish community under the Nazis, Doron Rabinovici has written, "Individuals could resign, report for deportation, or commit suicide."[137] And indeed, after the war, depending on the accusations against them and subsequent consequences, many also stepped back from positions, emigrated abroad on their own, or considered the option of ending their own lives.

As Austrian Jews reemerged from different forms of hiding and as concentration camp survivors began to make their ways home, newspapers

---

134. Tom Segev, *Simon Wiesenthal: The Life and Legends* (New York: Doubleday, 2010), 134.
135. George Clare, *Last Waltz in Vienna: The Rise and Destruction of a Family, 1842–1942* (New York: Holt, Rinehart, and Winston, 1980), 223–24.
136. Rabinovici, *Instanzen der Ohnmacht*, 394.
137. Ibid., 354.

reported to an international audience that Jews did not actually wish to remain in Austria. A letter written by US Army Lieutenant William Perl and published in *Aufbau* in August 1945 related Perl's observation that returnees came only to find relatives and that hardly any wanted to stay in Vienna.[138] The *New York Times* related a January 1946 poll of Viennese Jews that stated that two-thirds of them wished to emigrate from Europe as soon as possible.[139] The *Jüdisches Echo*, an Austrian Jewish cultural and political magazine founded by a Jewish university student association, characterized the immediate postwar Kultusgemeinde as going about its work bureaucratically and claimed it lacked heart.[140]

In fact, Austrian Jews who survived the war in Vienna had "returned" to reestablish their lives, and the IKG reconstituted with its first postwar open elections in the context of the foreign and domestic policies of the Austrian government gelling under the eagerly assumed victim myth. Accustomed to navigating varying degrees of hostility and discrimination before the Anschluss, Viennese Jews had skillfully maneuvered pervasive antisemitism, overt and otherwise, as highly assimilated and acculturated members of society. When the Nazis were finally defeated, Jews who returned reemerged into life in a suddenly occupied Austria, first by the Soviets alone and then with the additional three Western Allies a few months later, where the Allied forces helped ensure them a level of acceptance. Once again, they learned which battles to take on and which to ignore as they assessed the realities of compromises they would have to make to live under a government and among a people that had never intended their return.

Many who survived in the capital never faced an actual or even a philosophical decision about their return home. They simply resurfaced into the society from which the Nazis had brutally thrust them years before and went about tending to immediate daily needs, reestablishing their lives in

---

138. "Besuch in Wien: Ein Brief von Lt. William R. Perl," *Aufbau*, August 3, 1945, 1. Perl fled Vienna to the United States in 1940 and returned to Europe and ultimately Vienna with the US Army as a military intelligence officer. He never returned permanently and lived in the United States for the rest of his life.

139. "3,028 Jews in Vienna Would Quit Austria," *New York Times*, February 14, 1946, 9.

140. Embacher, *Neubeginn ohne Illusionen*, 29.

the only home they had ever known. They were, after all, Viennese, and they navigated politics and society with Viennese sensibilities to coexist in a precarious situation. "Yes," Trude Berger said in an interview, "and that was 'peace,' and relatively speaking it was naturally not yet peaceful, but it was the end of the war."[141]

---

141. Berger interview.

3

KZ RÜCKKEHRER

Coming Home from Concentration Camps

Members of a Soviet infantry brigade liberated the Gross-Rosen concentration camp on February 13, 1945. There, among the smoldering ruins of barracks, they found a handful of exhausted, sick, and starving prisoners. Less than a week before, the Nazis had evacuated the majority of inmates by train or forced death march and burned many of the camp buildings. They left behind those who were too weak to attempt the journey, and among those remaining were Edith and Anni Holzer, twenty-five-year-old twins from Vienna. They had been deported with their parents and partners to Terezín, and all six had been transferred onward to other camps; only Edith and Anni survived.[1] After two years of incarceration in multiple concentration camps, each weighed less than eighty-five pounds at the time of their liberation. With nothing and no one but each other, they shared a vision of their reunion with family and friends in Vienna.[2]

---

1. Dieter J. Hecht, Eleonore Lappin-Eppel, and Michaela Raggam-Blesch, *Topographie der Shoah: Gedächnisorte das zerstörten jüdischen Wien* (Vienna: Mandelbaum Verlag, 2015), 257.
2. Edith (Holzer) Auerhahn and Anni (Holzer) Drill, interview, 495, Dokumentationsarchiv des österreichischen Widerstandes (DÖW), Vienna, Austria.

Their trek back began when the Red Army locked them in a hospital train bound for Minsk, where ostensibly survivors would be provided with much-needed medical care. The atmosphere remained tense and dangerous, however, because of the constant threat of sexual violence. Soviet soldiers had made unwanted advances toward female prisoners from the first moments after liberation. At best, the soldiers propositioned them; more "reasonable" soldiers complained, "I gave you freedom. Aren't you willing to give me anything?"[3] Many others simply raped the women.[4] Over the course of Edith and Anni's train journey, they observed drunken Red Army soldiers' regular visits to the wagons to prey on the female passengers.

When the train stopped at a station in Krakow, the twins escaped and continued toward home on foot, asking for food at farmhouses along the way. They walked as far as Bratislava, where two Austrian men driving a truck to Vienna picked them up. Their new travel companions showed signs of being no less aggressive than their liberators, though, and when they stopped for gas just outside the city, the sisters ran from them and walked the last few miles. Edith and Anni arrived in their hometown on April 20, 1945, more than two months after their liberation and among the first concentration camp survivors to return to Vienna.[5]

The IKG counted fewer than 5,000 official members at the end of 1945. Among them were 1,727 concentration camp survivors.[6] This starved, tortured, and psychologically traumatized group constituted the second wave of Jewish returnees to Vienna, following the reemergence of those who had

---

3. Bella Gutterman, *A Narrow Bridge to Life: Jewish Forced Labor and Survival in the Gross-Rosen Camp System, 1940–1945* (Jerusalem: Yad Vashem Jerusalem, 2008), 225.

4. For more about Soviet liberators raping the Jewish women they had freed and their assertion that the Jewish women owed them something, see Nomi Levenkron, "'Prostitution,' Rape, and Sexual Slavery during World War II," in *Sexual Violence against Jewish Women during the Holocaust*, ed. Sonja Maria Hedgepeth and Rochelle G. Saidel (Lebanon, NH: University Press of New England, 2010), 18.

5. Auerhahn and Drill interview.

6. F. Wilder-Okladek, *The Return Movement of Jews to Austria after the Second World War* (The Hague: Martinus Nijhoff, 1969), 114.

survived in the capital. Although some already harbored hopes of emigrating onward from their country of origin, most camp survivors conceived only of returning to the last place they had been together with family and friends. Returning to a *familial home* formed the core of camp survivors' motivation and drive to go back to Vienna. Reunions would occur at home, whether or not the survivors chose to remain there. And in any case, as Auschwitz survivor Marianne Windholm succinctly stated, "I had nothing ... nowhere else to go."[7] Vienna was home—the only home she and so many others had ever known or could imagine.

RETURN JOURNEYS

Camp survivors found no time for extended celebration after their liberation. Suddenly free but far from home and with neither money nor possessions, they watched fellow prisoners continue to die from disease and malnutrition and began to comprehend the size and scale of the devastation to European Jewry. Basic needs were of their immediate interest, and those with sufficient strength thought of nourishment, a clean place to stay, and the welfare of relatives and friends.

Liberated in camps far from Austria, Viennese Jews had to find passage home. As the Austrian government made no move to help them, survivors relied on their liberators and on their own resourcefulness. Some traveled back on Allied-organized repatriation transports, while others made their own way through a continent still at war. They navigated destroyed roads and railways as they traveled through territories hostile to Jews, and women felt the constant threat of rape in chaotic wartime and postwar situations. Along the way, chance meetings with acquaintances, friends, and relatives almost always brought heartbreaking news. And as survivors approached Vienna, disillusionment and fear increased with their worries about what and who they would—and would not—find upon arrival.

---

7. Marianne Windholm, oral history, RG 50.030*0503, United States Holocaust Memorial Museum (USHMM).

Repatriation Transports

The majority of camp survivors who returned to Vienna traveled back from Terezín, where more than fifteen thousand Austrian Jews had been deported.[8] Terezín, also referred to in German as Theresienstadt, was located outside Prague and served as both camp and ghetto. It opened on November 24, 1941, and first functioned as a transit camp for Czech Jews whom the Nazis later transported to killing centers, concentration camps, and forced-labor camps in the east. Starting with the arrival of fifty Berlin Jews on June 2, 1942, it took the function of ghetto and labor camp to house German, Austrian, and Czech Jews of select categories including those who enjoyed a particular cultural or artistic celebrity, those of certain age groups (both young and old), and German and Austrian military veterans. Toward the end of the war, Terezín received mostly Jewish prisoners (although some non-Jews) who arrived with death marches from many different concentration camps, most from Buchenwald and Gross-Rosen. In all, the Nazis deported 15,266 Austrian Jews to Terezín during the course of its operation.[9]

The high number of elderly prisoners in Terezín became a key part of Nazi propaganda aimed at eliding the true nature of the deportations. They speciously described it as a "spa town" for German Jews' retirement and even staged the town as a seemingly desirable destination in preparation for a Red Cross visit in June 1944. In reality, the aforementioned categories of Jews were collected there for intended deportation to ghettos and killing centers in the east. Operations in Terezín also resembled those of a ghetto. Prisoners wore civilian clothes, took part in cultural and educational events, and labored in a number of workshops. Others maintained and cleaned the buildings, worked in a garden, and served as nurses and orderlies in an infirmary.

---

8. Martin Niklas, "... *Die schönste Stadt der Welt*": *Österreichische Jüdinnen und Juden in Theresienstadt* (Vienna: Dokumentationsarchiv des österreichischen Widerstandes, 2009), 45.

9. USHMM, "Theresienstadt," accessed February 25, 2018, https://www.ushmm.org/wlc/en/article.php?ModuleId=10005424.

Another important ghetto-like aspect was the Jewish council, or *Judenrat*, which the Nazis forced to carry out their orders and policies as they administered the operations of Terezín. The *Judenrat* organized all municipal services, as well as labor detachments and deportations. Many of the members were former Jewish community leaders or Ältestenrat employees from Vienna, and they continued their work after the Red Army liberated the camp on May 8, 1945. In addition to the challenges associated with the management of the needs of a group of ill, malnourished, and traumatized people, they struggled to help organize departures for freed inmates. Two days after the liberation of former IKG employee Paul Stux at Terezín, he wrote to Dr. Josef Löwenherz, head of the Ältestenrat in Vienna. Many Jews had already left the camp for home, he stated, but the freed Austrian and German prisoners sat there waiting for some action on their behalf. He reported that about 10 percent of the Austrian Jews originally deported to Terezín remained, including some four hundred elderly and infirm.[10] Another former IKG employee in Terezín, Salomon Süss, wrote to Löwenherz just one day later to ask him to intervene on their behalf.[11] Former Terezín *Judenrat* functionaries like Stux and Süss composed lists of survivors, sorted them by nationality and hometown, and then sent them to the appropriate authorities with the request that the respective government arrange for the repatriation of its citizens. Buses from locations across Germany soon arrived, but the failure of Austria and the city of Vienna to reply to their appeal forced the Soviets to take over, and they organized buses to carry Viennese survivors home.[12]

The first such transport of approximately 650 Austrian Jewish survivors from Terezín arrived on July 7, 1945, and, about one month later, more than 300 followed them home to Vienna.[13] A correspondent for the

---

10. Paul Stux, Neuegasse 12, Theresienstadt, to Dr. Josef Löwenherz, May 10, 1945, A/W 4035, Central Archives for the History of the Jewish People (CAHJP), Jerusalem, Israel.

11. Salomon Süss, Neuegasse 12, Theresienstadt, to Dr. Josef Löwenherz, May 11, 1945, A/W 4035, CAHJP.

12. George Berkeley, *Hitler's Gift: The Story of Theresienstadt* (Boston: Branden Books, 1993), 252. Susanne Kriss mentions her return to Vienna from Terezín on buses provided by the Soviets. See Kriss, interview, 378, DÖW.

13. Niklas, *Die schönste Stadt der Welt*, 151.

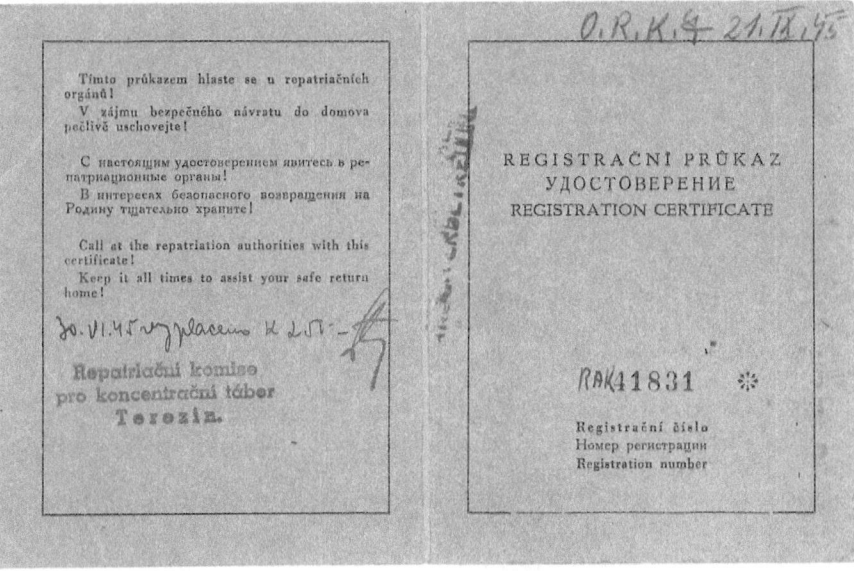

Repatriation certificate issued by the Czechoslovak Ministry of Defense to Terezín survivor Jeanette Porges to return home to Vienna. (US Holocaust Memorial Museum; courtesy of Paul Peter and Lucie Porges)

Jewish Telegraphic Agency (JTA) witnessed the early-August arrival and described the returnees' excitement: "Despite the fact that half of them were ill . . . [they] laughed and chattered like children when they reached the Vienna railroad station. They called greetings to the few fellow-Viennese who were on hand to greet them." The same correspondent also specified that everyone interviewed reportedly sought to emigrate elsewhere.[14] More than 400 traced the same path home in the subsequent weeks, and by September 20, 1945, a total of 1,368 Austrian Jewish survivors of Terezín were once again living in Vienna.[15]

Independent Return and Dangers to Women

Some concentration camp survivors, like Edith and Anni Holzer, organized their return without the assistance of Allied forces. Not wanting to wait for the repair of railways or for their turn on a waiting list, they pieced together their own journeys home. Their modes of transportation ranged from horse-drawn carts to crowded trains to any available vehicle moving in the general direction of Vienna. Alexander Rabinowicz was one of many who simply started out on foot. After surviving Auschwitz,[16] a death march, and Buchenwald,[17] he escaped from a moving train bound for Terezín in April 1945 and began his six-week trek home by walking toward Austria. He reached Brno, Czechoslovakia, where he found a ride in a truck the rest of the way to Vienna.[18] Soviet troops liberated Marianne Windholm at Auschwitz, where they found her in the camp infirmary, very ill and

---

14. "Austrian Jews Return from Theresienstadt to Vienna; Jewish Population Reaches 8,000," Jewish Telegraphic Agency, August 2, 1945.

15. List "Heimkehrer aus Theresienstadt," September 20, 1945, 3.1.1.3/78805385–78805407/ITS Digital Archive, USHMM.

16. Transportliste des Sammellagers Malines, postwar compilation, 1.1.24.1/1269542/ITS Digital Archive, USHMM. The cited document shows that Rabinowicz was transported to Auschwitz from Malines on Transport XI/1228 on September 26, 1942.

17. Häftlings-Personal-Karte Alexander Rabinowicz, January 22, 1945, 1.1.5.3/6971088/ITS Digital Archive, USHMM.

18. Alexander Rabinowicz, interview, 487, DÖW.

badly beaten.[19] Despite the physical ailments and illnesses of Windholm and other prisoners from the camp, they walked together over the wintry Carpathian Mountains and slept in the streets and in bus stations along the way. Although they possessed neither tickets nor passports, they finally arranged seats on a packed train and arrived in Vienna after four months of travel.[20]

Like Anni and Edith Holzer, many women journeying homeward encountered the particular horror of sexual assault. In Germany and Austria, all women were potential victims of rape by Soviet soldiers. The soldiers held Austrians and Germans collectively responsible for mass murder and rape committed against their families and communities during the Nazi invasion of the Soviet Union, and their rage and vengeance motivated them. And, as the twins' experience revealed, even physically and mentally traumatized Jewish women who clearly had taken no part in Nazi crimes were at risk. And, as we have seen, women did not face such danger only from Red Army troops. After bicycling part of the way from the Ravensbrück concentration camp, located about fifty miles north of Berlin, Irene Musik teamed up with two Viennese Jewish men also making their way home. They protected her from Red Army soldiers' advances during their trip, but they too pressured her for sex. When she denied them, they abandoned her at the Czech border.[21]

Elderly among the Survivors

There were no children among the more than three hundred Austrian Jews arriving in Vienna on a August 1, 1945, repatriation transport. Most were middle-aged and elderly.[22] This sample represented a particular of Vienna's

---

19. Namensverzeichnisse ehemaliger Häftling (nach der Befreiung aufgest. Listen über den Gesundheitszustand und haftbed. Erkrankungen), 1.1.2.1/534797, 534798/ITS Digital Archive, USHMM.
20. Windholm oral history.
21. Irene Musik, interview, 212, DÖW.
22. "Austrian Jews Return from Theresienstadt to Vienna," Jewish Telegraphic Agency, August 2, 1945.

postwar Jewish population: its demographic distribution differed greatly from that of European Jewry as a whole. More than half of the Austrian Jewish survivors in immediate postwar Vienna were forty-five years old or older. The same age group constituted only 10 percent of all of Europe's surviving Jews.[23] A number of factors account for this difference. Historian C. Gwyn Moser has reported that of the 619 files of *U-Boote* survivors that she studied, nearly 60 percent had gone into hiding at the age of forty or older.[24] This constitutes a significant percentage of *U-Boote* survivors but represents only 361 individuals. If, as Brigitte Ungar-Klein has estimated, there were a total of some 800 *U-Boote*, and 60 percent were forty or older, the number would increase to 500,[25] yet it would still be less than 10 percent of the estimated number of surviving Jews in Vienna at war's end.[26] A number of Viennese "Mischlinge" and Jews over the age of forty-five who were married to gentiles surely survived the war in the city, but the extent to which they joined the IKG—or were permitted to join it—remains unclear.

The most important factor that shaped the postwar demographic appears to have been wartime emigration efforts. Thanks to the unflagging efforts of the Viennese Jewish community working under the intense pressure of the Nazis' forced emigration policies, about two-thirds of Viennese Jews emigrated from Austria after the Anschluss. Most of them young and physically capable, they left to begin anew in other countries, and many left behind elderly relatives—temporarily, or so they thought. They planned to orchestrate their family members' escape from abroad, but most of these efforts

---

23. Zorach Wahrhaftig, *Uprooted: Jewish Refugees and Displaced Persons After Liberation* (New York: Institute of Jewish Affairs of the American Jewish Congress and World Jewish Congress, 1946), 53.

24. C. Gwyn Moser, "Jewish *U-Boote* in Austria, 1938–1945," *Simon Wiesenthal Center Annual* 2 (1985): 56.

25. Brigitte Ungar-Klein, "Überleben im Versteck—Rückkehr in die Normalität?," in *Überleben der Shoah—und danach*, ed. Alexander Friedmann, Elvira Glück, and David Vyssoki (Vienna: Picus Verlag, 1999), 35.

26. Historian Jonny Moser calculated that 5,538 Jews survived the war in Vienna, and Gertrude Schneider estimated a slightly higher 5,600. See Moser, *Demographie der jüdischen Bevölkerung Österreichs, 1938–1945* (Vienna: Dokumentationsarchiv des österreichischen Widerstandes, 1999), 55; and Gertrude Schneider, *Exile and Destruction: The Fate of Austrian Jews, 1938–1945* (Westport, CT: Praeger, 1995), 157.

proved unsuccessful. Thus, a disproportionate number of middle-aged and elderly constituted the city's Jews subject to deportations. The Nazis sent many of Vienna's older Jews to Terezín. The particular history of that camp afforded the aged a greater possibility of survival, and thus a relative prevalence of elderly Viennese were still alive at the end of the war and returned. Of the 15,351 Austrian Jews deported to Terezín, 1,270 were still there on May 5, 1945, awaiting repatriation, and many were of advanced age.[27]

ARRIVING HOME

Exhausted, malnourished, and often gravely ill, camp survivors came back to a partially destroyed Vienna with nearly eighty-seven thousand uninhabitable apartments.[28] Marianne Windholm arrived in the city after dark with a group of other returning camp survivors, and they spent their first night home in a cellar. She only saw the destruction the next morning and did not recognize her hometown. "I went out and I did not . . . know where I [was]. The buildings were bombed. I had no idea in which district I [was]. It was terrible."[29] War damage in the capital included destroyed and impaired bridges, sewers, and gas and water pipes, as well as massive food shortages. The conquering Soviets placed first priority on bringing the city to working order and feeding the population, and they tasked the former chancellor of the First Austrian Republic and the last president of Parliament before the Austrofascist period, Dr. Karl Renner, to lead the establishment of a provisional Austrian government. Returnees from concentration camps arrived to find these problems but held tight to their more specific personal

---

27. Schneider, *Exile and Destruction*, 176–94. Another 154 Austrian Jews survived Terezín but had been sent to Switzerland on February 5, 1945; 149 Austrian Jews were liberated at other camps to which they had been sent from Terezín.

28. Government of the City of Vienna, "The Years of the Allied Forces in Vienna (1945 to 1955)—History of Vienna," accessed November 14, 2011, http://www.wien.gv.at/english/history/overview/reconstruction.html. Walter Kleindel reports that 28 percent of Vienna's buildings had been destroyed in Allied air raids. See Kleindel, *Die Chronik Österreichs* (Dortmund: Chronik Verlag, 1984), 537.

29. Windholm oral history.

intentions. Their first thoughts turned to locating family members and friends, finding places to live, and securing other basic life necessities.

Locating Family and Friends

Upon arrival in Vienna, camp returnees confronted the immediate question of where and how to locate other survivors. Some went directly to their prewar residences; others visited the IKG office for guidance and assistance. Ralph Segalman, a relief worker with the American Jewish Joint Distribution Committee (JDC or Joint), arrived in Vienna in November 1945 and described such efforts in his unpublished memoir: "At that time . . . about 1000 Jews had returned from the concentration camps and most of them were old. The few younger and middle age Jews were not around when we visited. We found that the younger people were trying to pull the threads of their families together, to find their loved ones and to figure out how and what to do with their lives. I met with many of them later when I began to see them at meetings and gatherings of Jews."[30]

A fortunate few did reunite with relatives in Vienna. Alexander Rabinowicz stumbled through the unrecognizable streets when he first arrived and wondered what to do first. He made his way to his sister- and (gentile) brother-in-law's tenth-district apartment; his sister-in-law initially did not recognize him. Once the couple realized who stood before them, they immediately welcomed Alexander to their home. He slept on their kitchen floor for a few days, while his brother-in-law helped ease his reentry to life in the changed city. He took Alexander for delousing and used personal connections to help him secure an apartment.[31]

Other camp survivors miraculously found family members waiting for them at their homes or in new ones. Susanne Kriss's non-Jewish grandmother survived the war in Vienna, although the Nazis had evicted her

---

30. Ralph Segalman, "Letters to My Grandchildren," unpublished memoir (Northridge, CA, 2001), 76. Special thanks to Professor Harold Marcuse for bringing this memoir to my attention and for providing me with a copy. Mr. Segalman's memoirs can also be accessed at the Jacob Rader Marcus Center of the American Jewish Archives, Marcus Repository, SC-14902.

31. Rabinowicz interview.

from the home Susanne had known; they had grown suspicious of her frequent postal contact with Jewish relatives interned in Terezín. Susanne found her grandmother in the new home nonetheless, and the two set up house together.[32] Most returnees, though, arrived to have their worst fears confirmed, as they searched and found no surviving relatives in Vienna. A deep connection to a familial home had motivated camp survivors' return, and the loss felt upon finding that home empty left them heartbroken and haunted. JDC relief worker Ralph Segalman observed that many of the Jewish survivors he worked with had been "psychologically shaken" by their experiences and what they learned of the fates of their families. Segalman's meetings with survivors about even practical matters like housing involved providing support to survivors in their grief and their sense of being lost and alone.[33] "It was as if around every corner, my mother or sisters or husband would be coming," wrote Trude Binder of her anguish in this situation. "I saw their ghosts everywhere."[34]

Survivors registered with the IKG and sought the community's assistance to find others. A bulletin board displayed notices to connect people, and many created new support networks by banding together with friends and distant relatives, as well as by marrying and starting families anew. There, on the IKG bulletin board, Marianne Windholm found her friend Anna Vietner's message directing anyone who knew the Vietner family to an address in Vienna's fifteenth district.[35] Anna and her mother had survived the Nazis in the city in hiding, protected by their family's non-Jewish maid. After the war, they were assigned an apartment that had been abandoned by Nazi residents who fled from the Red Army. Marianne made her way to the address and reunited with Anna, who opened her home to Marianne as she regained her footing in the city.[36]

---

32. Kriss interview.
33. Segalman, "Letters to My Grandchildren," 78.
34. Trude Binder, "A Survivor's Memoirs of the Holocaust 1942–1946," 30, 426179, MM III 17, ME 1480, Leo Baeck Institute, New York, NY.
35. Glaubensjuden in Wien, 1946, 3.1.1.3/78805492/ITS Digital Archive, USHMM. According to the cited list, Windholm was living at Kranzgasse 7/4 in Vienna's fifteenth district.
36. Windholm oral history.

Other returnees met family and friends by chance. In Edith and Anni Holzer's first hours back in Vienna, they fortuitously ran into a physician they had known before the war. He told them that their friend and former nursing colleague Mignon Langnas had survived working as a nurse in a Jewish hospital.[37] The three women reconnected, and Langnas took the sisters in at her tiny one-room apartment, where they lived together and took care of one another until Edith and Anni fell ill with typhus and required hospitalization.[38]

Rebuilding kinship connections and establishing new ones became important in reclaiming one's familial home, especially in light of the immense loss to the Jewish community. A wedding could provide joyous events for a grieving people working hard to reestablish lives. Despite enduring nearly three years in concentration camps, including Terezín,[39] Auschwitz,[40] and Flossenbürg,[41] Lili Asch had been fortunate. After a short stint in the Deggendorf DP camp in Bavaria, she was back in Vienna and living with her sister and both of her parents, all also concentration camp survivors, by September 20, 1945.[42] Lili married Alexander Asch, an Auschwitz survivor from Łódź, Poland, in December 1947 at the Seitenstettengasse Stadttempel, the city's main synagogue and the only one left standing in Vienna after the massive destruction of the Reichspogromnacht. She wore a rented bridal gown and later fondly recalled the reception at her parents' home. She marveled at her mother's ingenuity at arranging eggs for the baker at

---

37. Auerhahn and Drill interview.

38. "Biographien," in *Mignon: Tagebücher und Briefe einer jüdischen Krankenschwester in Wien, 1938–1949*, ed. Elisabeth Fraller and George Langnas (Innsbruck: Studien Verlag, 2010), 473.

39. On August 8, 1942, the Gestapo deported Lili to Terezín on Gestapo transport number 35. See 35. Transport vom 13.8.1942 nach Theresienstadt, 1.2.1.1/11203728/ITS Digital Archive, USHMM.

40. On October 23, 1944, Lili was sent from Terezín to Auschwitz on Transport "Et." See Alphabetisches Verzeichnis zum Transport Et, abgegangen am 23.10.1944, 1.1.42.1/11203728/ITS Digital Archive, USHMM.

41. On October 27, 1944, Lili was sent from Auschwitz to Flossenbürg with a group of more than two hundred other female prisoners. See Transportliste über 200 jüdische Häftlingsfrauen, 1.1.8.1/10799564/ITS Digital Archive, USHMM.

42. List of Austrians who returned to Vienna from Theresienstadt, September 20, 1945, 3.1.1.3/78805385/ITS Digital Archive, USHMM.

the famous Demel pastry shop; securing a special wedding cake in a city ravaged by food shortages was no small feat and indicated the importance of and reverence with which her family regarded the union.[43] Weddings and other family celebrations, however, did not always ensure a sustained sense of home in the city. Later that same year and with the support of an affidavit from Alexander's well-known uncle, the writer Sholem Asch, the couple immigrated to the United States.

Finding Housing and Work

Many Viennese Jews arrived to find their apartments confiscated and occupied by gentile Austrians, many of them yesterday's Nazis. In the first few months of occupation, the Soviet authorities tried to help with the distribution of housing to Vienna residents. Once the government established a *Wohnungsamt* (housing office) to serve all residents of the partially destroyed city, the Soviets had no say, and survivors depended on municipal functionaries for housing assignments. Jews encountered antisemitic discrimination during the application process and while competing for housing with the general population, and in the summer of 1946, the IKG made an official agreement with the city of Vienna to work in partnership to provide its returning members with the abandoned apartments of Nazis who had left or fled the city.[44] As previously mentioned, even before the 1946 agreement, the Soviets and the Austrian provisional government had assigned some survivors to such homes, which often had been stolen outright from Jewish families, or "Aryanized." Overall, however, the Austrian courts restored many such properties. In 1946, 8,400 victims occupied Nazis' abandoned or otherwise empty homes, but in 1950, only 730 still lived in them.[45]

---

43. Lili Asch, interview 20995, Visual History Archive (VHA), USC Shoah Foundation, Los Angeles, CA, accessed at USHMM, August 16, 2011.
44. *Bericht des Präsidiums der Israelitischen Kultusgemeinde Wien über die Tätigkeit in den Jahren 1945 bis 1948* (Vienna: Israelitische Kultusgemeinde Wien, 1948), 25.
45. Brigitte Bailer, Florian Freund, Elisabeth Klamper, Wolfgang Neugebauer, Gerhard Ungar, and Brigitte Ungar-Klein, *Erzählte Geschichte: Berichte von Widerstandskämpfern und Verfolgten*, vol. 3, *Jüdische Schicksale* (Vienna: Österreichischer Bundesverlag, 1992), 269n26.

Connections—both through private channels and through the city government—helped accelerate the process of obtaining apartments and furniture. A visit to the housing office with a friend or relative in Allied uniform ensured more prompt attention.[46] Returnees also found that although revealing one's status as a camp survivor could elicit antisemitic reactions, on other occasions it could be wielded to arouse sympathy or even shame.[47] Camp survivor Frances Tritt worked in a pharmacy after the war and benefited from the good nature of a regular customer.[48] When the customer asked Tritt about her wartime experiences, she told him that she had been in Terezín, and he immediately arranged to help her secure furnishings for her apartment through his governmental role as distributor to people in need in Vienna.[49]

Homeless camp survivors turned to the IKG, which operated three KZ Rückkehrerheime (homes for returning camp survivors) in different locations across the city—two in the second district (Tempelhofgasse 3 and Untere Augartenstrasse 35) and one in the ninth (Seegasse 9). Hundreds of returnees, most of them elderly, lived in these facilities, run by the Jewish community with financial and logistical help from the Allies, the JDC, and eventually from the city of Vienna.

Finding work often depended on personal connections, as well as specialized skills and abilities, and survivors were resourceful in identifying ways to earn a living. Returnees with the appropriate language proficiencies secured translation and other work with the Allied occupation forces. Others found jobs with the Jewish community. Many found positions in medical facilities associated with the Kultusgemeinde. A chance meeting with a friend on the street led Marianne Windholm to obtain a job at the

---

46. For example, see Dr. Franz Hahn, interview, 510, DÖW.
47. For example, see Rabinowicz interview.
48. The Gestapo deported Fanny Tritt to Terezín on Transport 45 from Vienna. 45. Transport vom 9.10.1942 nach Theresienstadt, 1.2.1.1/11204145/ITS Digital Archive, USHMM. Tritt was liberated there and had returned to Vienna by September 20, 1945. List of Austrians who returned to Vienna from Theresienstadt, September 20, 1945, 3.1.1.3/78805403/ITS Digital Archive, USHMM.
49. Frances Tritt, "Meine Lebensgeschichte. Das Wunder des Überlebens 1918–1971," 90, MM 78, ME 650, Leo Baeck Institute, New York, NY.

Rothschild Hospital DP camp in the American Zone.[50] After the Holzer sisters recovered from typhus and convalescence, they worked for the IKG, assisting other returnees. Anni served as a nurse in a Jewish community clinic, and Edith worked first registering returnees and later as a social worker and cashier for the IKG.[51] Dr. Franz Hahn had worked at the Rothschild Hospital from 1938 through 1943, and when he returned to Vienna in mid-August 1945, he almost immediately began work at the Jewish hospital on the Malzgasse.[52]

Interacting with Gentiles

Returning camp survivors quickly realized that they were not welcome and learned to refrain from sharing their experiences with gentile Austrians. When they did, they frequently confronted listeners' expressions of doubt and disbelief. Few gentile Austrians showed sympathy or appreciation for Jews' ordeals under Nazi oppression, and some displayed outright hostility. The building superintendent at Marianne Windholm's former family home greeted her with, "Oh, you're still alive?"[53]

Jewish returnees became targets for new and renewed antisemitism in Vienna, as their presence threatened the feeble construction of the myth of Austria as the Nazis' first victim. Survivors knew that a large part of the gentile population had been—and still were—enthusiastic Nazis and antisemites. Austrian Jews knew that their gentile neighbors had exploited Jewish citizens' dire situations to benefit from Nazi "Aryanization" policies and that some had participated in the mass murder of their families, friends, and community members. Gertrude Schneider wrote that it seemed that "everyone, except the survivors, suffered from a convenient kind of amnesia."[54] In addition, postwar antisemitism facilitated non-Jews' defensive reasoning that prisoners of concentration camps must have broken laws and that they

---

50. Windholm oral history.
51. Auerhahn and Drill interview.
52. Hahn interview.
53. Windholm oral history.
54. Schneider, *Exile and Destruction*, 159.

had deserved incarceration as criminals.⁵⁵ Schneider described her disappointment upon her June 1, 1945, return to Vienna: "We were not greeted with open arms, as some incorrigible optimists, myself included, had hoped for. The reception we had dreamed about in those long, cruel years that had robbed us of our youth, sapped our strength, and taken away our loved ones, was not forthcoming. There were no kind words; instead, there was the typical exclamation, something like 'you people always come back,' and with that we had to be satisfied."⁵⁶ Recounting camp experiences to gentile Austrians also prompted their attempts to match stories of suffering with descriptions of air raids and marauding Soviet liberators.

Gentiles in Vienna perceived returning survivors as contemptible competitors in a postwar housing crisis. Allied bombs had damaged 28 percent of the city's buildings, rendering tens of thousands of apartments uninhabitable, and homeless returnees competed for shelter with bombed-out gentiles.⁵⁷ In addition, some sixty thousand apartments in Vienna had been "Aryanized," and those who were in possession of Jews' former homes and businesses feared the possibility of losing them to the rightful owners.⁵⁸ When laws about the return of property went into effect in 1947, so-called Aryanizers formed official advocacy associations to protect themselves and the property they held from Jews' claims.⁵⁹

Although Jews encountered predominantly negative reactions from Austrian gentiles, intermittent kindness sparked. Some gentiles recognized and vividly recalled the experiences of their Jewish friends and neighbors. They refused to take part in the exploitation of Jews' unfortunate situations and tried to help. Trude Binder emphasized while describing her first visit with non-Jewish friends after the war, "To show you how good people can be, they presented me with some money entrusted to them by my mother. It

---

55. Helga Embacher, "Unwelcome in Austria: Returnees and Concentration Camp Survivors," in *When the War Was Over: Women, War and Peace in Europe, 1940–1956*, ed. Claire Duchen and Irene Bandhauer-Schöffmann (London: Leicester University Press, 2000), 196.
56. Schneider, *Exile and Destruction*, 159.
57. Kleindel, *Die Chronik Österreichs*, 537.
58. Embacher, "Unwelcome in Austria," 198.
59. For an analysis of such organizations' activities, see chapter 6.

was still in the same package. They themselves had been plundered by the Russians but had managed to save my money."[60]

Occasionally gentiles provided returnees with much-needed support upon their return. When Auschwitz survivor Kurt Herzog arrived in Vienna,[61] he already knew that the Nazis had murdered his parents, so instead of going to his prewar home, he went directly to the Pollack family's apartment. This non-Jewish family had assisted him even after the Anschluss and until his deportation. He knew they would welcome him, and indeed they housed him and provided care during his first few weeks in Vienna. In an interview decades later, Herzog explained that he eventually grew frustrated with the difficulties of reestablishing himself in Vienna and immigrated to Australia. In light of this, he sought to be clear about the Pollacks: "Now, I have to mention this because those people were small people and they behaved in a way which is absolutely fantastic."[62]

Not all seemingly sympathetic actions sprang from idealistic origins. Kind treatment was sometimes superficial and part of a deeper agenda. Trude Binder (née Weiner) ran into a carpenter and former neighbor soon after her return, and he greeted her with contrived warmth: "Oh, Fraulein Weiner, I'm so glad you're back!" Trude knew that he was a former member of the Sturmabteilung (SA) and that he still held possession of an "Aryanized" carpentry workshop. She caught on to his fear of her denunciation when he offered to build her any furniture she wanted and used it to her advantage to furnish her apartment.[63]

Such opportunities for retaliation presented themselves to survivors, but many chose not to seek retribution against individuals. Their decisions not to denounce former Nazis may have sprung from a sense of forgiveness, but testimonies suggest that the returnees felt such compromises to have been in their best interest. Bringing difficulties to the non-Jewish neighbors among whom they consciously decided to resettle might serve only

---

60. Binder, "Survivor's Memoirs of the Holocaust," 32.
61. ITS Certificate of Incarceration Kurt Herzog, May 28, 1958, 6.3.3.2/104356374/ITS Digital Archive, USHMM.
62. Kurt Herzog, interview, RG 50.583*0003, USHMM.
63. Binder, "Survivor's Memoirs of the Holocaust," 33.

to create further problems for returnees, their families, and the Jewish community. Residency in postwar Vienna required an acceptance of living among perpetrators, and coping mechanisms that returnees developed and utilized involved discretion. A woman who had denounced Susanne Kriss's mother to the Nazis for appearing in public without the required Star of David sought her out after the war and begged her not to inform the authorities of this act. Kriss's mother brought no complaint against her. Kriss disagreed with the decision because, she said, she blamed exactly this kind of person for what had happened to them.[64] Kriss's mother, however, must have felt that she could better protect herself and her daughter by keeping silent.

Franz Hahn faced more than one opportunity for reprisal, but, despite a wartime path of persecution that included more than two years internment in Terezín[65] and shorter stints in Auschwitz,[66] Sachsenhausen, and Dachau,[67] he exhibited restraint. He elected not to attempt the recovery of his former home when he found a gentile Austrian woman living there after she had been bombed out of her apartment. Hahn realized that she had not been the original "Aryanizer" and viewed her as less of a perpetrator and more of a victim. She had not stolen his apartment, he rationalized; why take it from her?[68] At a later date, the father of an SS camp guard named Hartl approached Hahn and some of his survivor friends to ask them to write a letter on behalf of his son awaiting trial by the Allies. The young officer Hartl had shown great kindness to them in the camp, Hahn and his friends recalled, and they agreed. Their formal statement secured Hartl's

---

64. Kriss interview.

65. Hahn was arrested in Vienna on September 30, 1942, and deported to Terezín the following day. 43. Transport vom 1.10.1942 nach Theresienstadt, 1.2.1.1/11204049/ITS Digital Archive, USHMM.

66. After two years in Terezín, Hahn was deported to Auschwitz. Alphabetisches Verzeichnis zum Transport Et, abgegangen an 23.10.1944, 1.1.42.1/4959507/ITS Digital Archive, USHMM.

67. Hahn arrived in Dachau on November 17, 1944, after a short time in Sachsenhausen. Häftlingspersonalbogen Franz Hahn, Dachau, 1.1.6.2/10084760/ITS Digital Archive, USHMM. By September 1945, Hahn was back in Vienna and was residing at the Hotel Alserbach. Aus den Konzentrationslagern nach Wien Zurückgekehrte Juden, September 1945, 3.1.1.3/78805176/ITS Digital Archive, USHMM.

68. Rabinowicz interview.

acquittal, and although Hahn and his friends had no further contact with the officer, Hahn told his interviewer that he held no resentment. They had known Hartl to be the most decent and upstanding of all the guards they had encountered during the war and felt it the honorable thing to help him go free.[69]

Others felt that to gain some measure of justice outweighed potential future problems and, with no mitigating factors in the balance, chose to pursue legal channels. A Nazi neighbor wrongfully accused Alexander Rabinowicz of criminal activity, and an altercation ensued. Rabinowicz was arrested. Once released, he learned that the arresting officer had also been a Nazi, presumably conspiring with his neighbor. He filed a complaint that resulted in the officer's suspension.[70]

Though Viennese returnees encountered widespread hostility, they were mostly spared the violence that met many returning Polish Jews in their hometowns, which has become the dominant narrative about return. The Jewish population in Poland grew from 42,662 on May 1, 1945, to a peak of 240,489 by July 1, 1946, but antisemitic assaults and massacres, which had started in the last half of 1944 and continued through the summer of 1946, caused that number to drop sharply by 1947 to a total of 89,000.[71] After the Kielce pogrom on July 4, 1946, through the autumn of the same year, approximately one hundred thousand Jews left Poland, most for DP camps in Germany and Austria.[72] Gentile Poles, unlike non-Jewish Austrians, had suffered as victims of the Nazis, who viewed them as a source of wartime and future slave labor. Most Poles, though, felt neither connection with nor empathy for the experiences of their Jewish compatriots. And unlike Austrian Jewish returnees, the majority of Polish Jews found that permanent resettlement in their former homes, towns, and cities proved impossible.

---

69. Hahn interview.
70. Rabinowicz interview.
71. Lucjan Dobroszycki, *Survivors of the Holocaust in Poland: A Portrait Based on Jewish Community Records, 1944–1947* (New York: M. E. Sharpe, 1994), 10.
72. Laura Jockusch, *Collect and Record! Jewish Holocaust Documentation in Early Postwar Europe* (Oxford: Oxford University Press, 2012), 123.

THE AUSTRIAN GOVERNMENT AND THE RECEPTION OF CAMP SURVIVORS

Just as interactions with gentile Austrians taught most returning camp survivors to turn to Jewish friends and acquaintances for support, so the formal reception by their government communicated that for institutional assistance they could depend only on the IKG. Politicians and bureaucrats transmitted messages explicitly and implicitly that proved that postwar Austrian consciousness was permeated by Austria's assumed victim identity, a lack of responsibility for the persecution and genocide of European Jewry, and outright antisemitic hostility.

Postwar Austrian Government and the Victim Myth

At the end of July 1945, American, British, and French forces joined the Soviets in Vienna to assume control of agreed-on zones of occupation in Austria and in the capital city. All four powers also shared control of the Inter-Allied zone in the first district. By October, the wary Western Allies had officially recognized the Renner government, which was composed of politicians working diligently to shape a new national identity for Austria. This provisional government included a number of Communist Party representatives, as Renner and other leaders were wary of offending the Soviets.[73] They seized important opportunities in the development of Cold War politics to define the country and its citizens as the particularly *non-German* first victims of the Nazis. This permitted Austrian individuals to emerge from World War II as innocent casualties rather than as perpetrators and aggressors, and Austria as a country could evade its share of responsibility for Nazi crimes by highlighting the nation's technical nonexistence from March 1938 to May 1945.

The Austrian government's attitude toward Jewish concentration camp returnees remained staunchly unsympathetic, and it denied culpability for

---

73. Günter Bischof, "Allied Plans and Policies for the Occupation of Austria, 1938–1955," in *Austria in the Twentieth Century*, ed. Rolf Steininger, Günter Bischof, and Michael Gehler (New Brunswick, NJ: Transaction, 2002), 176.

any part of their persecution under the Germans. Many government officials simply refused to believe their descriptions of camp conditions and their experiences, suggesting to survivors, "it couldn't have been that bad, or you wouldn't even be here now."[74] The few instances of efforts made by the Renner government to welcome or assist with Jews' repatriation consisted of exceptions. Renner shifted narrative gears to suit the situation and his audience, but he did not veer from his position of utter disinterest in Austria's Jews, current or former. In January 1946, the Association of Jewish Refugees in the United Kingdom reported that Renner had promised to eliminate Nazis from leading industrial and trade positions, which he said in response to revelations that "Aryanizers" still owned and ran many former Jewish grocery and textile businesses.[75] No such action was taken.

Renner was in good company. All postwar political parties sought to embrace former Nazis and the beneficiaries of "Aryanization," as they constituted an important segment of the electorate. Parties strove to include them by maintaining a second line of domestic discussion—or domestic silence—about the Nazi past,[76] which involved avoiding enflaming animosity that would result from an official welcome of Jewish citizens' return. Restoring former Nazis' professional and social status became a main theme in domestic politics, and Austrian leaders simultaneously distanced themselves and their nation from responsibility for or association with Nazi crimes, while they also courted former Nazi Party members with political, professional, and social reconciliation.[77]

Such contradictions made sense as the Renner government sought to refashion a postwar Austrian national identity that differed for international and domestic audiences. Austrian leaders recognized that in 1946,

---

74. Embacher, "Unwelcome in Austria," 197.

75. "News in Brief: Austria's Industries Still in Nazi Hands," *Association of Jewish Refugees Information*, January 1946, 8.

76. Peter Pulzer, "Between Collectivism and Liberalism: The Political Evolution of Austria since 1945," in *Austria 1945–95: Fifty Years of the Second Republic*, ed. Kurt Richard Luther and Peter Pulzer (Aldershot, UK: Ashgate, 1998), 229.

77. Heidemarie Uhl, "The Politics of Memory: Austria's Perception of the Second World War and the National Socialist Period," in *Austrian Historical Memory and National Identity*, Contemporary Austrian Studies 5, ed. Günter Bischof and Anton Pelinka (New Brunswick, NJ: Transaction, 1997), 68.

after the first strict phase of Allied control following war's end, pressure to bring Nazis and war criminals to justice eased. The priority of rooting out and punishing Austrian Nazis waned as tensions between the Soviets and the Western powers increased. And the Austrian government exploited the situation to solidify the Moscow Declaration's promise of victim identity. The nation sought to stress its innocence and to underscore Germany's sole responsibility for Nazi crimes, and thus for reparations, on the world stage. At the same time, denazification as administered by the Renner government involved controlling the consequences for a large group of potential voters and took place as a series of amnesties.[78] All postwar parties claimed that the Austrian populace included few committed Nazi Party members, and Renner posited that many had just caved to economic, social, and personal pressures. In 1946, some 90 percent of former Nazi Party members were amnestied, reinstated to their jobs, and paid compensation for material and financial losses after 1945.[79] Such pardons led to the creation of the Federation of Independents (Verband der Unabhängigen, or VdU), the predecessor party to Austria's current-day far-right Freedom Party (Freiheitliche Partei Österreich, or FPÖ).[80]

In the immediate postwar years, those who were active in the resistance movement received heroes' honors, and memorials to those who were killed in the struggle for Austria's "liberation" were erected in Vienna and the provinces. The government strove to define most all Austrian citizens as victims and promoted its view of Austria as victim nation with an antifascist exhibition at Vienna's Künstlerhaus and the publication of the *Rot-Weiss-Rot Buch: Gerechtigkeit für Österreich! Darstellungen, Dokumente und Nachweise zur Vorgeschichte und Geschichte der Okkupation Österreichs (nach amtlichen*

---

78. Peter Utgaard, *Remembering and Forgetting Nazism: Education, National Identity, and the Victim Myth in Postwar Austria* (New York: Berghahn Books, 2003), 31.

79. Uhl, "Politics of Memory," 71–72.

80. Utgaard, *Remembering and Forgetting Nazism*, 31. The VdU changed its name to the Freedom Party in 1956 and continues to serve today as Austria's far-right political party. An ÖVP and FPÖ coalition in 2000 brought the Freedom Party and its then-leader, Jörg Haider, to worldwide attention, as the European Union initiated and maintained a diplomatic boycott with Austria for seven months in reaction to the leadership of a xenophobic party with known Nazi ties.

Quellen).⁸¹ An English version carried the same title in direct translation, including its reference to the national flag: *Red-White-Red Book: Justice for Austria; Descriptions, Documents and Proofs to the Antecedents and History of the Occupation of Austria.*⁸²

The 224-page *Rot-Weiss-Rot Buch* represented the foreign ministry's determined attempt to highlight Austrian patriotism and to solidify the nation's victimhood and innocence. Its intended audience was the Allied occupiers and indeed the world, and the lengthy subtitle emphasized that the collection of official documents and the accompanying narrative were evidence of the German Reich's forced occupation of Austria. The book justified the lack of Austrian resistance by likening the Anschluss to the Nazi annexation of Czechoslovakia. As no other country offered military might in support of either nation (Austria or Czechoslovakia), the book reasoned, resistance to German "occupation" would have been senseless.⁸³ It also presents the case that Austria as a country did not exist politically and economically after the Anschluss and thus could not be responsible for Nazi crimes.⁸⁴

With this official position, the Austrian government endeavored to define or redefine nearly all other Austrian citizens as victims and, in doing so, elided the most oppressed group. Government benefits to concentration camp survivors persecuted on political grounds included the provision of housing, clothing, and food. Those mistreated "on racial grounds only" were specifically excluded.⁸⁵ The nongovernmental KZ-Verband (concentration camp survivor association), established in 1945, also refused membership to Jews, as well as to Roma and Sinti, homosexuals, and those who were

---

81. Uhl, "Politics of Memory," 66.

82. *Red-White-Red Book: Justice for Austria; Descriptions, Documents and Proofs to the Antecedents and History of the Occupation of Austria, from Official Sources* (Vienna: Austrian State Printing House, 1947).

83. *Rot-Weiss-Rot Buch: Gerechtigkeit für Österreich! Darstellungen, Dokumente und Nachweise zur Vorgeschichte und Geschichte der Okkupation Österreichs (nach amtlichen Quellen)* (Vienna: Druck und Verlag der österreichischen Staatsdruckerei, 1946), 69.

84. Ibid., 94.

85. Bailer et al., *Erzählte Geschichte*, 672.

punished for helping slave laborers.[86] Jewish survivors could turn only to the devastated IKG and foreign Jewish organizations conducting relief work in the city.

The government's explicit and implicit antisemitism regarding victim status and subsequent welfare benefits affected some non-Jews as well, as the government refused to recognize as resistance the aid and rescue of Jewish Austrians. The Gestapo arrested Dr. Ella Lingens, her husband, and a friend in September 1942, after an informant reported them for helping Jews flee Austria. The Nazis held Dr. Lingens in a Gestapo prison until February 1943 and then deported her to Auschwitz, where she served as a camp doctor and continued to help Jews at great personal risk.[87] She survived and, after liberation, returned to her native Vienna, where she applied for an *Amtsbescheinigung*, the official certification of her victim status that would permit her benefits. A government official denied her request on the grounds that "having hidden Jews [was] a private matter and not a form of resistance."[88] Despite her arrest, deportation, and suffering at the infamous Nazi death camp, Lingens was not categorized as a victim because helping Jews did nothing in the supposed movement for a free Austria.

The case of Theresia H. illustrates a similarly appalling contradiction that took place in the context of the developing postwar national narrative. In 1962, the Austrian government denied her application for support as a victim, although the Nazis had arrested and imprisoned her in Eisenstadt in August 1942 for providing assistance to Polish prisoners of war. She was later interned from March 20, 1943, to February 20, 1945, in Ravensbrück, where she wore a red badge that identified her as a political prisoner. Yet the postwar Austrian authorities did not categorize her as a victim of the

---

86. Helga Embacher, *Neubeginn ohne Illusionen: Juden in Österreich nach 1945* (Vienna: Picus Verlag, 1995), 196–98.

87. Yad Vashem: The Holocaust Martyrs' and Heroes' Remembrance Authority, "Flickers of Light: The Stories of Six Righteous Among the Nations in Auschwitz. Dr. Ella Lingens," accessed September 23, 2012, http://www1.yadvashem.org/yv/en/exhibitions/flickers_of_light/ella_lingens.asp. On January 3, 1980, Yad Vashem honored Dr. Ella Lingens and Dr. Kurt Lingens as "Righteous Among the Nations" for their extraordinary efforts rescuing Jews during the Holocaust.

88. Bailer et al., *Erzählte Geschichte*, 634.

Nazis, although they had considered Theresia H. a political opponent and imprisoned her for it. On the contrary, the authorities upheld the legislation used to imprison her in the first place as a traitor or saboteur. In response to her postwar claim, the Austrian government deemed the January 25, 1939, Nazi law that banned the provision of help to prisoners of war to be similar to laws of other countries at war and not a particularly National Socialist regulation. With this, they upheld Theresia H.'s guilt and at the same time dodged qualifying her as a politically persecuted victim.[89] She had helped others oppressed by the Nazis and, in particular, members of an army of a nation opposed to the Third Reich and genuinely a "victim," one in the group of countries to which Austria aspired to belong. This should have been seen as resistance, in favor of a supposedly oppressed Austria. Instead, the government handled her case in a way that clearly represented their true alliance.

In both of the preceding cases, the Austrian government denied victims' benefits to *women*. Both Lingens and Theresia H. had provided aid to others whom the Nazis had oppressed, and they did so in traditionally female ways. The concept of resistance stood as a debated and controversial one in postwar Austria. An understanding of "resister" included "taking gun in hand" to protect the country, as more conventionally masculine and aggressive forms of opposition constituted "resistance." Thus, in addition to the blatant contradictions involved in denying the women assistance as victims themselves, expectations and norms related to gender also guided an Austrian postwar understanding of resistance.

Restitution of Property

Despite Allied supervision, returning Jewish survivors encountered hostility in postwar Vienna, especially regarding the recovery of real estate and businesses stolen under Nazi "Aryanization" laws. Those who were in possession of Jews' assets resisted relinquishing the property and often

---

89. Brigitte Bailer, *Wiedergutmachung kein Thema: Österreich und die Opfer des Nationalsozialismus* (Vienna: Löcker Verlag, 1993), 165.

succeeded in retaining it, as the provisional government had no interest in antagonizing this important group of voters. As we have seen, the postwar government made no secret of its lack of interest in or responsibility for Jewish citizens, and this held true with regard to restitution as well.

The provisional government formally addressed the issue of stolen property restitution on May 10, 1945, at the Fifth Cabinet Council meeting on "Aryanized" assets. Despite its title, the minutes of the meeting reveal that leaders focused on the return of the property of the Social Democratic Party (SPÖ) and associated organizations, stolen under the Austrofascist dictatorship in the mid-1930s. It was inconceivable, Renner stated, to compensate every "small Jewish merchant or peddler for his loss" when the SPÖ had not regained its confiscated assets.[90] His responsibility was to, and his reputation relied on, the 47 percent of the population he estimated that the SPÖ represented. For postwar Austrian politicians, satisfying the Jewish sliver of the electorate provided no advantage. On the contrary, *not* satisfying them but rather caring for the needs and wants of "Aryanizers" proved beneficial. Jews who had been racially defined by and persecuted under Nuremberg Laws had constituted less than 3 percent of the pre-Anschluss population of Austria.[91] Jews alive in Austria after war's end in 1945 constituted less than one-tenth of 1 percent of the population, and the many tens of thousands of Austrian Jews living abroad had lost their citizenship under Nazi law and were not entitled to regain it. Politicians identified their electoral base and looked no farther.

On November 3, 1945, representatives of the Viennese Jewish community submitted a memorandum to the offices of General Mark Clark, the US representative of the Allied control commission for Austria. They officially requested American assistance in the return of Jews' property and in obtaining one hundred former IKG-owned buildings in the possession of

---

90. Robert Knight, *"Ich bin dafür, die Sache in die Länge zu ziehen": Wortprotokolle der österreichischen Bundesregierung von 1945–52 über die Entschädigung der Juden* (Frankfurt am Main: Athenäum, 1988), 83.

91. The 1934 Austrian census reported a total population of 6,760,044. "Population Census Data since 1869 by Age and Provinces," Statistik Austria: Die Informationsmanager, accessed August 3, 2012, http://sdb.statistik.at/superwebguest/login.do?guest=guest&db=defi174.

the Austrian government. Their statement outlined the Austrian provisional government's turpitude with regard to provisions for the compensation of Jews and described the antisemitic discrimination that public officials directed at returning camp survivors. The memo stressed that immediately after conquering Vienna, the Soviets had named many former Jewish owners as "temporary administrators" of their prior businesses, a move that seemed in the direction of the return of rightful property. But just a few months later, the Renner government had gained official recognition and more power, and many "Aryanizers" of such establishments resumed control. The municipality controlled Jewish theaters stolen during the Nazi regime rather than restoring them to the rightful owners, and more than one hundred former Jewish community buildings were still the property of the Austrian government.[92] A little over a month after sending General Clark the memo, Jewish community leaders followed up with a letter of thanks and appreciation for Clark's "unparalleled kindness" and "judicious insight and respect for human rights and dignity."[93] Clark and US forces clearly expressed support and wanted to help the Jewish community, but as the provisional government gained and then increased in power, prospects for the recovery of former property looked bleak.

Although Chancellor Renner had promised to eliminate Nazis from leading positions in industry and trade, Aaron Ehrlich, president of the Jewish Chamber of Commerce in Vienna, reported in January 1946 that "seventy per cent of the food stores in Austria and at least 80 per cent of its clothing industry [were] still in the hands of former Nazis."[94] Ehrlich also emphasized that trade associations denied camp survivors the licenses they needed to establish businesses or to engage in trade. Then, too, Jews struggled, he pointed out, unable to secure accommodation, and all the while Nazis retained and enjoyed luxurious apartments.

---

92. "Vienna Jews Appeal to US Authorities for Aid in Obtaining Their Confiscated Property," Jewish Telegraphic Agency, November 5, 1945.

93. "Vienna Jews Thank Gen. Clark for His Interest in Bettering Conditions of Jews," Jewish Telegraphic Agency, December 13, 1945.

94. "News in Brief: Austria's Industries Still in Nazi Hands," Association of Jewish Refugees Information, January 1946, 8.

The Austrian government's first restitution act went into effect on July 26, 1946, and dealt with the restitution of property that had been seized by the Nazis and was still held and administered by the Austrian federal or a provincial government as successor and beneficiary of the Nazi regime.[95] The second restitution act on February 6, 1947, standardized the restitution of property still in the hands of the Austrian government as a result of seizure under the Nazis.[96] The same day, Parliament passed a third restitution act, which dealt with the return of Jews' and other victims' property and dealt with reclaiming property not taken and held by a public authority but held by individuals and organizations.[97] Despite the possibility created by such legislation to support victims' rights with regard to the return of their illegally appropriated property, with time, legal interpretations and judicial outcomes increasingly favored former Nazis and "Aryanizers."

CAMP SURVIVORS AND THE IKG

Viennese Jews read the situation and quickly got the message. They learned to trust mainly one another and to surround themselves with mostly Jewish friends. They knew that they could not rely on their government for compensation, assistance, or sympathy. Jewish returnees depended on the IKG for food, housing, communication, and other resources, while international Jewish organizations provided goods to supplement the IKG's assistance. Returning camp survivors who were left homeless turned to the IKG-run KZ Rückkehrerheime.

---

95. Bundesgesetz vom 26. Juli 1946 über die Rückstellung entzogener Vermögen, die sich in Verwaltung des Bundes oder der Bundesländer befinden (Erstes Rückstellungsgesetz), *RIS—Bundesgesetzblatt von 1945–2003*, 156/1946.

96. Bundesgesetz vom 6. Februar 1947 über die Rückstellung entzogener Vermögen, die sic him Eigentum der Republik Österreich befinden (Zweites Rückstellungsgesetz), *RIS—Bundesgesetzblatt von 1945–2003*, 53/1947.

97. Bundesgesetz vom 6. Februar 1947 über die Nichtigkeit von Vermögensentziehungen (Drittes Rückstellungsgesetz), *RIS—Bundesgesetzblatt von 1945–2003*, 54/1947.

Provisions and Communication through the Kultusgemeinde

Many returning camp survivors obtained meals from Kultusgemeinde soup kitchens and depended on supplies from foreign Jewish organizations.[98] In fact, most survivors credited the Joint with providing their basic necessities. With provisions limited for everyone in Vienna, some returnees relied on wartime black-market trading skills to organize supplies. Gertrude Schneider's mother traveled back and forth to Hungary to secure basic foodstuffs,[99] and Marianne Windholm recalled using chocolate as currency to purchase meat from a butcher.[100]

Returnees depended on the IKG for communication with their compatriots and family members not yet in Vienna. Many made a daily ritual of visiting the Jewish community's offices, looking for news of relatives and friends across the continent and, with any luck, among the small but steady trickle of returnees arriving in Vienna. Like Jewish communities and organizations throughout Europe, the IKG compiled and distributed lists of survivors living in the city to displaced persons' assembly centers and camps, as well as to Jewish community leadership in cities and countries around the globe. The compilation and dissemination of such information, coupled with tracing services facilitated by international organizations in the immediate aftermath of the war, allowed relatives and friends to search for one another in the chaos of postwar Europe.

Many Jews believed at first that an increase in the Jewish population would improve their situation.[101] As we have seen, governmental, professional, and social organizations disappointed them, but the Jewish community worked hard to meet its members' needs and to represent them. As the IKG reconstituted, it found the US occupation forces particularly helpful. Individuals also recognized that the American zone had some of the best conditions in Vienna and sought to move there, and postwar relief worker Ralph Segalman and his Joint colleagues urged those surviving Jews living

---

98. Schneider, *Exile and Destruction*, 161.
99. Ibid., 160.
100. Windholm oral history.
101. Schneider, *Exile and Destruction*, 160.

in the former Jewish district of Vienna—which fell in the Soviet zone of occupation—to move to another zone. But, Segalman observed,

> We were concerned that we might not be able to protect them in the Russian sector and who knew how long the Russians would remain friendly to the Jews? But these [many] elderly people wanted to remain in that quarter, near the old Jewish hospital, the old synagogue, and the Jewish old age home. Many of their friends lived there and the Jewish cafeteria with kosher food subsidized by the AJDC was located there. There was also a kosher bakery, subsidized with flour from the AJDC, and a pharmacy sponsored by the AJDC. This sector was not far from the Kultusgemeinde building where many cultural and Jewish political meetings were held. It was the place where Jews could meet on the street and exchange news about Palestine and emigration.[102]

Jewish survivors in Vienna benefited from the active involvement of Jewish organizations like the Joint in reestablishing their lives there. They also appreciated the Jewish soldiers among the occupation forces. Gertrude Schneider went to an IKG-organized Chanukah Ball in Vienna in 1945, the attendees of which included mostly Jewish survivors but also a number of Jewish soldiers from the various occupation forces. After some entertainment, ball-goers lit traditional candles and sang the "Maos Zur," a customary Chanukah song. "There was not a dry eye among us," recalled Schneider, "even though we should have been very happy, for our survival was indeed a great miracle, too."[103] It might be hard to expect a true "happiness" at such an occasion, as any such feeling would have been tempered with an ambivalent optimism after having lost so much and at best a sort of joy filled with relief and mixed with profound pain.

---

102. Segalman, "Letters to My Grandchildren," 85.
103. Schneider, *Exile and Destruction*, 162.

Profile of Cooperation: The KZ Rückkehrerheim at Seegasse 9

At the end of the war, the Ältestenrat controlled and ran one Jewish hospital in Vienna. The Nazis had systematically appropriated its other properties, but soon after taking the city, the Allies began to enforce the return of IKG medical facilities. By October 1945, the IKG operated five KZ Rückkehrerheime to meet the particular needs of camp survivors requiring housing, medical services, and food.[104] As we have seen, many returnees found their former homes occupied, had no one with whom they could stay, and needed immediate shelter. A number turned to KZ Rückkehrerheime for accommodation and services.

The KZ Rückkehrerheim at Seegasse 9 in Vienna's ninth district represented an example of IKG cooperation with and reliance on the US occupation forces to work toward the reconstruction of the Jewish community, starting with providing care for the IKG's most vulnerable members. The home's postwar history reveals ways the United States Forces-Austria (USFA) worked officially and unofficially to assist the Jewish community while the Austrian government—whose job it should have been—failed to do so.

At the time of the Anschluss, Vienna's Servitenviertel (a small quarter named for the Catholic Serviten order and the church located there) in the ninth district was home to a thriving middle- and upper-class Jewish community. Many Jewish organizations and religious institutions had been situated in the magnificent turn-of-the-century buildings along the picturesque cobblestone streets, including the grand Müllnergasse temple, which the Nazis burned to the ground during the November Pogrom.

For nearly three hundred years, with the exception of 1942–45, a Jewish medical facility stood at Seegasse 9. In 1698, Samuel Oppenheimer built a private Jewish hospital on the grounds alongside Vienna's oldest Jewish cemetery, and in 1793, the Jewish community took over its formal

---

104. Memo from Major Judah Nadich, US Army, to Commanding General, USFA, APO 777, US Army, October 23, 1945, Folder 104–105, Box 16, Int Affairs/DP Div., DP Section, General Records 1945–50, RG 260, United States National Archives and Records Administration (NARA), College Park, MD.

ownership. The Kultusgemeinde constructed a then-modern nursing home on the grounds in 1890 and dedicated it to Emperor Franz Joseph I. Further modernized with an addition of a two-story annex in 1935, the home contained 454 beds for patients in 1936.[105]

The facility at Seegasse 9 served the city's elderly Jews until mid-1943 and was the last Jewish nursing home closed and emptied of residents in Nazi Vienna.[106] On August 25, 1942, the German Reich purchased the building from the IKG for 622,000 Reichsmark and transferred the monies to a fund intended to finance forced emigration from Bohemia and Moravia.[107] On May 25, 1943, the last 122 residents of the nursing home were evacuated, most of them to Terezín, although some were resettled at the Swedish Mission across the street at Seegasse 16.[108] The Swedish Lutheran Church had established the Swedish Mission in 1920 with the specific intent of converting and baptizing Jews. From the time of the Anschluss through 1941, however, the staff served "non-Aryan Christians" persecuted under the Nuremberg Laws and some Jews, helping with their social welfare and emigration needs. Once deportations to the east began, the home at Seegasse 16 served under the management of the IKG as a hospital and nursing home for Jews and Christians with Jewish family backgrounds, and from June 1943, the Nazis permitted it to continue in existence as a home for couples in "mixed marriages."[109] In all, the Swedish Mission helped some three thousand Jews and Christians with Jewish family backgrounds to emigrate from Nazi Vienna.[110] After the war, Seegasse 16 also served as a

---

105. Angelika Shoshana Duizend-Jensen, *Jüdische Gemeinden, Vereine, Stiftungen und Fonds. "Arisierung" und Restitution* (Vienna: Historikerkommission, 2002), 12.

106. Ibid., 61.

107. Elizabeth Anthony and Dirk Rupnow, "Wien IX, Seegasse 9: Ein österreichisch-jüdischer Geschichtsort," in *Nurinst Jahrbuch 2010, Beiträge zur deutschen und jüdischen Geschichte, Schwerpunktthema: Leben danach—Jüdischer Neubeginn im Land der Täter*, ed. Jim G. Tobias and Peter Zinke (Nürnberg: Antogo Verlag, 2010), 107.

108. Bericht über die Tätigkeit des Ältestenrates der Juden in Wien im Jahre 1943, p. 11, A/W 117, CAHJP.

109. Duizend-Jensen, *Jüdische Gemeinden*, 63.

110. Ulrich Trinks, "Die schwedische Mission in der Seegasse," Koordinierungsausschuss für christlich-jüdische Zusammenarbeit, accessed July 25, 2020, https://www.christenundjuden.org/index_files/b9db2b368f00956c4e0e699f6f08c64b-19.html.

KZ Rückkehrerheim and often worked in coordination with the home at Seegasse 9 across the street.[111]

The building at Seegasse 9 was handed over to the German Reich on May 27, 1943.[112] The Waffen-SS moved in about a week later (June 4, 1943)[113] and used the home to billet troops until the end of the war.[114] An immediate postwar witness statement dated June 3, 1945, also mentioned that under Nazi possession it had housed a jail, either specifically for or at least also used to detain some Wehrmacht deserters.[115] The Nazis forcibly relocated those who remained at the Swedish Mission at Seegasse 16 to the Jewish hospital at Malzgasse 7 on June 21, 1943.[116] The IKG resumed operation of the nursing home at Seegasse 9 under the Soviets, and although the IKG had not yet regained ownership of the building, it reopened the building as a KZ Rückkehrerheim on July 7, 1945.[117] On that same day, the first large repatriation transport from Terezín arrived with five hundred survivors, four hundred of whom became Seegasse 9's first residents.[118] The Rückkehrerheim manager Nicholas Lazarowitsch, who had survived the war in Vienna,[119] reported that upon the facility's opening, its furnishings scarcely accommodated the new arrivals. Properly feeding them also proved difficult for the first eight weeks, but the home's ration assignment from the US forces gradually improved. By the middle of September, residents received

---

111. Bailer et al., *Erzählte Geschichte*, 173.

112. Duizend-Jensen, *Jüdische Gemeinden*, 63.

113. Ältestenrat der Juden in Wien, 22. Wochenbericht, June 1, 1943, DÖW.

114. Max Birnstein to the director of the Ältestenrat, May 28, 1943, A/W 275 and 1827, CAHJP.

115. "Postwar Witness Statements concerning the Formation of the Special Detachment Dirlewanger," June 3, 1945, 1.1.0.6/82326879/ITS Digital Archive, USHMM.

116. Bericht über die Tätigkeit des Ältestenrates der Juden in Wien im Jahre 1943, p. 11.

117. Seegasse 9 KZ-Rückkehrerheim director Lazarowitsch to the IKG Amtsdirektion at Schottenring 25, 1010 Wien, August 21, 1948, XXVII, B, e, B31, Das Archiv der Israelitischen Kultusgemeinde Wien (IKG Archive), Vienna, Austria.

118. Report by Nicholas Lazarowitsch, manager of the Seegasse 9 KZ-Rückkehrerheim, December 22, 1945, Lazarowitsch briefcase (not catalogued), 1, IKG Archive.

119. It is unclear exactly how Lazarowitsch survived the war. As shown on a "List of homeinmates" of Seegasse 9 (January 2, 1947, 3.1.1.2/82048263/ITS Digital Archive, USHMM), he presumably self-reported that he survived the war in Vienna. His name, however, does not appear on a list of "Austrian Jews residing in Vienna during the occupation" (November 30, 1945, 3.1.1.3/78804734–78804758/ITS Digital Archive, USHMM).

forty grams of bread daily with some meat, cheese, or jam, plus a breakfast of coffee with forty milliliters of milk, a half liter of *Eintopf* (a hearty Viennese meat and vegetable soup) for lunch, and dinner of forty milliliters of broth with various traditional Viennese *Einlage* (noodles, meat, strips of crepes, or dumplings added to soup).[120] By October 1945, Seegasse 9 was the largest of the five shelters for returning concentration camp survivors in Vienna, one of two in the US sector.[121]

The USFA assumed official oversight of Seegasse 9 on November 15, 1945, and officially classified it as a Displaced Persons Camp under the supervision of its DP Section.[122] This was unusual, and a phenomenon particular to Vienna, as the United Nations Relief and Rehabilitation Agency (UNRRA) defined a "displaced person" as one displaced *outside* his or her country of origin. Brigadier General Ralph Tate, deputy commander to General Clark, had interceded to change the status of Viennese Jews from "refugees" to "displaced persons," which entitled them to medical aid, food, shelter, and other support from US Army sources.[123] Without this, 90 percent of Seegasse 9's residents would have been excluded from the benefits afforded displaced persons.[124] The fact that USFA formally qualified all Viennese Jews as "displaced persons" points to American efforts to provide assistance to the Jewish community by making a special allowance, actually bending rules to accommodate them with funds allocated for DPs. In addition, General Mark Clark, although baptized Episcopalian during his time at West Point, descended from a Jewish mother,[125] and there has been speculation that this affected his interest in the surviving Jews living in areas under his command. Policies regarding Jews appeared more strictly enforced

---

120. Report by Lazarowitsch, 1.
121. Nadich to Commanding General, October 23, 1945.
122. Nicholas Lazarowitsch to the IKG Amtsdirektion, August 21, 1948, IKG Archive.
123. Report by Harry A. Freidenberg, Administrative Officer, Military Government Section, Vienna Area Command, US Army, to Rabbi Max Nussbaum, May 25, 1947, 2, AR 45/54–143, Archives of the American Jewish Joint Distribution Committee, New York, NY.
124. Report by Lazarowitsch, 1.
125. Benjamin Ginsberg, *How the Jews Defeated Hitler: Exploding the Myth of Jewish Passivity in the Face of Nazism* (Lanham, MD: Rowman and Littlefield, 2013), 56.

in Austria under Clark,[126] and he was certainly quite vocal and supportive about the contributions of the Jewish soldiers who served under him.

In addition to funding and overseeing the medical care, US Army officials assisted residents in pursuing the return of former property. In a December 22, 1945, report, Lazarowitsch stated that none of his facility's residents who had lived in Vienna before the Anschluss had regained his or her home.[127] Many found their homes occupied by the Austrians who bought or received them under Nazi "Aryanization" policies. Army officials kept records of progress made toward regaining such property, but, according to the residents' documentation, few if any had regained their homes even four years after the end of the war.[128] Restitution legislation did not cover rented apartments. As residents of Seegasse 9 physically recovered and sought to reestablish independent lives in Vienna, they looked for housing outside the Rückkehrerheim, and many gave up on the possibility of regaining past residences. If they were not to recoup property with the support of the US Army, they reasoned, they would never recover anything.

In December 1945, about 60 percent of the population of mainly camp survivors at the KZ Rückkehrerheim at Seegasse 9 were over the age of sixty, reflecting the demographic pattern of the Jewish population of postwar Vienna.[129] Two years later, a census record dated October 16, 1947, listed a total of 291 residents, 43 between the ages of sixty and sixty-nine, 85 over the age of seventy, and 26 over the age of eighty. One was eighty-seven.[130] Like the general population at Seegasse 9, these 291 were almost without exception concentration camp survivors, most from Terezín. The institution's history as an IKG nursing home might contribute to the high concentration of elderly at Seegasse 9, but the percentages nonetheless closely resemble the significantly high proportion of aged Jews in Vienna.

---

126. Joseph W. Bendersky, *The "Jewish Threat": Anti-Semitic Politics of the U.S. Army* (New York: Basic Books, 2000), 360.
127. Report by Lazarowitsch, 2.
128. Applications filed by residents, folder "Wohnungen," B13, AD, Rückkehrerheime, Seegasse 9, 1949, IKG Archive.
129. Report by Lazarowitsch, 2.
130. List of all residents of Seegasse 9 KZ-Rückkehrerheim, folder "Diverse," B13, AD, Rückkehrerheime, Seegasse 9, October 16, 1947, IKG Archive.

The KZ-Rückkehrerheim at Seegasse 9 employed many of its residents in its daily operations. Many housed there were of advanced age and unable to assume outside jobs, while others encountered difficulties regaining trade and business licenses and therefore were delayed or prevented in their efforts to return to work.[131] The home paid wages to residents for peeling potatoes and for helping needy roommates.[132] In October 1945, seventy-seven-year-old Jella Caro, a survivor of Terezín,[133] lived in a large room at Seegasse 9 with fourteen roommates. She received compensation for her assistance with daily activities with the elderly and the partially blind or deaf among them.[134] In addition, the central kitchen that supported IKG-run facilities across Vienna operated from the neighboring house at Seegasse 11 and employed many of the homes' residents. Workers at both Seegasse 9 and 11 received either cash or points to be used for purchase within the DP camp system, or a combination of the two.[135] The aged, the physically impaired, mothers, and those who were caring for young relatives or other dependents also received work exemptions and were allotted a certain amount of money to live.

The US Army, as supervising and organizing power, oversaw and funded many of the home's activities until 1950.[136] Initially it provided food, including special items for Jewish holidays, and undertook renovations to

---

131. Report by Lazarowitsch, 2.

132. List of payments in currency and points to camp residents, AD, Rückkehrerheime, Seegasse 9, 1949, B13, folder II, Punkte 1948, IKG Archive.

133. The Gestapo deported Gabriele Caro from Vienna to Terezín on Transport 28 on June 20, 1942. Abgangsliste des. 28. Transportes, 1.2.1.1/11203480/ITS Digital Archive, USHMM. Caro was liberated in Terezín and had returned to Vienna by September 20, 1945. List of Austrians who returned to Vienna from Theresienstadt, 3.1.1.3/78805387/ITS Digital Archive, USHMM. She was listed as residing at Seegasse 9 in September 1945 (Aus den Konzentrationslagern nach Wien Zurückgekehrte, September 1945, 3.1.1.3/78805180/ITS Digital Archive, USHMM), in 1946 (Liste der in Wien lebenden Glaubensjuden, 1946, 3.1.1.3/78805419/ITS Digital Archive, USHMM), and on January 2, 1947 (List of home-inmates, 3.1.1.2/82048260/ITS Digital Archive, USHMM).

134. Jella Caro to "Meine Lieben," October 25, 1945, accession number 70867, document 1339/1, Wiener Library for the Study of the Holocaust & Genocide, London, UK.

135. File "Kultusgemeinde Korrespondenz," AD, Rückkehrerheime, Seegasse, 1949, B13, IKG Archive.

136. List of payments in currency and points to camp residents, Punkte 1948, IKG Archive.

the building, including the installation of central heating and the repair of broken windows.[137] The Joint also supported activities in the KZ-Rückkehrerheim at Seegasse 9, as it did in many DP camps. Private individuals around the world sent "care packages" of food and relief supplies for survivors through Joint-organized channels, as well as through other international Jewish organizations. Others supported the home with direct gifts. Max Hirschmann, formerly of Vienna, corresponded directly with Lazarowitsch to offer his and other former Viennese Jews' assistance from their host country, Australia. Over a number of months, Hirschmann and his group provided many basic supplies for Seegasse 9.[138]

The Joint funded a *Kindergarten* (day-care center and preschool) for children residing in the home and for community members desiring a Jewish program. Participants learned arts and crafts and music, played sports in the garden (the old Jewish cemetery next to which the home was situated), and took walks around the neighborhood. Seegasse 9 also hosted holiday parties and games for children.[139]

Religious observances took place for young and old residents alike and included Purim and Chanukah parties, Passover Seders, and services for the High Holidays. A 1948 Chanukah party included song and dance performances and plays put on by the children of the kindergarten, each of whom also received a gift.[140] The Swedish Mission across the street provided Easter eggs and Christmas trees for the few non-Jewish residents. US Army reports to the DP Section reveal that USFA personnel were involved in both oversight of and participation in such activities. They also placed a priority on ensuring that higher-ranking officers were aware of such events.[141]

---

137. Report by Lazarowitsch, 2.
138. AD, Rückkehrerheime, Seegasse 9, B13, folder "Max Hirschmann," IKG Archive.
139. AD, Rückkehrerheime, Seegasse 9, 1949, B13, folder "Rapporte: Joint, IKG," IKG Archive.
140. Report of December 31, 1948, AD, Rückkehrerheime, Seegasse 9, 1949, B13, folder "Rapport Woche," IKG Archive.
141. Mentioned on various reports from 1948 and 1949, AD, Rückkehrerheime, Seegasse 9, 1949, B13, folder "Rapport Woche," IKG Archive. Amusing to today's reader, American soldiers' accounts tell of residents celebrating Passover, "the Jewish Easter," and Chanukah, "the Jewish Christmas."

The USFA and the IKG tried to accommodate residents' social and cultural needs in addition to religious observances. Visiting guests and celebrities performed concerts to entertain residents. An administrative report of activities in the home specified that Peter Herz and a cast of London actors and singers delivered a "great music hall performance" for a number of important guests (presumably representatives from the US Army) in attendance on June 28, 1949.[142] On April 12, 1946, residents also showed their gratitude to their American benefactors with an observance of the first anniversary of the death of Franklin Delano Roosevelt at an event that included a formal gathering with guest speakers.[143]

The USFA oversaw operations of the facility until 1948. The IKG regained official ownership and control of the building at Seegasse 9 in 1947,[144] and by March 1, 1948, the home was completely self-administered and covered its costs with revenues generated from the residents and from the surplus of the Seegasse 11 refugee kitchen.[145] In addition to its initial and stated purpose as a home for those who were returning from concentration camps, Seegasse 9 opened its doors in later years to include other DPs and refugees, mostly Jews. The home received, for example, a number of Jewish refugees returning in 1949 after many years in exile in Shanghai.[146] The IKG took complete control of the house in 1950 with funding from the city of Vienna, and it returned to its previous role as a Jewish nursing home. Seegasse 9 also retained its Rückkehrerheim function in part until the end of 1953, and former concentration camp prisoners resided there until the mid-1960s.[147] The IKG finally sold the building to the city of Vienna in 1978, ending the

---

142. Report on Seegasse 9 to Mr. Healy, July 1, 1949, AD, Rückkehrerheime, Seegasse 9, 1949, B13, folder "Rapport," IKG Archive.

143. Various photos, captioned and dated April 12, 1946, Lazarowitsch briefcase (not catalogued), IKG Archive.

144. 1.3.2.119.A41—VEAV—Vermögensentzug-Anmeldungsverordnung, 1947, 9. Bez., C 3, Wiener Stadt- und Landesarchiv, MA 8, Vienna, Austria.

145. Lazarowitsch to the IKG Amtsdirektion, August 21, 1948.

146. Report on Seegasse 9 to Mr. Healy, April 7, 1949, AD, Rückkehrerheime, Seegasse 9, 1949, B13, folder "Rapport," IKG Archive.

147. *Der Lebensbaum: Der Wiener Israelitischen Kultusgemeine, 1960–1964* (Vienna: Israelitishche Kultusgemeinde Wien, Fritz Molden Grossdruckerei und Verlag Gesellschaft m.b.H., 1964), 133.

centuries-long Jewish ownership of the property (except for the few years between 1942 and 1945), and opened a new community-run nursing home in another part of the city.

After years of torture, deprivation, and starvation, many concentration camp survivors thought only of returning to their familial homes. Austrian Jews made their way back to Vienna independently or with assistance from their liberators. Few found the people they had so long yearned to see. As they sought to establish a toehold in what they fondly thought of as their hometown, they found that neither the Austrian public nor the government welcomed them. In their partially destroyed city, returnees confronted the loss of their family and community members, as well as their homes and businesses. As Austrian national consciousness formed around the "victim myth," returning camp survivors turned to the IKG and international Jewish organizations for assistance as they struggled to reestablish lives.

A desire to return to one's familial home motivated camp survivors to go back to Vienna, but in the face of the many obstacles and disappointments, some felt that no sense of "home" remained. When Gertrude Chandler was liberated from a concentration camp in Poland, she thought only of going back to Vienna. Once returned, however, she learned that none of her family members had survived. She recovered from tuberculosis contracted in the camp but was unable to bear the emotional pain and the hostile atmosphere she felt surrounding her. Chandler emigrated to Palestine in 1947.[148]

Still, many did stay. Camp survivor Susanne Lamberg was among them. The Nazis had deported her and her parents to Terezín on October 1, 1942.[149] She survived Terezín, Auschwitz, a death march, and Bergen Belsen.[150] Of her decision to return, Lamberg said, "In 1945, I was 20 and at

---

148. Gertrude Chandler, interview 42583, Visual History Archive (VHA), USC Shoah Foundation, Los Angeles, CA, accessed at USHMM, August 16, 2011.
149. 43. Transport vom 1.10.1942 nach Theresienstadt, 1.2.1.1/11204058/ITS Digital Archive, USHMM.
150. Nominal Roll of German Nationals, May 10, 1945, 1.1.3.1/3395393/ITS Digital Archive, USHMM.

the end. I was deathly ill, weighed 35 kilograms. I had lost my family. I had seen more dead bodies than anyone. But I wanted to live. And to go home. Austria and Vienna were my home. Despite it all. And because I had no other home. So I came back. And I stayed."[151]

---

151. Susanne Lamberg, "Nacht des Schweigens" (speech, Vienna, Austria, March 12, 2008), A Letter to the Stars, accessed November 12, 2011, http://www.lettertothestars.at/lastwitnesses_pers.php?ctype=1&uid=2637.

4

TO RECLAIM *THEIR* AUSTRIA

Hansi Tausig spent the war years in exile in Great Britain, where she became active in the youth group of the Austrian Communist Party (Kommunistische Partei Österreichs, or KPÖ), Young Austria.[1] As war's end drew near, she and her comrades—many of them Jewish, like Hansi—conducted a book drive. Armed with lists of the names and addresses of German and Austrian Jewish refugees, they knocked on doors across the city. In the early years of the Nazi regime, many families had escaped with complete household inventories that included massive collections of books. As the young Austrian Jews greeted their fellow refugees, they asked them to donate titles banned by the Nazis. They explained that they planned to send the books to Vienna to replenish libraries and to reeducate a generation of young people conditioned by years of Nazi propaganda and censorship.

The idealistic young Communists learned that not all refugees shared their hopeful vision of a postwar Austria. Some told them that they would rather burn their books or throw them in the River Thames than give them to Germans or Austrians. The rehabilitation of those who were connected in

---

[1]. For a summary of Young Austria's activities and biographies of former members, see Sonja Frank, ed., *Young Austria: Österreicherinnen im Britsischen Exil, 1938–1947; Für ein freies, demokratisches und unabhängiges Österreich* (Vienna: ÖGB Verlag, 2012). See pages 419–26 for a biography of Hansi's husband, Otto Tausig (mentioned later in this chapter), which also includes information about and a photograph of Hansi.

any way to the mass murder of their families and friends ranked low among refugee Jews' priorities. Unlike the politically committed and convinced youths who greeted them at their doors, they foresaw no place for themselves in postwar Germany or Austria and wanted nothing to do with their former neighbors. Still, Hansi and her friends managed to gather hundreds of books, which they shipped to Vienna. For them, the book drive was part of a larger vision of reclaiming their homeland and securing Austria as an autonomous, democratic state. The youth group planned to distribute the materials once their members arrived home to begin the work of correcting the influence of years of Nazi antisemitic and anticommunist ideology.

In spring 1946, Hansi, her husband, Otto, and some other Young Austria members arrived in Vienna eager to begin their work. The Tausigs spent their first night back in their hometown on the floor of the Communist Party's youth offices, where, to their dismay, they happened upon the books that they had so diligently collected in London. They had been neither circulated nor read. Abandoned and forgotten, the entire collection sat in a moldy, disorganized pile in a storage room. They had sent the books to Vienna more than six months before, but in the face of the more immediate, basic needs of the city's postwar disaster situation, the distribution of reeducation and cultural material held little importance.

Hansi pinpointed the moment of finding the discarded books as the symbolic start of the disappointment and disillusionment that followed. All they had discussed and planned in great detail for the reeducation of Austrian youth proved unrealistic in the midst of a chaotic and partially destroyed Vienna. The neglected, crumbling pile of ruined books, Hansi said, "was all a lot of rubbish," and, similarly, many of their idealistic expectations and plans for a significant role in postwar Austria were also relegated to a figurative garbage heap.[2]

During the war years, the Austrian Communist and Social Democratic Parties operated in the various countries of Austrian refugees' exile; both had

---

2. Hansi Tausig, interview by author, Vienna, Austria, December 13, 2010.

a significant presence in London, but other hubs of émigré political activity included Washington, DC, Stockholm, Paris (until 1940), and Moscow. They organized their groups and recruited members, provided activities and events, and otherwise gave refugees in foreign lands an adopted family and home with which to identify. They provided a vision for their members' return to their *political home*, as both parties planned for and worked toward a day when they would return to reclaim *their* Austria.

A firm belief that both country and government had been forcibly taken from the Austrian populace guided the efforts of these party members. From the start, the Austrian Communist Party saw this as a two-part violation.[3] In the view of party members, the Austrofascists first had assumed dictatorial control with the installation of a new constitution in May 1934, which continued until the time of the Anschluss. Based in part on Italian fascism and Catholic national politics, the Austrofascist regime opposed the National Socialist sentiment brewing in Austria and imprisoned Nazi Party members, but it incarcerated Social Democrats and Communists too, deeming them political opponents as well. The Anschluss ushered in a second round of oppression for the latter two groups, as the Nazis too imprisoned their political enemies. Former "illegal" Nazis (illegal under the terms of the Austrofascist regime) became important members of the Nazi Party in Austria, while supporters of Karl von Schuschnigg and the ousted Catholic fascist leaders found themselves in concentration camps alongside the Communists and Social Democrats they had jailed.

The Social Democratic Party (then, the Sozialdemokratische Arbeiterpartei Österreichs, or SDAPÖ) had initially endorsed union with Germany. After the Allies signed the 1943 Moscow Declaration that, among other things, clearly stated the official position that Austria was the first victim of Nazi aggression and implying that the Anschluss was an invasion and occupation by a foreign power, the Social Democrats came to concur with the KPÖ's opposition.[4] By the end of the war, both groups had

---

3. Free Austrian Movement, *The Case of Austria* (London: New Europe, 1942).
4. Marietta Bearman, "'Austria Tomorrow?' Planning for a Post-war Austria," in *Out of Austria: The Austrian Centre in London in World War II*, ed. Marietta Bearman, Charmian Brinson, Richard Dove, Anthony Grenville, and Jennifer Taylor (London: Tauris Academic Studies, 2008), 213.

instructed their members abroad that Austria and their fellow Austrians eagerly awaited and welcomed their return. These directives included the assertion that, once the Allies forced out the Germans, the exiles would be needed to take part in the reclamation and reconstruction of the country. In the meantime, they should work and prepare for that time from their positions abroad.

Bruno Kreisky, an Austrian Jew who survived the war in Sweden, later became the Socialist chancellor of Austria from 1970 to 1983. He wrote that even before the Nazi regime, the Socialist movement had been a "true home" for many people. "It enabled them to feel that their life, even with all its misery, still had human dignity."[5] In the same way, the Social Democrat and the Communist Parties provided continuity for their members in exile by fashioning such homes and surrogate families abroad. Both parties impressed their vision for postwar Austria on their members, and Kreisky specified that one of his primary political concepts in the immediate postwar years was to found a new Austrian patriotism and to make Austria "into a good homeland for its people."[6] For him and for other convinced Communists and Social Democrats—many of them Jews—their commitment was as *Austrians* who had a role in and a responsibility for their nation after the war. Their political activity in exile prepared them to return, reclaim, and reshape their political home.

In *Reclaiming Heimat*, a literary analysis of memoirs written by Jewish Austrian reémigrés, language and literature scholar Jacqueline Vansant has described returnees' motivation as a desire to reattach to an Austrian collective, a "we." She specifies that Socialist and Communist political beliefs provided a concept of the "we" that one could hope to rejoin.[7] Austrian-born writer and Holocaust survivor Jean Améry never returned to live in his homeland, but he also suggested the significance of a connection to a collective identity through his discussion of finding its absence. In his essay

---

5. Bruno Kreisky, Matthew Paul Berg, Jill Lewis, and Oliver Rathkolb, *The Struggle for a Democratic Austria: Bruno Kreisky on Peace and Social Justice* (New York: Berghahn Books, 2000), 69.

6. Bruno Kreisky, *Zwischen den Zeiten* (Berlin: Siedler, 1986), 136.

7. Jacqueline Vansant, *Reclaiming Heimat: Trauma and Mourning in Memoirs by Jewish Austrian Reémigrés* (Detroit: Wayne State University Press, 2001), 42.

"Wieviel Heimat braucht der Mensch?" (How much home does a person need?), he wrote about the loss he felt of both an individual and a collective identity. "I was no longer an I and did not live within a we."[8] Rather than returning to reclaim a lost home, Améry's experiences had taught him that his deep bonds to his homeland had been an "existential misunderstanding." As Améry understood it, he and other Austrian Jews forced into exile had to realize that they had not lost their country; rather, they needed to recognize that it had never belonged to them.[9] Each perspective exhibits an aspect of the importance of a concept of home to which one feels a belonging. One elucidates the hunt for something fundamental and meaningful, while the other stresses the failure to find or the outright loss of the same. The Social Democrat and the Communist Parties in exile kindled and stoked their members' desire for a "we" and drew them to return to Vienna with hopes of home, even after the devastation of their families and communities.

Both parties' fundamental beliefs rested on the premise that Germany had invaded and occupied Austria against its will, a perspective that was first advanced by Austrian exile groups abroad and that later gained official weight with the Moscow Declaration. A little heard and less acknowledged portion of the Declaration was the further stipulation that Austria carried "responsibility for its participation in the war on Hitler's side." Many of the large proportion of Jews among both the Social Democrats and the Communists shared the belief in this early iteration of the victim myth. Their acceptance of it paved the way for many to return to and reclaim their *political home*, an idea fostered—and, for some, created—during their time abroad. Refugees' identification with these parties also permitted an interpretation of their persecution as a manifestation of political strife rather than as the oppression of a cultural or ethnic group.[10]

---

8. Jean Améry, "Ich war kein Ich mehr und lebte nicht in einem Wir," in *Jenseits von Schuld und Sühne: Bewältigungsversuche eines Überwältigten* (Stuttgart: Klett-Cotta Verlag, 1977), 78.

9. "Wir aber hatten nicht das Land verloren, sondern mußten erkennen, daß es niemals unser Besitz gewesen war. Für uns war, was mit diesem Land und seinen Menschen zusammenhing, ein Lebensmißverständnis." Ibid., 86.

10. Christoph Reinprecht, "Jewish Identity in Postwar Austria: Experiences and Dilemmas," in *Jewish Studies at the Central European University: Public Lectures, 1996–1999*, ed. András Kovács and Eszter Andor (Budapest: Central European University, 2000), 207.

Reémigré Jewish Communists and Social Democrats faced antisemitism and clear evidence that they in fact were not wanted, but their political commitment guided them through the difficult postwar years of reconstructing an independent nation. They believed in the home that their parties had provided them during the years of Austrofascist suppression in Austria and throughout their wartime exile abroad, as well as the home promised to await them in Vienna after the war. The surrogate families they had formed abroad solidified the sense of political home and belonging in Vienna. Accepting the idea that Austria had been the Nazis' first victim, many returned assured that the Germans' departure also meant the departure of the Nazis and that home awaited them. For Hannah Fischer, a young Viennese Jewish Communist who survived the war in England, going back to her hometown was key. "I was born here, I was brought up here, I went to school here, and though I [experienced] quite some antisemitism . . . I also had friends who were friendly and interested and so on. . . . I didn't feel that the town was at fault. It was just the Nazis."[11] Hannah and those like her returned home, to *their* Austria.

AUSTRIAN COMMUNISTS AND SOCIAL DEMOCRATS BEFORE THE ANSCHLUSS

Austrian Communists' and Social Democrats' political commitment throughout and after World War II flowed from their parties' histories, particularly their role in the political past of Austria—and specifically Vienna—after World War I and during the Austrofascist dictatorship of 1933–38. The significant part played by Social Democrats in "Red Vienna," the disastrous results of the short civil war in 1934, and the Austrofascists' persecution and arrest of members of both the Austrian Communist and Social Democratic Parties shaped both groups' commitment to a nation that they viewed as having been usurped by a hostile power. Then, too, Austrofascist political oppression had led many to flee Austria even before

---

11. Hannah Fischer, interview by author, Vienna, Austria, June 25, 2011.

the arrival of the Germans. Communist Prive Friedjung, for example, left Vienna for Moscow in November 1934 and returned in September 1947.[12] Dollfuss banned both the Communist and Nazi Parties and, after the civil war in February 1934, eventually also declared the Social Democratic Party illegal. In July of the same year, Nazi revolutionaries assassinated Chancellor Engelbert Dollfuss in an unsuccessful attempted coup, and Schuschnigg succeeded him to stave off National Socialism for another four years.

Czechoslovakia became the center of Austrian Communist and Social Democrat activity in exile. The Social Democrats established a foreign bureau in Brünn, and the KPÖ set up offices in Prague.[13] With the Germans' invasion of the Sudetenland and subsequent annexation of Bohemia and Moravia, many Austrian Communists continued their journey eastward to seek security in the Soviet Union, where they felt they could live according to their beliefs with like-minded comrades. Others, both Communists and Social Democrats, found safety in Yugoslavia, Switzerland, Belgium, France, and the Scandinavian countries.[14] Communist and Social Democrat Austrian Jews, persecuted for political reasons under Dollfuss and Schuschnigg, found refuge in Palestine too. Max Tauber's father, a member of the Social Democratic Party, was threatened with arrest after he refused to join the Fatherland Front. He fled to Palestine, and his family joined him there. Thus, Max was not in Vienna at the time of the Anschluss, and he and his family survived the Nazis in exile in Palestine.[15]

The Austrian Communist and Social Democrat Parties took different positions on unification with Germany. The Social Democrats favored Anschluss and considered it a viable option for their party's political and strategic future. After the Germans' arrival in Austria, however, the Nazis maintained the ban on the Social Democrats and the Communists and added to their list of targets the leaders of the Schuschnigg government.

---

12. Prive Friedjung, *"Wir wollten nur das Paradies auf Erden": Die Erinnerungen einer jüdischen Kommunisten aus der Bukowina* (Vienna: Böhlau Verlag, 1995), 185, 256.

13. Max Lotteraner, *Österreicher im Exil, 1934–1945* (Linz: Kammer für Arbeiter und Angestellte für Oberösterreich, 1977), 11.

14. Ibid.

15. Max Tauber, interview by author, Vienna, Austria, October 22, 2010.

The Nazis deported their political opponents to concentration camps, where former enemies suddenly found themselves imprisoned together. Increased antisemitic measures and rhetoric also accompanied the Nazis' arrival in Austria, and many Jews, along with Communists and Social Democrats (both Jewish and gentile), fled Austria.

WARTIME IN EXILE

Once the Nazis' threat and intentions became clear, many Jewish members of both the Social Democrat and Communist Parties fled to nearby countries. Some Austrian Communist volunteers had fought with the International Brigades in the Spanish Civil War (July 17, 1936–April 1, 1939) and, after Franco's victory in April 1939, had remained in perceived safety in France rather than return to Nazi Austria.[16] Other Social Democrats and Communists fled from Austria to France. Anni Friedler married a French friend she had met in a Socialist youth camp years before in order to escape. She remained in Paris until the Nazis marched in and then fled south, where she worked with the Communist Party until February 1943.[17] A number of Austrian Social Democrats, such as Bruno Kreisky, who decades after the war would become Austrian chancellor, found safety in Scandinavia. Like Kreisky, some of these refugees later found their paths of remigration via the Soviet Union[18] or by passing through eastern Europe to enter Austria.[19] Some Communists fled east to the Soviet Union, both for security and to join their ideological comrades.

A significant number of Austrian Social Democrats and Communists—among them, politically active Jews—fled to Great Britain, where prewar

---

16. An estimated combined total of five thousand German and Austrian volunteers fought on the side of the Spanish Republicans with International Brigades. See Hugh Thomas, *The Spanish Civil War* (London: Penguin, 2001), 637.

17. Anni Friedler, interview, 173, Dokumentationsarchiv des österreichischen Widerstandes (DÖW), Vienna, Austria. Their marriage did not last, but as it seemed to have been a union meant to ensure Anni's safety, it was nonetheless successful.

18. See Walter Neuhaus, interview, 300, DÖW.

19. See Kurt Hahn, interview, 210, DÖW.

governmental policies provided some opportunity for resettlement. An IKG and Reichsvereinigung der Juden Deutschlands (Reich's Association of Jews in Germany) report on Jewish emigration, as submitted on November 11, 1941, to the Reichssicherheitshauptamt (Reich Security Head Office), stated that 146,816 of the 206,000[20] Austrian Jews estimated as of May 2, 1938, had emigrated to other countries, including 27,293 to Great Britain.[21] Postwar statistics of the Kultusgemeinde and the Jewish Historical Commission for a similar period (March 13, 1938, to mid-November 1941) quoted a slightly higher total of 30,850.[22] Not all of these people began as politically engaged members of the Communist or Social Democratic Parties in exile, but their sheer number created a meaningful pool of disenfranchised and isolated recruits seeking group identification and a feeling of home with other Austrians. In addition to these Jewish refugees, some 3,000 non-Jewish Austrian political exiles resided in Great Britain and took part in maintaining Austrian political activity abroad. Jews thus constituted about 90 percent of all Austrian exiles in Great Britain during World War II.[23]

Some Jews had arrived in Great Britain as unaccompanied children on the *Kindertransport*, while a number of young women had come with special permits to work as domestic help. Others found asylum through their own means or the IKG's unflagging efforts to help them emigrate. We shall follow politically active Austrian Jews who survived the war in exile in Great Britain, paying particular attention to the wartime and postwar experiences of members of the KPÖ in exile and their activities as members of the Austrian Centre and its youth group, Young Austria. A close analysis provides

---

20. Jonny Moser calculated the estimate of 206,000 Austrian Jews to be about 5,000 too high and came to the total of 201,000. See his calculations and explanation in Moser, *Demographie der jüdischen Bevölkerung Österreichs, 1938–1945* (Vienna: Dokumentationsarchiv des österreichischen Widerstandes, 1999), 18–19.

21. Wolfgang Muchitsch, *Österreicher im Exil: Großbritannien 1938–1945; Eine Dokumentation*, ed. Dokumentationsarchiv des österreichischen Widerstandes (Vienna: Österreicher Bundesverlag, 1992), 8.

22. Herbert Rosenkranz, *Verfolgung und Selbstbehauptung: Die Juden in Österreich, 1938–1945* (Vienna: Herold Verlag, 1978), 270.

23. Muchitsch, *Österreicher im Exil*, 8.

insight into their reasons for and expectations about returning to postwar Vienna, which were similar to those of other politically active Austrian Jewish reémigrés. As we shall see, ideology was a key motivation for their decisions to go back to Vienna.

The Austrian Centre and Young Austria

After fleeing Nazi Vienna and arriving in Britain, many Austrians sought to combat isolation and to maintain some tie to their home country by connecting with other refugees in the same situation. Various cultural groups sprouted in Great Britain to provide exiles places to gather and events in which to take part, and to offer a feeling of home. Because British authorities had imposed restrictions on refugees' political activity and organization,[24] some such groups provided a substitute for political activity by continuing engagement through other means. The Austrian Centre was one important Austrian cultural group that also operated unofficially as an organ of the KPÖ. Originally established in early 1939, the Centre opened its doors on March 15, 1939.[25] The founders conceived of and created a community center to serve as a place for Austrians to gather and also aimed to help the economically ailing Austrian Self-Aid charitable organization provide assistance and guidance to Austrian refugees.[26] Like most Austrian refugees in Great Britain, the majority of the Centre's members were Jewish.

By 1941, the Centre maintained a head office and two branches in London, plus one each in Birmingham and Glasgow. Members enjoyed access to club rooms and reading rooms, attended organized lectures, and even dined in an Austrian restaurant. Socials and dances were held, in addition to many other activities including a Jewish study circle, a literary debating club, and a knitting group. The Centre-affiliated Viennese Theatre, The Lantern, provided a venue for the drama group's performances, and the publishing arm of the Austrian Centre, Free Austrian Books, operated out of the

---

24. Anthony Grenville, "The Politics of the Austrian Centre," in Bearman et al., *Out of Austria*, 25.

25. Charmian Brinson, "'A Very Ambitious Plan': The Early Days of the Austrian Centre," in Bearman et al., *Out of Austria*, 9.

26. Ibid., 7.

Performance by the "Young Austria" choir on June 28, 1942, at the Stoll Theatre in London, an example of the many cultural activities offered by the Austrian Centre. (DÖW)

main London branch. The Centre offered refugees help and advice about war matters and issues surrounding the internment of family members.[27] It even offered membership to interested English citizens, and, as of January 1, 1943, the Centre counted a total of three thousand dues-paying members.[28]

Attracted by cultural events, attendees soon recognized that the Austrian Communist Party guided and ran the organization. In addition to social and cultural offerings, the Centre offered opportunities to participate in political discussions and organizing. The youth arm of the Austrian Centre, Young Austria, was founded in 1939 with twenty members and worked closely with its parent organization.[29] The primary concerns of both were to plan for postwar Austria and to recruit returnees. Young Austria, for example, offered a Jugendführerschule des Jungen Österreich (Young Austria

---

27. Austrian Centre, *This Is Austria* (London: Austrian Centre, 1943), back cover.
28. Ibid., 6.
29. Sonja Frank, introduction to *Young Austria: Österreicherinnen im Britsischen Exil, 1938–1947; Für ein freies, demokratisches und unabhängiges Österreich*, ed. Sonja Frank (Vienna: ÖGB Verlag, 2012), 17.

School for Youth Leaders) to prepare young leaders to deal with practical and ideological matters after their return. These courses lasted three to four months, included exams, and provided diplomas for those who passed.[30]

At the same time, Austrian Jewish men who were interned as "enemy aliens" in the United Kingdom also found their way to the KPÖ and to Young Austria through the groups' activities in internment camps. With the fall of France in 1940 and the subsequent end of the "phoney war,"[31] the British government initiated a policy of internment of foreigners who were deemed potential threats to national security. This resulted in the confinement of around twenty-seven thousand so-called enemy aliens, including Jewish refugees along with non-Jewish Germans, Austrians, and Italians. Of these, over seven thousand were deported to Canada and Australia.[32] Most internees were men, but some four thousand women also found themselves temporarily in such camps—most in the Rushen camp on the Isle of Man—until the end of July 1940.[33] Although interned Jews were detained and in some cases humiliated and denigrated by guards, the treatment they experienced paled in comparison to what they knew was taking place in their home countries. Then, too, rather than languish passively, many of the internees took advantage of suddenly imposed spare time to organize cultural and intellectual activities. The many scholars, artists, and other leaders among them organized cabarets, concerts, and art exhibitions; wrote and distributed internal camp newspapers; and developed camp universities and libraries.

Austrian Communists were among the most ambitious and resourceful of such organizers, and in addition to providing activities for internees,

---

30. Bearman, "Austria Tomorrow?," 226.

31. The term "phoney war" refers to the period between September 1939 and May 1940. Germany invaded Poland on September 1, 1939, thus triggering World War II. England and France formally declared war at that time but did little else until May 10, 1940, when the German Army marched into Belgium, the Netherlands, and Luxembourg.

32. Tony Kushner, *The Persistence of Prejudice* (Manchester: Manchester University Press, 1989), 145.

33. Miriam Kochan, "Women's Experiences of Internment," in *The Internment of Aliens in Twentieth Century Britain*, ed. David Cesarani and Tony Kushner (London: Frank Cass, 1993), 148.

they also sought to recruit and indoctrinate new members. Many inmates thus came to the Party and remained active after their release, which began to occur in January 1941 and continued throughout 1942. (Only a few "hardcore of people" remained interned to the end of the war.)[34] Max Schneider became a member of the Party during his confinement on the Isle of Man and continued his activity later in similar detention in Canada. Communists seemed to enjoy a great deal of authority in both camps, he recalled. The ideology guided him upon his release and subsequent enlistment in the British Army, in which he fought eagerly "to free Austria from fascist control."[35]

The KPÖ continued its work through the Austrian Centre and its Young Austria youth group and, from its position in exile, pushed on toward its main political goal of a free state. The Party sought the Allies' official recognition of Austria as an invaded and occupied country in need of liberation, solidifying and formalizing its endorsement and promotion of the "victim myth" as a main principle for postwar recovery and reconstruction. It encouraged its members to do everything possible to support the British war effort and to work toward an Allied victory, including volunteering to fight in the British armed forces. It planned for return to Vienna after war's end and strove to prepare its members for postwar work, reeducation, and political involvement in Vienna. It did so through a combination of programs and services that fostered the dual purposes of keeping émigrés occupied and active while indoctrinating them with the Communist Party's ideological and political plan.

Social Democrats in exile in Britain also formed political groups but were less overtly active in their organizing and enjoyed less success. Party leadership had been located in Paris from the start of the war and moved to New York City with the collapse of France in 1940. London-based Social Democrats formed the Austrian Labour Club but remained quite insular, with support only from their approximately one hundred members, and

---

34. Ronald Stent, *A Bespattered Page? The Internment of "His Majesty's Most Loyal Enemy Aliens"* (London: Andre Deutsch, 1980), 248.
35. Max Schneider, interview, 287, DÖW.

barely tried to recruit new members among the refugees.[36] Their activities did, however, include providing advice to the British Labour Party about the situation in Austria and making contact with British government offices and politicians, trade unionists, and journalists.[37]

But the Social Democrats and the Communists took different positions on their ideas and plans for Austria's postwar fate. The main issue dividing the two was the Social Democrats' refusal to support an independent postwar Austria. Until 1943 and the Allies' Moscow Declaration, the SPÖ still held onto some remnants of its post-1918 position of favoring Austria's Anschluss with Germany, which left it open to the accusation of endorsing a policy that was not too different from the Nazis.[38] In addition, the Communists based their platform on the concept that their organization served as the mouthpiece in exile of a strong resistance in Austria, the extent of which the Social Democrats doubted, which further distanced the two.[39]

The Free Austrian Movement (FAM) and Austria as "First Victim"

The KPÖ was one of the Austrian groups in exile operating in the United Kingdom that officially formed the Free Austrian Movement (FAM) in London on December 3, 1941.[40] Initially the FAM consisted of the Austrian Centre, the Council of Austrians, the Monarchists organized in the Austrian League, the Austrian Democratic Union (a small bourgeois group led by Emil Müller-Sturmheim and Julius Meinl), the Association of Austrian Social Democrats (a breakaway group organized by Heinrich Allina), Marie Köstler's League of Austrian Communists in Great Britain, and a number of youth, professional, and regional organizations: fifteen member

---

36. Grenville, "Politics of the Austrian Centre," 24.
37. Andrea Reiter, "Political Exile and Exile Politics in Britain: Introduction," in *Political Exile and Exile Politics in Britain after 1933*, ed. Anthony Grenville and Andrea Reiter (Amsterdam: Rodopi, 2011), xix.
38. Grenville, "Politics of the Austrian Centre," 38, 24.
39. Ibid., 40.
40. Free Austrian Movement, *Case of Austria*, 6.

organizations in all.⁴¹ Germany had invaded the Soviet Union in June of that year, and these Austrian organizations, heavily influenced by the Communist Party, joined to create the FAM in response. Members signed a resolution that clearly stated their position: Nazi Germany had annexed Austria by force, and *all* Austrians desired a free, democratic nation within the 1918 borders.⁴² The FAM sought to secure the Allies' official acknowledgment and acceptance of the concepts that united its members: that Austria had been the first victim of Nazi aggression and that they represented the true, pre-Nazi Austria.⁴³ The organization wanted the British government to refuse to accept the Anschluss and to assure Austrian citizens the right to self-determination as per the Atlantic Charter, the Allies' official statement of intended goals for postwar policy, which among its many aims included the intention of restoring self-government to those who had been deprived of it. Further, the FAM sought to mobilize all Austrians in the United Kingdom to work for the Allied cause through service in the military, civil defense, and war production and pointed out that this required a change from their "enemy alien" status.⁴⁴

The 1942 publication *The Case of Austria* outlined the interests of the FAM and stressed what the group claimed to be an inherent Austrian opposition to Nazism. The support of the British government, this slim volume posited, would strengthen Austrian resistance. This booklet portrayed Austrians as a united people opposed from the start to the Nazis' "foreign, military occupation." It subjectively and emotionally asserted that Austrian sensibilities and patriotism simply could not have permitted Austrians to allow Anschluss. *The Case of Austria* presented this innate Austrian inability to embrace unification with Nazi Germany as proof that the smaller nation had been forcibly occupied by a foreign military power. The FAM urged the Allies to accept its view and to embrace Austria as one of the Allies.⁴⁵

---

41. Grenville, "Politics of the Austrian Centre," 36.
42. Free Austrian Movement, *Case of Austria*, 32.
43. Ibid., 30.
44. Ibid., 27.
45. Ibid., 25.

The book went on to point out that combating the Nazi enemy had brought together groups with previously divergent missions, as evinced by FAM membership composed of Catholics, Social Democrats, and Communists. Austrians living in the United Kingdom felt it to be their duty to do all they could to assist their compatriots at home in their struggle for freedom. They wanted to devote their energy and efforts to an Allied victory, including creating a Free Austrian Fighting Unit to fight the Germans.[46] In summary, *The Case for Austria* specified,

> The idea of the Free Austrian Movement sprang from the desire of all freedom loving Austrians for the restoration of Austria's liberty and independence and from the will to fight for freedom, to help to win it, and not simply to accept it as a gift. The idea of the Free Austrian Movement was born out of the realization that the active part played by Austrians in this country could help to bring nearer the hour of liberation in Austria itself. The Free Austrian Movement will, it is hoped, finally clear away all the obstacles which have hitherto prevented and still prevent the full utilization of Austrians in the active struggle at the side of the Allies.[47]

At the same time, the Austrian Social Democrats in exile in Great Britain organized their members. After some increased activity in 1940, they founded the London Bureau of the Austrian Socialists in Great Britain in April 1941.[48] But the bulk of the group's activity consisted of attacks on Communist successes, like the creation of the FAM, a most important example of Communist strength in coordinating a united front of diverse groups from different backgrounds.[49] The London Bureau was the main group of Austrians missing from the FAM, and, determined not to be drawn in, they created the rival Austrian Representative Body (österreichischen Vertretungskörperschaft) after the 1943 Moscow Declaration and asserted their representation of all Austrian exiles. The FAM naturally rejected this

---

46. Ibid., 29.
47. Ibid., 26.
48. Muchitsch, *Österreicher im Exil*, 157.
49. Grenville, "Politics of the Austrian Centre," 25.

claim, and fighting continued.⁵⁰ The Austrian Representative Body in the end served only to cut off Social Democrats from the other groups of Austrians incorporated in the FAM.⁵¹

The FAM began organizing for return in 1943 and reported in *Austrian News* that it had assembled a committee of experts to negotiate planning with the Allies for an independent Austria—and presumably a new Austrian government—and to deal with postwar problems.⁵² *Austrian News* emphasized the broad political representation of the FAM and nimbly and diplomatically addressed its hosts in exile and anticipated occupiers by phrasing its plans as provisional and tentative, to be carried out with and by the Austrian population. Another of the FAM's publications, *Das Free Austrian Movement in Großbritannien und der Wiederaufbau Österreichs* (The Free Austrian Movement in Great Britain and the reconstruction of Austria), described the FAM's vision for postwar Austria and attempted to engage the Allies in reconstruction. Fashioning its plan after that of the Czech government-in-exile, the FAM aspired to secure the same Allied recognition and acceptance as the Czechs had.⁵³ Such official status never came to be, but the wording and ratification of the Moscow Declaration that underscored Austrian victimhood encouraged the FAM and the Austrian Communist Party. With this, the KPÖ's mission solidified: once the Allies "liberated" *their* Austria, Communists in exile would return and take part in rebuilding a democratic society.

Preparing Austrian Communists for Return to Their Political Home

Well before the Moscow Declaration, a KPÖ and Austrian Centre top priority was to persuade and prepare members to return to Austria once the war ended. The Centre's president, Franz Carl West, gave a speech in spring 1942 with a title that both reflected the organization's intentions and played on the English cultural environment in which the refugees lived. "Zurück

---

50. Ibid., 40.
51. Ibid., 38.
52. Bearman, "Austria Tomorrow?," 215.
53. Ibid., 216.

oder nicht zurück—das ist keine Frage" (To return or not to return—There is no question) made the case for going back to rebuild Austria as Communist Party members and specifically as *Austrian* citizens. West also encouraged all Austrian refugees in Britain to take part in the war effort,[54] as they had the opportunity as residents in their Allied host country to show their support and to contribute to the defeat of Nazi Germany.

KPÖ instructions and expectations competed with the message of Zionist group leaders, who told their members "that the return to Austria would be the way to certain death" and that "for Austria's youth every path would be better than the one leading back to Austria." Jews constituted the vast majority of the membership of the Austrian Centre and the Austrian Communist Party operating in wartime Great Britain, but the great majority of Austrian Jewish refugees in the United Kingdom were neither communists nor Communist Party members, and many were loath to return to Austria after Nazi persecution and genocide, not to mention Austria's long history of antisemitism.[55] Addressing these issues, the general secretary of the Austrian Centre, Willi Scholz, penned a pamphlet that appeared in February 1943, *Ein Weg ins Leben: Das neue Österreich und die Judenfrage* (A way into life: The new Austria and the Jewish question), that countered the Zionist argument and attributed antisemitism to the German nationalist and pan-German movement in Austria.[56] Under a new government, he declared, a newly conceived and reconstructed democratic nation would have starkly different qualities that allowed no place for antisemitism.

A May 1943 survey of two Young Austria groups in London revealed that 70 percent of respondents desired to return to Austria.[57] Young Austria depended on this enthusiasm and commitment and envisioned that its young members would take up the task of undoing years of Nazi ideological programming, especially among former members of the Hitler Jugend

---

54. Franz Carl West, *Zurück oder nicht zurück?* (London: Free Austrian Movement / Austrian Centre, 1942).
55. Bearman, "Austria Tomorrow?," 214.
56. Wilhelm Scholz, *Ein Weg ins Leben: Das neue Österreich und die Judenfrage* (London: Free Austrian Books, 1943).
57. Bearman, "Austria Tomorrow?," 215.

(Hitler Youth).[58] Young Austria trained its young leaders and prepared them to organize and lead Communist youth groups after their return home. In this, the Party was successful; its greatest achievement in postwar Vienna was its youth arm.[59]

The war ended in Europe two years later, on May 8, 1945, and the Allied occupation of Austria began. The time had come for the KPÖ to set its plans into action. Its members would return as Austrians to a land in which they foresaw no place for antisemitism and where they were needed to help undo the effects of Nazi propaganda and indoctrination. The Austrian Centre closed its doors at the beginning of 1947 after organizationally and financially suffering when key members returned to Austria.[60]

RETURN TO VIENNA

The Austrian Communist Party in exile had informed its members of their duty to help at home and pushed them to return to take part in the nation's political and physical reconstruction. Many Social Democrats also went home for the same reasons, despite the original wavering and ambiguous positions of their party. This largely Jewish group of returnees viewed themselves as Austrians and specifically as Communist and Social Democratic Austrians. They also viewed their compatriots as victims, with few exceptions. Their parties ultimately had led them to believe, and they expected, that their countrymen and women awaited and welcomed their return. "We wanted to live and work as Austrian *Socialists* in Austria ... personally, professionally, politically," wrote Stella Klein-Löw. "We wanted to adapt the life that had been interrupted by exile to the new circumstances, revive old friendships, deepen existing relationships.... And we would have also been ashamed to have abandoned Austria, Vienna, Socialism at this juncture to wait for better times."[61]

---

58. Ibid., 221.
59. Ibid., 228.
60. Richard Dove, introduction to Bearman et al., *Out of Austria*, 2.
61. Stella Klein-Löw, *Erinnerungen: Erlebtes und Gedachtes* (Vienna: Jugend und Volk, 1980), 165.

Whether a prewar decision or a determination made during the course of political activity abroad, Austrian Centre and Young Austria members consciously chose to return to Vienna as Austrians and committed Communists. They sought to reclaim their homeland and to take part in its political and physical reconstruction and, in doing so, supported the victim myth, or at least some part of it. As Communists, they found that the myth fit their Party's ideological instruction and guided their way back. As Jews, their acceptance of Austria's and Austrians' victimhood permitted them to return to a land and a people with whom they felt they shared the horror of the past and a promise of a future.

Expectation Encounters Reality

Actualizing the goal of returning home, however, was more complicated than simple desire. To go to Vienna, returnees needed the official approval of the Allied occupiers, which was not easily granted, particularly in the first days after war's end. Initially, the Allies banned repatriation, attributing their decision to food shortages in the city and the disruption of transportation. One exception to this prohibition, however, was the entry of the leading member of the Social Democrats' London Bureau, Oscar Pollak, in September 1945. When the Communist-dominated FAM inquired whether Pollack's approved return meant that the general ban was lifted, it received a negative reply. Remarks by an official of the British Foreign Office illuminated the Western Allies' perspective: "It is in our interest to strengthen the Social Democrat and Christian Social elements in Austria against the Communists."[62] The occupying forces saw the value of supporting Social Democrats in their return and the resumption of political activity on behalf of Austria. Cold War politics had begun to brew, and a strong Communist presence in a partially Soviet-occupied Vienna was not attractive to the Western Allies.

---

62. Minutes of William Mack, August 16, 1945, FO 371/46659, National Archives of the United Kingdom, London, UK.

The assessments and opinions of other organizations and officials and their impressions of life in Austria bolstered the Allies' reluctance to grant permission for Communists to return to Vienna, especially as such a large proportion of Austrian refugees in Great Britain were Jewish. Dr. J. Benson Saks, the head of Austrian Operations for the Joint, clearly stated in a February 20, 1946, letter that he felt that Jews should be discouraged from going back to Vienna. He argued that an antisemitic atmosphere in Austria compounded the general postwar social and economic problems and made for a particularly hostile place for Jews. He also recommended that the Joint officially discourage repatriation, although he admitted that he believed that the Austrian government itself was willing and prepared to protect the rights of Jews:

> In this regard, however, I state emphatically, and in doing so I am supported by a considerable weight of opinion, that insofar as the Jewish problem is concerned, the Austrian Government does not reflect the sentiments, the attitude or the tenor of the great mass of Austrian people. It cannot be denied that antisemitism is endemic to Austria. Nor can the recent twelve or so years of intensive anti-Jewish indoctrination of the Hitler program be eradicated from the minds of the populace over night, or by efforts of the new Government. The great and predominant mass of Austrians have been and are intensely anti-Semitic. The preponderant majority, if they would reveal to you the true state of their feelings, would state that one of their greatest regrets is the fact that Hitler did not finish the job entirely, and liquidate every single member of the Jewish community.[63]

At least in the early months of Allied occupation, a Joint representative could be convinced that the newly formed postwar Austrian government sought to protect and advocate for all its citizens—even Jews. Although Saks officially discouraged Austrian Jews' return, the atmosphere in which

---

63. Dr. J. Benson Saks, Austrian Operations, AJDC, to Mr. Richard H. S. Crossman, Anglo-American Committee of Inquiry, Headquarters United States Forces Austria, New York City, February 20, 1946, Frames 0221–0222, File 146, Collection AR45/54, Archives of the American Jewish Joint Distribution Committee (JDC Archives), New York, NY.

he formed such observations supported hopeful reémigrés' concept that, despite it all, they were needed in Austria for reconstruction and education. In theory and according to their belief, the government would support them.

Many Communist Party functionaries gave up on legal permission to repatriate and undertook unauthorized journeys back to Vienna. This often involved roundabout routes. Many traveled from London to Paris, where they met Party members who organized their next steps. Other members soon followed along similar routes and continued to do so well into 1946. Hansi Tausig and her husband, Otto, ostensibly attended a trade-union conference in Paris in April 1946. When they arrived, however, officials checked their luggage and found pots, pans, and household items, clear signs that they did not plan simply to stay a few days for meetings. Nonetheless, they were permitted transit through the country, and Party members in Paris helped them arrange their continued journey to Vienna without tickets. A colleague bribed the train conductor, and they enjoyed first-class accommodations all the way home.[64]

Immediately upon arrival or even on the journey home before reaching Vienna, returnees encountered the reality of postwar Austria and Austrians' attitudes. Viennese Jewish poet and Austrian Centre leader Eva Kolmer traveled to the capital in early 1946. Along the way, she observed the first indications that the Germans had not been the wholly unwanted occupiers that she and her comrades assumed. As her train passed through the station in Innsbruck, Kolmer witnessed distraught Tyrolean women bidding German soldiers a tearful farewell. "And then," she stated in an interview, "we saw that there was no dislike of the Germans and [that] there had been no resistance against them."[65]

Like so many Jewish political activists, Communist Gerda Geiringer had, in her words, "bought the line that Austria was Hitler's first victim. And when I returned to Austria in September 1946, I was very quickly disabused.... I didn't think that we would be greeted at the Westbahnhof with cheers. I didn't think the Communists would have a big following. I was

---

64. Tausig interview.
65. Eva Schmidt-Kolmer, interview, 719, DÖW.

one of the most realistic people. But coming to Vienna, I was more than surprised. I mean I was horrified and surprised."⁶⁶

For many who went back, the decision to return had been hardly a decision at all. Their Party instructed them to do so; then, too, many had always intended to return. Decades later, Hannah Fischer recalled the day in 1938 when her mother took her to Vienna's Westbahnhof to depart for England; she had thought with certainty, "I will come back!"⁶⁷ She returned to the same but much-destroyed train station in September 1946 with a few other Young Austrian group members. They had traveled via Paris, where they had waited a few days before moving on to Vienna, committed to rebuilding Austria through their work with the Communist Party.⁶⁸

Renewing Lives: Housing, Work, Education

Life in postwar Vienna was difficult for Jews and gentiles alike. With more than 25 percent of the city destroyed, the infrastructure damaged, and massive food shortages, those who went back faced a bleak landscape. Like other Jews who survived the war in the capital or returned from concentration and death camps, they confronted a lack of housing and a need to earn a living. They also encountered antisemitism and exclusion from Austrian civil servants and from their neighbors. Unlike other Jews, however, they had their Party and fellow Party members to rely on.

In 1946, Hansi and Otto Tausig were greeted at the Westbahnhof by a friend and Communist Party member whom they had known in London and who took them to the Young Austria headquarters, where they spent their first night in postwar Vienna. A friend's mother soon took them in, and they stayed with her for a few days until they happened to meet another old friend at a May Day demonstration. He lived in a large apartment that

---

66. Gerda Freistadt-Geiringer, oral history conducted by Debórah Dwork, Vienna, July 10, 12, and 15, 1991, transcript II, 8, 9, 37, quoted in Debórah Dwork and Robert Jan van Pelt, *Flight from the Reich: Refugee Jews, 1933–1946* (New York: Norton, 2009), 329–30.

67. Hannah Fischer, interview by Tanja Eckstein of Centropa, Vienna, Austria, July 2004, accessed June 20, 2011, http://at.centropa.org/index.php?nID=30&x=PXVuZGVmaW5lZD sgc2VhcmNoVHlwZT1CaW9EZXRhaWw7IHNlYXJjaFZhbHVlPTUxMTsgc2Vhcm NoU2tpcDow.

68. Hannah Fischer, interview by author, Vienna, Austria, June 25, 2011.

he sought to fill before government officials assigned strangers to the empty rooms, as was the practice of housing administrators in postwar Vienna. He welcomed Hansi and Otto to join him, and thus they secured a home for the next couple of years.[69]

In many ways, the Tausigs' search for a place to live speaks for a number of Jewish Communist and Social Democrat reémigrés' experiences. Prive Friedjung also secured her postwar apartment through the help of her Party comrades.[70] Connections and chance, often through or with Party contacts, combined to help these returnees solve problems with which other Jews struggled. Such networks also helped individuals find and secure jobs. Hannah Fischer worked with youngsters in the Communist Party's nursery school. She had begun to care for children while in exile in England, working with Anna Freud and, later, in the Austrian Centre's day nursery in London.[71] There, she came into contact with Young Austria and the KPÖ, and her affiliation with the Party enabled continuity in her political activity and professional life when she returned to Vienna. She also continued her education in Austria, passing the *Matura* exam in the summer of 1946 to qualify to attend the university. She obtained a *Magister* (master's degree) in education and a doctorate in psychology and education and, after studying medicine, became a psychologist at a children's home.[72] Her employment by and activity with the Communist Party fostered her career path.

Reconnecting within the reestablishing Party offices and groups provided these returnees with a sense of security and familiarity. Without a true home abroad, their parties had served as such, their fellow members an ersatz family. Many found themselves in what should have been the familiar streets and neighborhoods of their hometown but feeling alone and alien. A place to go and a group to turn to helped one to feel anchored again. "The first days were full of seeking and not finding, trying to settle in, realizing one was alone, a stranger," Stella Klein-Löw recalled. "Immediately after our

---

69. Tausig interview.
70. Friedjung, "Wir wollten nur das Paradies auf Erden," 259.
71. Dieter J. Hecht, Eleonore Lappin-Eppel, and Michaela Raggam-Blesch, *Topographie der Shoah: Gedächnisorte das zerstörten jüdischen Wien* (Vienna: Mandelbaum Verlag, 2015), 565.
72. Fischer, interview by author.

arrival, I went to the new Party [SPÖ] headquarters in Löwelstraße. The rooms were strange, but there were friends there. They knew me, I knew them. Hugs—happy smiling faces—memories—conversations—plans."[73]

Members of Young Austria found continuity and familiarity in the Freie Österreichische Jugend (FÖJ), the Communist Party's youth movement in Austria. FÖJ leaders maintained contact with those who were still in England, reminding them of their duty to their country with messages like, "When are you finally coming? Each individual is needed. Every right thinking young Austrian is welcome here. And still more so, our well trained youth leaders. There is work for everyone."[74]

As the Young Austria leaders had been trained, they returned and took positions heading the youth movement in Austria.[75] Robert Rosner and his wife, Elisabeth Rosner-Jellinek, got back to Vienna in 1946. Robert soon assumed a leadership role with Young Austria in the nearby town of St. Pölten, while Elisabeth worked there as a nurse in a factory and continued with the Party in her free time. Their Party-related functions and involvement enabled the Rosners to establish themselves anew in Austria, and the following year, they relocated to Vienna, where Robert began chemistry studies at the University of Vienna. Austrian obstacles, however, challenged his academic pursuits. British high school studies had not included Latin, which the Austrian *Matura* required. Experience and understanding "the Austrian way," as Robert said, helped him circumvent this obstacle. Perhaps "the Viennese way" would have been more specific; he and other Viennese Jews were, after all, Viennese. Socialized and conditioned in a more or less typical prewar Viennese childhood, Robert still had the awareness and understanding of how to get things accomplished in the framework of that society. With the help of a sympathetic official in the ministry of education who directed him to a *Frauen Oberschule* (a women's high school), Robert had his British diploma certified as equivalent to the Austrian *Matura* because the curriculum of girls' schools did not require Latin. Thus, he

---

73. Klein-Löw, *Erinnerungen*, 167–69.
74. "Fritz Walter schreibt," *Jung-Österreich*, December 1, 1945, 3.
75. Bearman, "Austria Tomorrow?," 215.

received his Austrian *Matura*, and his diploma shows that he officially graduated from a women's school. In his words, "Typically Austrian!"[76]

Other returnees found work with the Allied occupation forces, utilizing language and intercultural skills. Anny Friedler worked for the *Welt am Montag*, the French occupation forces' newspaper in Vienna.[77] Hansi Tausig worked with the youth section of the Austrian-Soviet Friendship Society the first year she returned, striving to build bridges between the Soviets and the locals. Later she was employed by the KPÖ as a secretary and organizer in the Party's nineteenth-district offices. Hansi recalled gaining a position quite easily, but this was due to her Party ties. She recalled working diligently in the community and in public places and remembered the bewilderment and confusion of former Nazis whom she and her colleagues engaged in conversation. They labored furiously to promote their ideals and to help shape politics and a future in their hometown, while Hansi remembers that "the old Nazis simply sat around" or looked at them with puzzled faces that seemed to say that only "the *meshuggeneh* [Yiddish for "crazy person"] would work so hard."[78]

Others sought to continue their prewar occupations or to reintegrate themselves into everyday Viennese business life. Unlike positions in the Party, work in private firms did not provide insulation from public opinion. A colleague told the Jewish Communist reémigré Walter Kammerling that surviving Jews had "slipped through the grates in the oven" and proceeded to outline the government's need to reengage the company to build them better.[79]

---

76. Robert Rosner, interview by author, Vienna, Austria, August 13, 2009. Dealing with his lack of Latin studies continued for Robert. After a long and successful career as a chemist, he retired and returned to the university to study the history of science. Instead of enrolling in the history department, he registered as a student of political science and made his sideline focus the history of science. Again, he avoided a Latin requirement in the "typically Austrian" way.

77. Anny Friedler, interview, 173, DÖW. *Welt am Montag* was published from February 18, 1946, to February 28, 1948, in Vienna.

78. Tausig interview.

79. Walter Kammerling (in London, UK), telephone interview by author (in Vienna, Austria), February 23, 2011.

Disappointing Responses from Gentiles

Like Kammerling, many returnees to Vienna encountered responses from non-Jewish Austrians that ranged from deep denial of their suffering to outright antisemitism. Jewish Communists and Social Democrats soon realized that, contrary to the information provided by their parties, neither the nation as a whole nor individual Austrians actually desired their return because they were Jewish. A 1946 poll of Austrian citizens indicated that only 28 percent of respondents wanted Austrian Jews abroad to come back, and 46 percent explicitly opposed it.[80]

Gentile Austrians perceived Jewish returnees as foreigners and no longer—and perhaps as never having been—Austrians.[81] At the same time, Jews returning from exile also frequently met the accusation of having abandoned Austria, despite the death sentence they would have faced had they remained.[82] Austrians even questioned Jews' motivations for return, as they held that life for the émigrés surely had been better in their lands of exile. Others praised them for their foresight in escaping the fate of *gentile* Viennese. The headwaiter at the Café Herrenhof greeted his former regular customer Hilde Spiel with, "The Frau Doctor did the right thing by getting out. The air raids alone, three times they set the entire city ablaze!"[83]

These responses from gentile Austrians reflected their unwillingness to confront the grim situation of Jews in Nazi Austria and expressed their denial of having been a part of the oppression and persecution of Jews. When Hannah Fischer visited her former home after the war, a neighbor greeted her as a long-lost friend. A convinced Nazi from the start, this man had been in the SA, yet he received Hannah as if she had been dear to his family and related fond memories of her parents. Unable to bear his denial, she never visited her old home again, although even in 2013, she lived

---

80. Bruce F. Pauley, "Austria," in *The World Reacts to the Holocaust*, ed. David S. Wyman (Baltimore: Johns Hopkins University Press, 1996), 493.
81. Christoph Reinprecht, *Zurückgekehrt: Identität und Bruch in der Biographie österreichischer Juden* (Vienna: Braumüller, 1992), 101.
82. Vansant, *Reclaiming Heimat*, 49.
83. Hilde Spiel, *Rückkehr nach Wien: Ein Tagebuch* (Vienna: Milena Verlag, 2009), 74.

nearby.[84] On another occasion, Walter Kammerling felt the emotional blow when he heard an acquaintance wax nostalgic for the Nazis on a snowy winter day. In the "good old days," the man lamented, they had been fortunate to have the Jews to clear the streets of the city.[85]

When gentile Austrians spoke with Jews of their wartime experiences in Vienna, they emphasized how frightened they had been of Allied bombings and the devastation these had wrought. At the same time, they utterly refused to recognize Jewish refugees' situations abroad, much less why they had fled. Returnees, by contrast, knew that their neighbors had welcomed the Nazis into Austria and had been Nazis themselves and that many had taken part willingly in the exploitation of Jews in "Aryanization" processes. The Jewish reémigré Hans Thalberg wrote of linguistic confusion in discussions with gentile Austrians in postwar Vienna—their reference to "catastrophe" meant something very different from his use of the word, he noted.[86] For Thalberg and other Jews, the Anschluss in 1938 had been the disaster; for many gentile Austrians, the disaster was the end of the war in 1945 and subsequent Allied occupation.

Larger, symbolic differences were apparent in Viennese society and culture and reflected the nation's and its citizens' struggle to secure a new and specifically *not* German postwar identity. Viennese survivor George Clare observed a new prevalence of Viennese dialect as evidence of this: even the educated citizen seemed to reject the softer, prewar Viennese version of Hochdeutsch (High German) for a working-class dialect that underscored their desire to be seen as utterly un-German.[87] Viennese survivor and Social Democrat Hilde Spiel survived the war in exile in London and returned to Vienna early in 1946 as a British correspondent. In her diary, she described a new postwar style of wearing Tyrolean hats as an outward sign of Austrian patriotism and as decidedly not German. Keenly aware of the superficiality of this trend and its part in the assumed pretense of Austrian innocence and

---

84. Fischer interview by author.
85. Kammerling interview.
86. Hans Thalberg, *Von der Kunst, Österreicher zu sein: Erinnerungen und Tagebuchnotizen* (Vienna: Böhlau Verlag, 1984), 153.
87. George Clare, *Before the Wall: Berlin Days, 1946–1948* (New York: Dutton, Penguin, 1990), 272–73.

naïveté, Spiel pointed out that their footwear gave them away. Before the war, she wrote, one wore galoshes in the rain; afterward, the Viennese wore boots that betrayed them. To Spiel, they looked like Nazi camp guards and 1920s Berlin prostitutes.[88]

Still, many Social Democrat and Communist returnees claimed that they did not encounter much antisemitism in the postwar years and little or none within their parties. Hansi Tausig recalled only one antisemitic remark from a comrade who expressed disgust when she realized that two new members were Jewish. Other than that, Tausig stressed, prejudice within the KPÖ posed no problem. In her view, "there were too many Jews among us" for antisemites in the Party to dare voice their opinions.[89] The critical mass of Jews in the Communist and Social Democrat Parties supported the repatriates, in addition to silencing antisemites. One woman who returned from Moscow and remained active with the KPÖ in postwar Vienna said, "I got together only with our people," specifying that by "our people" she meant not other Communists but rather Communists of Jewish descent. Such a great number of Jewish Communists had returned from England and had shared experiences that they were able to form a core and significant part of the Party.[90]

Many Jewish returnees also related a similar lack of antisemitism in postwar Austria. They knew it existed and suspected who among their friends and acquaintances had held Nazi sympathies and perhaps still harbored them after the war. But in the process of reconstructing a national identity in the postwar period and for many decades thereafter, silence and a refusal to discuss the activities and events between 1938 and 1945 contributed to insulating Austrian Jews from antisemitic sentiment as they rebuilt lives in Vienna. If the gentiles kept quiet, so did the Jews. Refusing to probe or question neighbors' wartime activities, returnees could cling to ignorance

---

88. Spiel, *Rückkehr nach Wien*, 37. It is important to note that, although Spiel maintained close postwar ties with Vienna, her permanent residence was in London (with a brief stint in Berlin) until 1963, when she returned to live in Austria. From 1955 on, however, she did own and use a second home in St. Wolfgang in Upper Austria.

89. Tausig interview.

90. Helga Embacher, "Unwelcome in Austria: Returnees and Concentration Camp Survivors," in *When the War Was Over: Women, War and Peace in Europe, 1940–1956*, ed. Claire Duchen and Irene Bandhauer-Schöffmann (London: Leicester University Press, 200), 203.

about the gentile Austrians around them. At the same time, Jews' discretion permitted gentile Austrians to ignore their neighbors' suffering and hardship and to focus on the present, thus allowing former Nazis or Nazi sympathizers to interact with and develop relationships with Jews as necessary or desired without confronting the issue of responsibility. Although many returnees reported that they heard and felt no direct antisemitism from the people around them, as we shall see in chapter 6, their recounting of difficulties with reparations and restitution, regaining homes and businesses, and struggles with the bureaucracy belie this narrative.

POSTWAR POLITICAL REALITY FOR JEWISH RETURNEES

The political climate in postwar Austria dashed KPÖ plans for serious involvement in reconstruction. Leaders watched as a coalition between the newly renamed Austrian Socialist Party (Sozialistischepartei Österreichs, or SPÖ) and the Austrian People's Party (Österreichische Volkspartei, or ÖVP), the successor to Austria's Catholic conservative Christian Social Party, took hold in the first elections held in November 1945, and they worried that this would affect the return of Austrian Communist Party members from exile abroad. The government proved unwilling to accommodate Jews in particular, despite their positions of disadvantage after the Holocaust and the destruction of their families and community. An official stated effort to show no "preferential treatment" for any particular group prompted Jews to turn to the Viennese Jewish Community for support, and even Communist Party members joined the IKG for the first time. Indeed, Communist members took a leading role in governing and guiding the rebuilding of the Jewish community.

The KPÖ lost ground with Jewish repatriates in the years that followed. Even the most devout Party members were bitterly disappointed by the brutal Soviet suppression of the Hungarian Uprising of 1956. The few who did not leave the Party disillusioned at that time withdrew their membership in 1968. The Soviet invasion of Czechoslovakia to put down the Prague

Spring liberalizations prompted most remaining Jewish Communist Party members to give up their affiliation.

Elections, Coalition Government, and a New Austrian Identity

At war's end, the possibilities for KPÖ participation in the new government appeared bright. In the provisional government ordered by the Soviet occupiers and headed by the Social Democrat Dr. Karl Renner, Communists held one-third of all offices. This initial, if temporary, constellation corresponded with the Free Austrian Movement's plan for the postwar government,[91] but elections held on November 25, 1945, proved to be the first official and public disappointment for the Communist Party, as it garnered only 5.2 percent of the vote and not the expected 20 to 25 percent. Years of anticommunist propaganda and the hardships of a brutal Red Army conquest of Austria had done their work: the KPÖ did not appeal to voters. Most Austrian Jewish exiles in Great Britain still lived there in November 1945, and Party officials worried that the poor electoral results would deter some from proceeding with plans to return to Vienna.[92] The Austrian Centre faithful had anticipated a very different Second Republic. "That was really the first shock," said Hansi Tausig. KPÖ leaders already in Austria sent messages of encouragement to their colleagues in Britain, Hansi among them. She recalled that they stressed that the disappointing results constituted all the more reason to repatriate and work hard toward their political goals in postwar Austria.[93]

The SPÖ, on the other hand, enjoyed tremendous electoral success. A new attitude had formed toward a party that was once on the margins. The populace no longer viewed the SPÖ as a revolutionary force as it had at the turn of the century and in the interwar period. Jewish Social Democrat returnees truly found a role in the reclaiming and rebuilding of postwar Austria. A coalition of the SPÖ and the ÖVP led the Austrian government

---

91. Bearman, "Austria Tomorrow?," 230.
92. Ibid., 233.
93. Tausig interview.

from November 1945 until 1966. Both groups used an antifascist narrative to anchor a national victim identity and competed for the votes of former Nazi Party members.[94] In the postwar setting of reconstruction and Allied occupation, the theme of national identity and presenting Austria as a victim on the world stage brought political parties together in rare consensus, but the competing ideologies of the interwar period that had led to violence and civil war had not disappeared. Rather, pragmatic Austrian leaders realized the need to avoid fierce partisan politics and devoted themselves to ideological reconciliation.[95] This and the commitment to re-create an Austrian Second Republic included reintegrating former Nazi Party members into professional and political society. Parties vied for the electoral support of former Nazis and determined that doing so required an official silence about the past that paralleled and fortified the silence taking root in society.[96] This reintegration took place during the denazification program, a process controlled by the Allies in occupied Germany. In Austria, however, the occupying forces gave the provisional government the responsibility of carrying out such investigations, hearings, and prosecutions and, in doing so, handed over any control over the imposition of any consequences on former Nazis, a large group of potential voters who were exonerated, regained their jobs, and received compensation for losses incurred postwar.

Politicians claiming that they sought to provide equally for all citizens—all victims of the Nazi regime—could do so while favoring former Nazis and refusing to acknowledge Jewish victims' particular suffering and loss. This amounted to extreme disadvantages for Jewish returnees. In the name of treating all Austrians equally, leaders opposed benefits or budget lines for the Jewish community. Agriculture minister Josef Kraus discouraged

---

94. Heidemarie Uhl, "From Victim Myth to Co-responsibility Thesis: Nazi Rule, World War II, and the Holocaust in Austrian Memory," in *The Politics of Memory in Postwar Europe*, ed. Richard Ned Lebow, Wulf Kansteiner, and Claudio Fogu (Durham, NC: Duke University Press, 2006), 67.

95. Peter Utgaard, *Remembering and Forgetting Nazism: Education, National Identity, and the Victim Myth in Postwar Austria* (New York: Berghahn Books, 2003), 31.

96. Peter Pulzer, "Between Collectivism and Liberalism: The Political Evolution of Austria since 1945," in *Austria 1945–95: Fifty Years of the Second Republic*, ed. Kurt Richard Luther and Peter Pulzer (Aldershot, UK: Ashgate, 1998), 229.

an advance of funds to be made to the IKG from a pool of heirless Jewish assets plundered by the Nazis, as he argued that this would give preferential treatment to a specific group.[97] Minister of internal affairs and SPÖ representative Oskar Helmer concurred, claiming it would contribute to "a perpetuation of distinctions" that the government aimed to avoid.[98]

Thus, the Austrian government, cloaked in the national innocence of "first victim," denied compensation or special benefits to Jewish victims but at the same time remunerated former Nazi Party affiliates for damages incurred through Allied-enforced anti-Nazi sanctions. By the logic of the victim myth, the *German* government carried responsibility for reparations and restitution to Jews. The *Austrian* government, however, assumed accountability to compensate former Austrian Nazis as theoretically victimized, like all Austrian citizens, by a German military occupation and then, again, a second time by the Allies. In the world of political maneuvering, this made sense, especially as it was rooted in Austria's long history of antisemitism. Gaining votes from a tiny Jewish community meant nothing; Austrian Nazis needed to be won over, appeased, and reintegrated.

As leading politicians in the postwar period set their sights on the large pool of Nazi sympathizers, they went beyond abandoning Jews who had returned. They castigated Jews for forsaking their country in its time of need. If gentile Austrian citizens took that position, their leaders reinforced their perspective. ÖVP politician Alfons Gorbach contrasted Jewish emigrants who sought refuge in comfort and safety abroad after the Anschluss with Austrian soldiers who had fought in the Wehrmacht on the front.[99] The *Vorarlberger Volksblatt* went so far as to blame world Jewry specifically for not coming to Austria's aid after the Anschluss.[100] For many gentile Austrians, the rationalization that Austrian Jews had deserted their country

---

97. Robert Knight, *"Ich bin dafür, die Sache in die Länge zu ziehen": Wortprotokolle der österreichischen Bundesregierung von 1945–52 über die Entschädigung der Juden* (Frankfurt am Main: Athenäum, 1988), 196.
98. Robert Knight, "'Neutrality,' Not Sympathy: Jews in Post-war Austria," in *Austrians and Jews in the Twentieth Century: From Franz Joseph to Waldheim*, ed. Robert S. Wistrich (New York: St. Martin's, 1992), 222.
99. Ibid., 226.
100. Ibid.

was further strengthened by the perception that Jews worldwide had supported them in doing so.

Despite the discouraging election results and negative attitudes of the government, Communist Party officials established the Free Austrian World Movement (FAWM) in Vienna by late 1945 and officially announced the opening of its offices in February 1946. With the initial political goal of the movement achieved—a free, independent, democratic Austria—they aimed to help organize relief and assistance for the country, to facilitate the return of their members, and to maintain representation in the newly formed government.[101]

Austrian Jewish exiles hoping for a gesture of welcome and invitation to return home would be disappointed. Communist city council member Viktor Matejka was the only member of the postwar government to extend an official invitation. In November 1945, the New York–based German-language publication of the American Federation of Austrian Democrats, the *Austro-American Tribune*, published his appeal to Jewish artists and other members of the intelligentsia to come back to Austria.[102] Incidents of invitation in most cases amounted to little more than a token and symbolic statement, but Social Democrat Ernst Lachs was one of very few émigrés to return in response to an offer to take a place in the postwar municipal government. He and his wife, Minna, had met before the Anschluss in a Socialist student group and remained committed to their party through their time in exile in the United States, where they and their son, Tommy, survived the war. Ernst began working toward their return to Vienna immediately after war's end, and indeed his initiative was the only thing that propelled Minna's decision to go back. Without his drive to rejoin compatriots in Austria for postwar reconstruction, she might have remained in the United States. Ernst departed for Vienna on January 24, 1947, and Minna and Tommy set sail from New York to join him at the end of August 1947.[103] Once back, Minna too resumed a career in local government as a

---

101. Marietta Bearman and Charmian Brinson, "'No Easy Matter': Closure and After," in Bearman et al., *Out of Austria*, 243.
102. Vansant, *Reclaiming Heimat*, 43.
103. Minna Lachs, *Zwischen zwei Welten* (Vienna: Löcker Verlag, 1992), 171, 177–78.

teacher and ultimately took an enterprising lead in introducing and incorporating the study of the persecution of Austrian Jews through exhibitions and programs on the topic.

Socialist success notwithstanding, a continued lack of support and assistance from the Austrian government prevailed. Before the Anschluss, many politically engaged Social Democrat and Communist Jews had been reluctant to join the IKG. But in the particular context of postwar Vienna, many turned to the Jewish community for backing and aid and took part as formal members.

The IKG and the SPÖ and KPÖ in Postwar Reconstruction

As the immediate postwar Austrian government policies and assistance benefited only those victims identifiable as resistance fighters, Jews turned to the IKG for sustenance. Of the many areligious and even antireligious Social Democrat and Communist returnees of Jewish heritage, a number joined the Viennese Jewish community as formal members. The IKG and foreign Jewish charities served as a means of support, while the Austrian government and the camp-survivor organization in Vienna helped only those who had been persecuted on political grounds. The community provided clothing, access to food (via the Joint), and assistance in securing housing.

As the IKG gained Communist members, KPÖ representatives played an increased role in Jewish community politics. The IKG fell under the purview of the Staatsamt für Volksaufklärung, Unterricht, Erziehung und Kultusangelegenheiten (State Office of Public Information, Education, and Religious Affairs, comparable to Austria's current Ministry of Education). The secretary of that office in September 1945 was Ernst Fischer, a longtime KPÖ member and politician, and he named his KPÖ colleague and journalist David Brill as provisional head of the IKG. A number of other KPÖ members helped advise Brill and worked in supporting roles.[104]

---

104. Helga Embacher, *Neubeginn ohne Illusionen: Juden in Österreich nach 1945* (Vienna: Picus Verlag, 1995), 37.

The community's first free elections took place on April 7, 1946, but KPÖ and SPÖ Jewish leaders had already established the Jüdische Komitee (Jewish Committee) to try to unite Vienna's Jews under one umbrella. They recognized the weak position of their community in postwar Austria and sought to overcome their differences. The voting members of the Jewish community elected Brill in April 1946 to continue as the IKG president.[105] Few of those who were elected even had affiliated publicly as Jews before 1938, and left-wing Jewish groups had held no influence over community politics previous to the Anschluss. Postwar reconstruction, however, took place under these leftist parties that formerly had been at the fringes of formal Jewish communal life and showed little interest in the religious needs of the community.[106]

Disillusionment with Communism

Steadfast conviction and dedication to Communist political and social values kept many Jewish Communists devoted to and active in their party. As the chasm between theory and practice visibly widened over the course of the next decade, however, such loyalty eroded, and many Austrian Jewish

---

105. Ibid., 41. See also Ralph Segalman, "Letters to My Grandchildren" (unpublished memoir, Northridge, CA, 2001), 85–88. Segalman, a social worker with the JDC in postwar Vienna, described his role as an election monitor and Joint representative and claimed that, in fact, the General Zionists had won the election and on that same day agreed to form a coalition administration with the Jewish Chamber of Commerce. By the following morning, Segalman reported, the Jewish Communist group had taken control of the IKG. He related reports from General Zionist and Jewish Chamber of Commerce leaders that a squad of Red Army soldiers had detained them in the middle of the night and threatened deportation to Siberia and harm to their families if they refused to sign over authority to the Jewish Communist group. They agreed and acquiesced; Segalman protested, he claimed, by refusing to hand over the Joint food and medicine warehouse to the IKG. Joseph Schwartz, then the head of Joint operations in Europe, overruled him, and Segalman resigned in protest. More than a decade later, however, Schwartz explained that the Soviets had threatened to close the borders to the east (to Hungary, Poland, Romania, Czechoslovakia, and East Germany) altogether if the Joint continued to refuse to work with the IKG's Communist leadership. He felt that it was his only choice, as it served a greater number of Jews in need.

106. Susanne Cohen-Weisz, *Jewish Life in Austria and Germany since 1945: Identity and Communal Reconstruction* (Budapest: Central European University Press, 2016), 89.

Communists left the Party. As the reality of the nature of the Soviet Union's brutal oppression in the name of Communism became clear, many grew disillusioned over the following decade. The Soviet suppression of the Hungarian Uprising in 1956 ultimately sparked an exodus of those who had lost faith in the system, and the Soviet invasion of Czechoslovakia following the 1968 Prague Spring prompted most of the rest to abandon the KPÖ. Many turned to the SPÖ to reroot themselves in their political home.

Hansi Tausig was one of the steadfast. Although disenchanted with Communism during the Hungarian Uprising, she remained loyal until 1968, when she let her membership lapse. "It just fizzled out," she said in reference to her official status with the Party but also in seeming metaphoric reference to her own convictions. "I didn't make a big deal of it."[107] At the time, Hansi worked at a firm run by people connected to the Party, and she felt it would have been unwise to make a scene about leaving and risk being fired. Many others, she said, left the KPÖ quietly, so as to avoid such repercussions. This was no easy decision. Hansi likened it to losing one's faith. "It was like a religion. . . . We were not religious [but the] Communist Party . . . was like a religion. And then all of a sudden you are without religion." Abruptly, former committed Communists lost their guiding ideology and found nothing to replace it. Hansi characterized the feeling as "a little bit like falling into a . . . nothing."[108]

Other KPÖ members found Austria impossible to bear without the foundation and commitment to their Party. Disillusionment with Communism and the Soviet activity in Hungary overtook Walter Kammerling in 1956, and he became ill. After two weeks in bed, he decided not only to give up the Communist Party but also to give up on Austria altogether. In 1957, he returned to England, where he had survived the war in exile, and never again lived in his hometown.[109]

---

107. Tausig interview.
108. Ibid. In our interview, Hansi admitted to avid support of the SPÖ chancellor Bruno Kreisky. Ties to her original party lingered as she confessed, "I still feel a little guilty saying that, but I truly did love him."
109. Kammerling interview.

Most returning Jewish Communists, however, stayed and reestablished homes once again in Vienna, with or without the KPÖ. Many Communists turned to the Socialist Party. Postwar Austria and Communism had failed to meet their expectations; but Vienna was their home, and they remained. And the SPÖ provided a strong continuity and possibility for representation and participation in the politics of the Second Republic.

A number of idealistic and committed young Jewish Social Democrats and Communists returned to Vienna beginning in the fall of 1945 and through 1946. All were eager to reclaim their home and to help rebuild an independent democratic republic. This commitment, along with pressure from their parties, guided their expectations and actions to remigrate to Vienna and to stay, even in the face of the disappointment and, for some, disillusionment that followed. Contrary to the assumptions they had held throughout the war years, Austrian society was not prepared to welcome Jewish returnees, no matter their political affiliation.

On the contrary, the victim myth that in large part traced its origins to the sentiments of Austrian refugee groups abroad—which included many Jews—had been further cemented with the wording of the 1943 Moscow Declaration and had taken hold in the postwar Austria in which they arrived. This allowed Austrians, from government officials to everyday men and women in the streets, to claim that Austrian Jews who fled the Nazis had abandoned their country in its time of need and had not suffered like the Austrian victims who had remained. Despite full knowledge that Austrian Jews had been stripped of their citizenship and robbed of their property, homes, and businesses, gentile Austrians and their leaders ignored the reality of Jews' forced emigration, resettlement, and deportation to concentration and death camps. Instead they considered Austrian Jews' flight unpatriotic and traitorous, employing a variant of an older disloyalty myth that viewed Jews as members of a separate nation and unable to be loyal to any other. They reasoned that they had suffered while Jews abroad had waited out the war in ease.

While the Austrian Communist Party in Britain had maintained a consistent platform of support for the reestablishment of an independent

Austria, the Social Democrat Party in exile had wavered and at least in part had continued a post-1918 endorsement of unification with Germany. With the turn of postwar Cold War politics, those Social Democrats who returned ironically had the opportunity with their party's success to take significant part in rebuilding the country. Reémigré Communists' intentions and plans met with both personal and organizational disappointment and a marginalization from national politics.

When I asked Hansi Tausig why she and her Jewish colleagues and friends returned to Vienna, she replied, "Because we were naïve!" She, like so many other politicized Jews living in exile, had believed the victim myth. It was not simply a right-wing creation to pardon former Nazis. The Left and even Jewish members of the Communist and Social Democratic Parties had believed it and with deep conviction. The myth helped motivate their return and justified the attachment and dedication they felt to a homeland that had forced their emigration, destroyed their communities, and robbed and murdered their families. Once disabused of their naïveté, why did they stay? When I reminded Hansi of her other options and asked why she neither returned to England nor joined family in the United States, she seemed puzzled: "Why would I do that? This is my home."[110]

---

110. Tausig interview.

5

(RE)ESTABLISHING CAREERS IN VIENNA

Friedrich Torberg returned home to Vienna in 1951. Born Friedrich Ephraim Kantor in the main capital of the dual monarchy of Austria-Hungary in 1908, Torberg was already a well-known writer in the German-speaking world when the Nazis banned his books in 1933. His flight after the Anschluss included stops in Prague, Zurich, and Paris and a detour through Spain to Portugal. After colleagues intervened to have his name included on the New York PEN Club's list of "Ten Outstanding German Anti-Nazi Writers," he secured the necessary visa for entry to the United States and sailed from Lisbon. He went first to New York and shortly thereafter to Los Angeles, where he earned his living under contract with Warner Brothers. He moved to New York in 1944 to work as a freelance journalist and translator.[1]

Torberg always wanted to return. He viewed Vienna as his professional home, a fact that financial struggles combined with the tiring life of an émigré only further reinforced. An essay printed in the November 1, 1940, issue of *Aufbau* titled "I Don't Believe It . . ." revealed his response to the naïve questions of new acquaintances about his impressions of New York

---

[1]. Olena Kotvytska, "Exilerfahrung und die Heimkehr österreichischer Autoren jüdischer Herkunft am Beispiel von Friedrich Torberg und Ernst Lothar," *Linguae Mundi* 5 (2010): 44–45.

just after his arrival and how clouded they were because of all he had been through as a refugee and because of all those whom he had left behind. He wished he could have seen the city with different eyes.[2] Later he wrote with disdain about American life, including the horrific phenomenon of frozen meals and children who watched far too much television, to list a few points of his objection.[3] He felt uncomfortable in the United States, although grateful that his life had been saved. After the war, he received a number of offers of employment in his hometown, and in 1951, he moved back to accept a position at *Die Presse* newspaper as an editor and theater critic. In 1954, Torberg founded *Forum*, a cultural and political magazine that was partially funded by the CIA. His work continued with an anticommunist focus but was silent about the Nazi years. His popular collection of short stories, *Die Tante Jolesch*,[4] much like his larger body of work, conveyed nostalgia about the loss of Jewish culture through anecdotes of Jewish life during the Habsburg monarchy. But Torberg's writing neither addressed Austria's Nazi past nor probed the reasons why that Viennese Jewish life no longer existed.

Torberg recognized the cultural void he found upon his return, and ten years after war's end, he questioned his role. In a 1955 letter to Max Brod, he wrote, "If I still have a Jewish function at all, then it is strictly this—that I shape my public activity such that as many non-Jews as possible experience the death of the last German-Jewish writer as a loss. Whether they are mourning or breathing a sigh of relief I don't care; they should just notice that something has come to an end for which they have no replacement."[5] He lamented the loss of Jewish contributions to literature and culture; but his own connection to Judaism and the Jewish community seemed tenuous, and he did not view it as his role to expose blatant or explicit injustices.

---

2. Friedrich Torberg, "I Don't Believe It . . . ," *Aufbau*, November 1, 1940, 7.
3. Walter Laqueur, *Generation Exodus: The Fate of Young Jewish Refugees from Nazi Germany* (Hanover, NH: Brandeis University Press, 2001), 158.
4. Friedrich Torberg, *Die Tante Jolesch oder der Untergang des Abendlandes in Anekdoten* (Munich: Georg Müller Verlag, 1975).
5. Friedrich Torberg to Max Brod, 1955, quoted in Hillary Hope Herzog, *"Vienna Is Different": Jewish Writers in Austria from the Fin-de-Siècle to the Present* (New York: Berghahn Books, 2013), 203.

Historian Lisa Silverman has argued that this may have been the price Torberg paid for achieving postwar success: he and many others "attempted to 'reclaim' the lost cultural property of prewar Jewish writers, artists, and entertainers by becoming active again in Austrian cultural life, albeit one without a flourishing Jewish component."[6] They sensed that, to rejoin the Viennese professionally and socially, their Jewish identity should be backgrounded, an obscure but potentially interesting bit of biographical trivia. Torberg's apparent struggle with his Jewish heritage and role within the Jewish, Austrian-Jewish, and Viennese facets of society and how he actively did and did not deal with these different aspects reveal the multiple nuances that constitute identity in general and postwar Viennese Jewish identity in particular.

Torberg's poem "Die Rückkehr" (The return) elucidates his difficulties coming home to Vienna:

> War ich denn jemals fort?
> War es denn jemals anders?
> ... Und jetzt erst,
> Jetzt, da die Zeit sich wieder in eins fügt,
> da dem Ablauf ich eingefügt bin,
> löst sich die Starre,
> löst sich der Schritt.
> Aber wo ich auch gehe,
> Flattern die dunklen Gewänder der Toten um mich.[7]

> [Was I ever gone?
> Was it ever different?
> And only now,
> Now, that time fits together again,

---

6. Lisa Silverman, "Repossessing the Past? Property, Memory and Austrian Jewish Narrative Histories," *Austrian Studies* 11 (2003): 151.

7. Friedrich Torberg, "Die Rückkehr," in *Lebenslied: Gedichte* (Munich: Langen-Müller Verlag, 1958), 57, as cited in Silverman, "Repossessing the Past?," 150. Translation from Silverman, with acknowledgment of Christoph Meinrenken.

that I fit into its passing,
the stiffness loosens
the step loosens.
But wherever I go,
the dark robes of the dead flutter around me.]

Published in 1958, the poem portrays his grief and the loss he both saw and felt in postwar Vienna. Like so many Austrian Jews who sought to regain their professional homes—and, for that matter, those reclaiming familial and political homes—Torberg longed for the city he remembered and, at the same time, felt haunted by his memories of it. Reclaiming a career may have been possible, but the social and political systems in operation militated against the fulfillment of expectations. As Torberg questioned the meaning of his return, he admitted that time made it easier to stay—but perhaps not easier overall.

After *U-Boote* and other Jews who survived in Nazi Vienna reemerged into the occupied capital city at the end of the war, after camp survivors came home, and after politically active Jewish reémigrés made their ways back, another wave of those who spent the Nazi era in exile followed. The returnees who began to arrive toward the end of 1946 by and large sought to reestablish their professional lives, along with families and social circles. Some among them also held the political goal of taking an active part in reshaping their homeland. For all, going back implied hope for a new future for their country. Most thought it only logical that normality would follow the removal of Nazi leaders and government and wanted to resume life as it had been—or as close to that as possible. Yet, as Torberg's poem indicates less than ten years after war's end, life as it had been would never be again. And for most, this revelation took far less than a decade to comprehend. Many realized it immediately.

This fourth wave of reémigrés held hopes of reclaiming their *professional home* in Vienna. As exiles, they had attempted to establish themselves in their lands of refuge, and many of them had done so successfully. Those

who eventually achieved some sense of home in their adopted countries—
or at least trusted that "home" lay in store for them there—felt secure and
comfortable staying on and continuing permanently. But some felt unsuccessful or dissatisfied with their accomplishments. Doctors, lawyers, and
writers, for example, were among those with training that tied them to their
homeland by certification, policy, and language. They sought to work and
live at a level to which they had been accustomed or to which they had
aspired before the Anschluss and felt they could do so only in Vienna.

Often men felt this professional need and persuaded or coerced wives
to join them. A number of these women followed with little enthusiasm or
willingness but ultimately did so with a dedication to their own sense of
home—in their case, a loyalty to their *familial home*. In that era, men made
most important household decisions, and if a husband decided to relocate, his wife was expected to go along with the children to keep the family
together. In these cases, the family was "home," and it was moving to Vienna.

This group of returning professionals was augmented by a number of
Austrian Jewish men who had fled the Nazis to the United Kingdom and
the United States and who found themselves in their home country at the
end of the war as members of the British or US Army. While still in the
uniforms of the Allied forces, they searched for surviving family members,
and some began to envision living there again and chose to remain after
their discharge from military service.

These returnees—the professionals and the soldiers—largely succeeded
in finding their place again in Vienna. Naïve hopes of a friendly welcome
were dashed as they confronted slogans such as "Rückkehr unerwünscht"—
return not desired. Some newspapers used the word "evil" to describe Jewish
reémigrés.[8] But even in the context of continued antisemitism and lingering
Nazi sentiment, returnees found ways to manage and to reestablish themselves. Why did they return and with what expectations? What did they
meet upon arrival in Vienna?

---

8. Christoph Reinprecht, "Jewish Identity in Postwar Austria: Experiences and Dilemmas," in *Jewish Studies at the Central European University: Public Lectures, 1996–1999*, ed. András Kovács and Eszter Andor (Budapest: Central European University, 2000), 206.

RETURN FROM AROUND THE GLOBE

The wave of returnees seeking to regain a professional home began to return to Vienna from all over the world in late 1946. Many of them felt bound to their hometown by training and language. Lawyers educated and certified to practice law in Austria found it difficult, if not impossible, to work in their chosen field outside the country. Journalists and other writers whose main professional tool was language also preferred to work in their native German. Some had always intended to go home; others had tried to make a professional home abroad but had failed to establish a work life that they found satisfying.

In July 1947, the director of Joint operations in Austria, Joseph Silber, estimated that ten thousand of the forty-five thousand Jews in the country were native-born Austrians; the majority of the rest were displaced persons originally from Poland.[9] Repatriation transports from Shanghai, Karaganda, and Palestine had reached Vienna with groups of survivors seeking to reestablish themselves in their homeland. Those who chose to go back did so consciously, knowing full well that working in their preferred city also meant living and working among former Nazis and Nazi sympathizers, shaping a newly emerging postwar Viennese Jewish identity that developed in the context of postwar Austrian nation building.

Helga Embacher has surmised that émigrés' readiness to return to Vienna from abroad was associated with difficulties and hardships encountered in countries of exile and professional problems incurred, as well as with age, illness, and some hope of regaining property. Embacher presents the example of the relatively few who came back from the United States—just 0.2 percent of exiles who had fled there—where comparatively more opportunities and comfortable conditions existed, in contrast to the relatively high rate of return from places of more difficult circumstances, such

---

9. Postwar Joint press release, July 30, 1947, translation of a July 16, 1947, press release, from Information Office in Jerusalem, AR 45/54-143, Records of the New York Office of the American Jewish Joint Distribution Committee, 1945–1954, Archives of the American Jewish Joint Distribution Committee (JDC Archives), New York, NY.

as Palestine and Shanghai.[10] Likewise, a number of Austrian Jews arrived in Vienna from Karaganda, the capital of the Karagandy province in Kazakhstan, also having chosen to return home.

Like many Austrian and German Jews, Ernst Csillag and his family had fled from the Nazis to the Baltic countries. Ernst, his sister Elisabeth, and their parents lived in Riga, Latvia, until Germany invaded the Soviet Union. At that time, the Soviets interned the German and Austrian citizens they found in Riga, and deported them—including the Csillags—to a Soviet forced-labor settlement in Karaganda.[11] Ernst, his sister, and his father lived there until late January 1947 (his mother unfortunately died during their internment), when the Soviet Army organized their repatriation.[12] The small family traveled on a train packed with Jewish repatriates that snaked through Ukraine, Romania, and Hungary to its destination. Thanks to the Joint, they enjoyed food rations better than those of the accompanying Soviet troops—a situation that caused some animosity. Csillag recalled that, when the transport reached the border between Hungary and Austria, the Austrians refused them entry, and the Red Army soldiers teased them that their countrymen obviously did not want them and that they would have to turn around and go to Siberia.[13] This joke proved rather a foreshadowing of the experience they and many other returnees would have in their return to Vienna, but the Csillags could not have yet known this. They finally arrived in their hometown on March 28, 1947. They, along with

---

10. Helga Embacher, "Unwelcome in Austria: Returnees and Concentration Camp Survivors," in *When the War Was Over: Women, War and Peace in Europe, 1940–1956*, ed. Claire Duchen and Irene Bandhauer-Schöffmann (London: Leicester University Press, 2000), 199.

11. List of people in Karaganda civilian internment camp, January 31, 1947, 3.1.1.3/78788168/ ITS Digital Archive, United States Holocaust Memorial Museum Library and Archive (USHMM), Washington, DC.

12. Ernst Csillag, interview, 490, Dokumentationsarchiv des österreichischen Widerstandes (DÖW), Vienna, Austria. In this interview, Csillag specifies that they left Karaganda on January 28, 1947. According to World Jewish Congress correspondence and a list in the ITS Digital Archive, the family was still living there (father, son, and daughter; mother died in Karaganda, as specified on list) on January 31, 1947. See List of people in Karaganda civilian internment camp, January 31, 1947.

13. Csillag interview.

204 other Jewish Austrians returning from Karaganda,[14] received no big or formal welcome, "just a mid-level official from city hall," Ernst Csillag said.[15]

After as many as six years of internment in work camps, the returnees were in poor condition. They needed help. Joint operations in the country were already taxed, and assistance was requested from its Paris office.[16] Meanwhile, the family was among those led from the Matzleinsdorfer train station to the Rothschild Hospital, an IKG-owned hospital located in the US zone of occupation that served as a displaced persons camp. There, they were disinfected with DDT and given a good meal and then were moved to a homeless shelter run by the Joint and the Kultusgemeinde as a temporary residence. All promptly began to search for a more permanent place to live and to reconnect with relatives. Lucky ones got packages from family members abroad. Everyone received clothing from the Joint and food from a Jewish soup kitchen on the Kleine Pfarrgasse in the city's second district. The Joint also arranged and paid for medical and dental care, as well as a stipend of one hundred schillings per month for repatriates (until one secured employment).[17] Most importantly, Csillag's father regained his position at the Anker insurance company, his prewar employer, and thus met one of his main goals: reestablishing his profession.[18]

If the Csillags returned as civilians, some Austrian Jewish men found themselves back in their home country with the British and US armed forces at the end of the war, and a few began to envision reestablishing lives there after discharge.[19] Most German and Austrian Jewish soldiers distin-

---

14. List of 207 people who have returned to Vienna from Karaganda, April 8, 1947, 3.1.1.3/78805335/ITS Digital Archive, USHMM.

15. Csillag interview.

16. JDC cable to Paris from Vienna, April 28, 1947, frame 0836, AR 45/54-143, Records of the New York Office of the American Jewish Joint Distribution Committee, 1945–1954, JDC Archives.

17. Joint cable to Paris, May 14, 1947, frame 0825, AR 45/54-143, Records of the New York Office of the American Jewish Joint Distribution Committee, 1945–1954, JDC Archives. The Joint in Paris then wired the same information to the Joint in New York City. See frame 0195, AR 45/54-146, JDC Archive.

18. Csillag interview.

19. Axel Corti's film *Welcome in Vienna* depicts this exact experience. One of the main characters fled Nazi Vienna to the United States and has returned with the US forces, naively

guished between Nazis and Germans or Nazis and Austrians, a difference that allowed them to maintain ties to their nations.[20] Austrian Jews had the additional benefit of the possibility of viewing Nazis as specifically *German*, much like their gentile compatriots. An internalization of this element of the "victim myth" enabled their return to a place where one could choose to see any Austrian citizen as some kind of victim of the Germans.

Actual experience often corrected this view. Kurt Fräser's is an extreme but telling example.[21] Fräser fled Nazi Vienna in 1939 for England, where he joined the British armed forces and took part in the invasion on the King Sector of Gold Beach at Normandy. He later found himself stationed in Germany as part of the postwar occupation and was back in Vienna for a visit at the end of 1947. Fräser went directly to his family's former apartment, where he found a strange couple in residence. His parents' dwelling had been assigned to this *Alter Kämpfer* (a pre-Anschluss, illegal Nazi Party member) and his wife after his parents' arrest and deportation. Despite knowing the cruel way that the two had snatched his family home, Fräser told them that he did not want to kick them out. The newly married Fräser instead explained that he intended to bring his bride to Vienna and suggested they all four live together in the small apartment until the Nazi couple found other quarters. They agreed, and the foursome carried out their plan, at least at the start. Unfortunately, with Fräser's discharge from the British Army one month later, his flatmates felt emboldened to oppose the restitution of the apartment to its rightful leaseholder. As soon as Fräser no longer had the support of an Allied occupation force, the Nazi filed a lawsuit to evict him. The case went to court, and during the course of the

---

imagining a "welcome in Vienna" but instead seeing the stark reality of lingering antisemitism and Nazi sentiment. Once discharged, he is faced with the dilemma of whether to return to the United States or stay in his hometown. See *Welcome in Vienna: Wohin und Zurück*, written by Georg Stefan Troller, directed by Axel Corti (Austria, 1986).

20. John P. Fox, "German and Austrian Jewish Volunteers in Britain's Armed Forces, 1939–1945," *Leo Baeck Institute Yearbook* 1995:24.

21. Thanks to Robert Rosner for alerting me to the identity of the anonymous man cited in Ruth Beckerman's documentary and its transcript *Jenseits des Krieges*. His name was Kurt Finkelstein, later Kenneth Fraser in the British Army, and then Kurt Fräser in postwar Vienna. See *Jenseits des Krieges*, written and directed by Ruth Beckerman (Hoanzl Vertrieb, 1996), DVD.

proceedings, the judge asked Fräser if he had been present at the time of his parents' arrest, although he knew full well that Fräser had been in the United Kingdom at the time. Because he had not been in residence there at the time of his parents' arrest and when the couple had taken the apartment, he technically had no claim on it. This moment signified more to Fräser than losing his family home. It was then that he realized that the Allies "may have won the war militarily but we were still far from democracy."[22] Indeed, Kurt never regained his family home, but nevertheless he remained in Vienna.

Otto Suschny also found himself in Austria with the British Army at the end of the war. He had fled the Nazis to Palestine, where he joined the British military. He was posted with the second contingent of British occupation forces in the Austrian province of Carinthia after the war and first went back to Vienna in 1945 to look for his family. He visited his former apartment and found on the doorstep an unopened letter—one that he had written to the Red Cross seeking information about his family members. Suschny then inquired at the *Meldeamt* (residency registration office) as to their whereabouts, and officials there simply informed him that they "had left" in 1942. In fact, the Gestapo deported Adele and Siegfried Suschny from Vienna to Minsk on August 17, 1942,[23] and they were murdered four days later in a pine forest near Maly Trostinec, a small village about eight miles east of Minsk.[24]

Suschny had never intended to stay in Palestine but rather had always planned to return to his family at home. When he found no one there, he considered emigrating to England with other relatives, but he learned that his matriculation exams qualified him to study in Austria and that he could receive a student stipend from the Joint. He also secured interesting and rewarding work helping to track down former Nazis with Tuviah Friedman, the head of the Haganah Wien's Documentation Center. Suschny

---

22. Ruth Beckerman, *Jenseits des Krieges* (Vienna: Löcker Verlag, 1998), 75–77.
23. Abgangelist des 36. Transportes, August 17, 1942, 1.2.1.1/11203795/ITS Digital Archive, USHMM.
24. Opfersuche (Victim Search) database of the Dokumentationsarchiv des österreichisches Widerstandes, accessed December 21, 2017, http://www.doew.at.

spent two years with Friedman's group, interviewing concentration camp survivors to accumulate evidence for war crimes trials. His income from this work, coupled with his stipend, made staying in Vienna financially feasible.

In addition to the academic and professional status Suschny achieved once back in Vienna, he also met his future wife, Kitty, at a Passover Seder in 1947. Although the two had grown up in the neighboring second and twentieth districts and only a few streets away from each other, and despite having been a part of the same Jewish youth group, they had never met. Kitty had fled the Nazis to England, where she survived the war, and returned to her hometown in October 1946 and worked as a translator for the US occupation forces.[25] After the two had made their own separate choices to live again in Vienna, they found each other, married, and started a family.

GENDERED EXPERIENCES AND IDENTITY IN EXILE AND RETURN

Unlike Kitty, not all women made their own choices to return. One female survivor who had fled to Shanghai and eventually made it to the United States would have been very happy to stay there, but her husband dreamed only of Vienna. "I would have gladly stayed in America! But in our marriage, there weren't any debates. That was what my husband wanted, and so we came back right after the end of the war."[26] Many women accompanied husbands who were dissatisfied with professional lives abroad. A number of these women had no interest in living in Austria again, but their dedication was to their families, in whatever geographic location. Their husbands had determined that Vienna was their professional home, which meant that these wives' familial home would be there too. And so they followed.

As we have seen (in chapter 1), many women organized their families' escape from the Nazis and in doing so had taken on tasks that men would

---

25. Kitty Suschny, interview with author, Vienna, Austria, December 22, 2010.
26. Anonymous resident of the Maimonides Zentrum, Vienna's Jewish old-age home, as quoted in *Gemeinde*, February 1984, 23.

have handled under different circumstances. Women suddenly had the responsibility and found the strength to support and provide for their families' needs of daily existence and flight to safety. Their men—emasculated and paralyzed by eviction from professional positions and social rank—were unable to act along traditional male gender norms to protect and care for their families. In addition to losing the means to make a living, men were also targeted with roundups, arrests, and deportation to concentration camps. Their wives and female relatives often took on the additional task of ensuring their release and the emigration of their families.

Women created new homes in countries of exile and achieved levels of success, some in resumed gender roles as mothers and caretakers and others as newly independent working women; a number of them *both* worked and cared for families. Wives and mothers established themselves and their families, engaged in their communities, and managed households. With family and home life at the core of their female identity and role—and, therefore, of their motivations and concerns—women by and large re-created their families' homes in their countries of exile, even when working to help support their families. Many of them creatively mixed cultures and styles to retain a typically Austrian flair. After successfully taking over traditional male tasks in Vienna, many wives' roles reverted to more stereotypically female functions, and their resilience and adaptability served them well.

For women who worked outside the home, levels of professional satisfaction or dissatisfaction tended to be very different from the bleak outlook of their male counterparts. At that time, most women had not received formal or specialty training, and thus few suffered from the loss of a professional life or the status that carried. As emigrants, they worked to support their families in whatever jobs they could arrange, and some enjoyed their newfound roles as working women. Anna Rattner described her time in Tel Aviv as her "seven years of plenty."[27] She had been a salesgirl in Vienna, but in Palestine she had been able to open her own Viennese clothing boutique. She raised her social and professional status while in exile, but her husband suffered unemployment after the founding of the State of Israel and the

---

27. Embacher, "Unwelcome in Austria," 200.

subsequent closing of the English-owned restaurant in which he had been employed. He wanted to return to Vienna, although Anna could have supported them with her shop.[28] "It's a big problem when the roles in a marriage are reversed, when the man isn't the boss anymore," Anna observed years later.[29]

Most male refugees living in exile found their professional and social status lagging and felt unable to support their families as they had before. They found it difficult or impossible to achieve professionally, as they were limited in their work sphere or unable to enter those domains at all, and this threatened the way they viewed themselves. They had developed professional and social identities over years of specialized Austrian training and experience. Many sought to live again in Vienna, their professional home, to try to attain or regain the status and positions they had enjoyed or had been working toward before the war.

Although exact numbers remain elusive, it has been estimated that some three thousand German and Austrian refugee doctors fled to the United Kingdom, most of them Jewish. The Austrian Association of Doctors in Great Britain was organized in 1941, and at the end of the war, its members wanted to return to Austria to practice medicine.[30] Young scholars who had received their doctoral degrees at German and Austrian universities found themselves pressed to enter other fields while in exile, such as taking work in libraries, as teachers, and at radio stations. Historian Heinrich Benedikt and professor of Arabic and Islamic studies Hans Ludwig Gottschalk were among those in exile in the United Kingdom, and both went to Austria immediately after the war, as they saw their home country as their only opportunity for scholarly activity.[31]

---

28. Anna Rattner and Lola Blonder, *1938—Zuflucht Palästina: Zwei Frauen berichten* (Vienna: Geyer, 1989), 15.

29. Embacher, "Unwelcome in Austria," 200.

30. Paul Weindling, "The Contribution of Central European Jews to Medical Science and Practice in Britain, the 1930s–1950s," in *Second Chance: Two Centuries of German-Speaking Jews in the United Kingdom*, ed. Werner Eugen Mosse and Julius Carlebach (Tübingen: J. C. B. Mohr, 1991), 251.

31. Christhard Hoffmann, "The Contribution of German-speaking Jewish Immigrants to British Historiography," in Mosse and Carlebach, *Second Chance*, 163.

Nazi persecution and mortal danger had led many Jewish exiles to positions well below their level of expertise and experience and in some cases to difficult manual labor and agricultural work in challenging climates and environments. With the end of the war and the threat to their lives, many wished to abandon jobs they deemed inferior or too difficult. Others who were unable to work in their fields of choice in lands of exile simply sought to resume their previous occupations and saw no other option. They envisioned that return would allow them to reconstruct what they had lost and to work and live as they had previously. Reestablishing oneself in Vienna, even if it meant coexisting with Nazis, seemed preferable to their lives abroad.

Exiled Jewish professionals largely took their decisions to return later than those who were motivated by the more emotional, instinctual impetuses for regaining a familial home and mostly after those who had gone back to Vienna out of a commitment to their political ideals of participating in the reconstruction of a democratic Austria. Jewish professionals abroad had more information than had been available to earlier waves of returnees about living and reestablishing oneself in postwar Vienna. Nonetheless, many made the decision to return. The promise of denazification, at least in principle, may have spurred many male professionals to come back to resume professions, although in practice it amounted to little or nothing. Yet at the same time, doctors, for example, knew that the government and professional organizations discouraged their homecoming. Still, come home they did, and as they assumed or resumed places in society, it did not take long to grasp the way to get along in postwar Vienna, living and working alongside former Nazis: to take part in a firmly rooted national silence on the issue of national and personal guilt for Nazi crimes.

Torberg's work demonstrates a version of this compromise. His refusal to comment on his nation's past and the perpetration of the Holocaust by Austrians serves as an example of a common situation: returnees realized what would serve them best to overlook in social, professional, and political situations. Torberg highlighted the social and cultural elements that his country had lost through the forced emigration, deportation, and mass murder of its Jews but specifically did not state *how* they were "lost."

Gentiles could read and enjoy his work, sympathizing with the absence he described but also without confronting their indirect or outright participation in Nazi persecution. In addition, if society assumed the perspective of having "lost" its Jewish component—rather than considering it taken, stolen, or intentionally annihilated—no blame had been assigned and certainly not to Austrians. This language and lack of discussion abetted the myth that culpability rested solely with the Germans—the *German* Nazis had invaded and occupied the country; as a result, Vienna had expelled its Jewish element. This not only stifled but also preempted discussion.

Returning Jews were not responsible for Austria's and Austrians' lack of reflection on and the failure to assume responsibility for the past. But it fell to them to find a way to cope with their countrymen's stance. After World War II and the Holocaust, Jewish returnees assessed the situation in Vienna and found ways to navigate the antisemitism in their midst, just as Jews in Austria had for centuries before, and part of that involved participation in the national silence on the Nazi past. This benefited both sides on macro and micro levels: returning Jews did not have to emotionally realize or "know" about their neighbors' post-Anschluss activities, and gentiles did not have to confront their participation in Nazi persecution.

Women were less likely to want to live among people who had robbed and persecuted them, forced their emigration, and deported and murdered family members. Going back to Vienna meant resuming traditional female interactions in the community, where women operated in social spheres, shopping for their families, managing their children's education, and running households—the same realm in which they had experienced hostility and antisemitism directly from Austrian neighbors. Men, by contrast, had experienced discrimination in the *public* sphere as ordered by *public* officials. This permitted them to consider the Germans' arrival and takeover as the cause of their unemployment and expulsion. Men could blame the Germans for the loss of their livelihoods and professions through some level of acceptance of the victim myth. With the end of "Greater Germany" and theoretical denazification in place, they could return with optimism to resume their professions, while women knew that they would return to social situations and communities where little had changed. In the community and in the informal dealings so prevalent in women's daily lives, not even theoretical denazification existed. They were well aware that their Austrian neighbors had inflicted their maltreatment and cruelty without any directive or demand from the Germans.

Maria Dorothea Simon spent the war years in exile in England, where she trained as a social worker and worked at Anna Freud's children's home. Later Simon served in the British Army, and at a New Year's Eve party 1943–44, she met the Viennese-born US citizen Joseph. They married in April 1944. After the war, Joseph was convinced that they could succeed in Vienna and wanted to return. Although Maria was born and raised in Vienna, she had been of Czech nationality but had lost her citizenship and was thus unable to accompany him. Instead, she went to the United States with her young son and sought citizenship there while furthering her social work training. Once a US citizen, she joined her husband in Vienna, but she found readjusting to life there and achieving a work-family balance difficult. She would have preferred to stay in the United States but returned to Vienna for Joseph. He proved to be more open-minded than his male peers, however, and in 1957, when Maria got an offer of a faculty position in the Department of Psychiatry of the University of Arkansas Medical School in Little Rock, he stayed in Austria to consider the move while she and the children went ahead. Maria enjoyed rewarding professional and personal experiences in Little Rock and wanted to make their permanent home in the United States, but in the end, Joseph refused to leave Vienna. Choosing family over career, Maria went back to Vienna in 1961, and eventually the whole family became Austrian citizens.[32]

Frau Fischer also loved the life she found in London after fleeing the Nazis, but her husband had the opportunity to regain his former job as a manager in Vienna's public transportation system after the war. He longed for his old life, and so they went back. But she found it hard to adapt and said it felt eerie to live among murderers. "My husband wanted to return. That's the way it goes when you are married, plus a little bit foolish and you

---

32. Maria Dorothea Simon, "Selbstzeugnis," in *Soziale Arbeit in Selbstzeugnissen*, vol. 2, ed. Hermann Heitkamp and Alfred Plewa (Freiburg in Breisgau: Lambertus, 2002), 248–51.

don't put up any resistance.... It was very difficult. Despite the fact that we were very happy, it almost ended up in a separation." Sadly, Frau Fischer felt in retrospect that she had been "defrauded of her life" and felt that she would have accomplished much more if she had stayed in England.[33]

Maria's and Frau Fischer's stories echo those of many wives and mothers who returned with their families to maintain the familial home, at least partially against their wishes. So many of them had found or created a new home elsewhere and did not desire to live again in the place from which they had been banished. But their home was relocating, back to Vienna. Even if against their will, they returned to Vienna for *home*.

PROFESSIONALS IN POSTWAR VIENNA

Of the more than fourteen thousand Austrian Jewish immigrants who fled from Nazi Austria to Palestine,[34] fewer than four hundred had come back to Vienna by 1947.[35] Stella Kadmon was among those to arrive in that year. Before she fled to Palestine, she had run a successful theater in Vienna and was well known for putting on political and satirical plays.[36] She had first escaped to Belgrade, where she stayed with cousins, and then eventually made it to Palestine. She barely spoke Hebrew, though, and thus was qualified only to undertake menial labor. After the war, she sought to return to Vienna as quickly as possible to pursue her work with the theater again.[37] After receiving her visa to go back to Austria, she stayed in a tent camp on

---

33. *Ich rege mich noch heute auf, wenn ich es erzählte: Frauen berichten über ihr Leben in der Zeit von 1934 bis 1945*, AUF-Eine Frauenzeitschrift Sonderheft zum Bedenkjahr 1988 (Vienna: Frauenzentrum, 1988).

34. Jonny Moser, *Demographie der jüdischen Bevölkerung Österreichs, 1938–1945* (Vienna: Dokumentationsarchiv des österreichischen Widerstandes, 1999), 76. Hugo Gold wrote that only 9,195 Austrian Jews emigrated to Palestine between March 13, 1938, and mid-November 1941. See Gold, *Geschichte der Juden in Wien: Ein Gedenkbuch* (Tel Aviv: Olamenu, 1966), 133.

35. Doron Niederland, "Die Immigration," in *Vertreibung und Neubeginn: Israelische Bürger österreichischer Herkunft*, ed. Erika Weinzierl and Otto D. Kulka (Vienna: Böhlau Verlag, 1992), 428.

36. Stella Kadmon interview, 284, DÖW.

37. Embacher, "Unwelcome in Austria," 199.

the Suez Canal for two months while waiting for a British troop-transport ship. Her journey took her to Venice, then Arnoldstein in the Austrian province of Carinthia, and finally home to Vienna. "For me, that was a happy day, although I was horrified at how my beloved Vienna looked. The devastation and everything. My apartment had also been destroyed and we stayed in an hourly hotel in the second district. That was less nice, but we were *home.* . . . Returning home was a happy time in my life."[38] In 1947, Kadmon reestablished her theater under the name Theater der Courage (Theater of Courage).

Many Viennese Jews arrived with ambitions of reestablishing themselves in their prewar careers, and some, like Kadmon, founded similar institutions or continued with careers influenced by their time in exile. The Paul Zsolnay Verlag had been one of the most successful publishing houses in Vienna during the interwar years. Owner Paul Zsolnay had tricked the Nazis for a short while after the Anschluss by utilizing an "Aryan" titular head to his firm, and in 1938, he fled to safety in London. Despite his efforts and those of his gentile colleague, the Gestapo investigated his business and closed his shop in April 1939, and the bookseller Karl H. Bischoff eventually took over the Paul Zsolnay Verlag.[39] In London, Zsolnay worked for the British publisher Heinemann, where he advanced quickly and eventually helped set up the imprint Heinemann & Zsolnay. When he returned to Vienna in 1946, he regained his business and renamed it the Heinemann & Zsolnay Verlag, in tribute to the London firm that had sustained him through the war.[40]

Others did not conceive of their professional home in Vienna until they got there. Erich Lessing fled the Nazis to Palestine in 1939 and worked there as a driver and later as a radio technician for the British Army. After the war, he worked on a fish farm and as a photographer, taking kindergarten-class pictures and tourist photos on the beach in Natanya. He knew

---

38. Kadmon interview (emphasis added).

39. Murray G. Hall, "Publishers and Institutions in Austria, 1918–45," in *A History of Austrian Literature, 1918–2000*, ed. Katrin Maria Kohl and Ritchie Robertson (Rochester, NY: Camden House, 2006), 79–80.

40. Uwe Westphal, "German, Czech and Austrian Jews in English Publishing," in Mosse and Carlebach, *Second Chance*, 206.

that no one from his family remained in Vienna and decided to go to Paris to study photography formally. Unable to obtain a visa for France in Jerusalem, he secured papers to go to Austria, sailed by boat to Naples, and finally arrived by train in Vienna in early 1947. He had hoped to gain a visa from the French occupation authorities but was unsuccessful. He found a place to stay and eventually took a position with the Associated Press (AP) in Vienna. Lessing was unable to regain his family's home in a *Gemeindebau* (public housing) in the city's eighth district, but he did reacquire some of their furniture with the help of informative neighbors.[41]

Despite Lessing's original plan, he stayed. He had secured satisfying work as an AP photographer and found himself in "interesting circles," in which he associated with young Austrians who believed in a different future for Viennese society, he said.[42] Although his original motivation to return to Vienna had not included staying or establishing a career there, the circumstances of the city in the postwar period opened opportunities, and he took advantage of them and established a new professional home.

THE RETURN OF JEWISH LAWYERS

The origins of the high number of Jewish lawyers in Vienna before the Anschluss can be traced back to the Habsburg monarchy. Starting in the middle of the nineteenth century, sending sons to university to study law or medicine had become fashionable among Jewish families across the empire. In addition, the civil service prohibited the entry of Jews into its employ, further contributing to a particular focus on these two fields. After World War I, lawyers from around the former empire swarmed into Vienna. With the 1929 stock market crisis, however, many lost their jobs in banking and other business enterprises and settled into positions as self-employed attorneys. By 1936, some 62 percent of lawyers in Vienna were Jewish.[43]

---

41. Erich Lessing, interview with author, Vienna, Austria, January 27, 2011.
42. Ibid.
43. Barbara Sauer and Ilse Reiter-Zatloukal, *Advokaten 1938: Das Schicksal der in den Jahren 1938 bis 1945 verfolgten österreichischen Rechtsanwältinnen und Rechtsanwälte* (Vienna: Manz, 2010), ix–x.

The Österreichischen Rechtsanwaltskammertag (Austrian Chamber of Lawyers) counted 2,541 registered lawyers at the time of the Anschluss in March 1938; by the end of that same year, 771 remained. Of those missing from the registry, 1,830 had been dismissed because of Jewish family background. The Nazis deported 388 of formerly registered lawyers, 303 of whom they ultimately murdered. Dozens of others committed suicide in the face of impending persecution.[44]

The majority, however, fled to safety in other countries, but most were unable to practice law due to differing legal systems and certifications. Many Viennese Jewish lawyers found themselves starting new careers, and a number resorted to manual labor and performing odd jobs. The loss of professional status caused them to suffer psychologically and to experience crises of personal identity. At least 249 Jewish lawyers returned to Austria after 1945. Most cited the difficulty of starting a new professional life in a new country as the main reason for return, but many also shared a desire to take part in the rebuilding of a democratic Austria.[45] Lawyer Anton Pick, for example, had been an active Social Democrat and a member of the Sozialistischen Arbeitsgemeinschaft für Wirtschaft und Politik (International Socialist Association for Business and Politics) from 1928. He defended revolutionary Social Democrats during the Austrofascist period in Vienna but seemingly suffered no persecution himself. After the Anschluss, however, he fled in fear of racist discrimination and maltreatment under the Nuremberg Laws, first to Prague and then to Palestine. He returned to his hometown in 1947, successfully resumed his career, recommenced his Social Democrat activity, and sought to take part in the reconstruction of his country. Pick later became the president of the IKG (1970–81) and was a board member of the Dokumentationsarchiv des österreichischen Widerstandes (DÖW),[46] a documentation and research institute focused on Austrofascist and Nazi persecution in Austria that was founded by Austrian resisters and survivors, both Jewish and non-Jewish. Not all returnees reintegrated

---

44. Ibid., xi.
45. Ibid., xiii–xiv.
46. "Anton Pick," Weblexikon der Wiener Socialdemokratie, accessed January 16, 2015, http://www.dasrotewien.at/pick-anton.html.

so well, however. Nearly 10 percent (23 of the 249) of them reemigrated at some point. Vienna, they found, was not home after all.

THE RETURN OF JEWISH DOCTORS

At the time of the Anschluss, Nazi race laws endangered some 3,500 of the 4,900 doctors in Austria because of Jewish family background.[47] Stripped of academic status, 372 were derogatorily termed "Krankenbehandler" (medic) and permitted to treat Jewish patients only.[48] Approximately 3,000 Austrian Jewish doctors found ways to emigrate, mostly to the United States or the United Kingdom.[49]

After the war, émigré Jewish doctors abroad expressed interest in returning to Vienna, but both the Ärztekammer (medical society) and the government encouraged them to stay overseas. Meanwhile, former Nazi doctors retained their posts in Austria. One Dr. A. Hartwich warned his Jewish colleagues of the economic hardships and limited possibilities in a 1946 article in the Austrian medical journal Österreichische Ärztezeitung (Austrian medical journal). He used friendly, if superficial, language to urge them to stay in their "hard-earned" medical jobs in other countries, rather than face the difficult struggle of working in the field in their hometown.[50] The government and political leaders also did nothing to support their remigration, even when it could have been of obvious benefit. In October 1945, for example, Chancellor Karl Renner reported Austria's shortage of doctors but proposed as a solution not the invitation of return for Jewish physicians living in exile but rather the relaxation of denazification regulations.[51]

---

47. Michael Hubenstorf, "Vertriebene Medizin—Finale des Niedergangs der Wiener Medizinischen Schule," in *Vertriebene Vernunft: Emigration und Exil der österreichischen Wissenschaft*, vol. 2, ed. Friedrich Stadler (Vienna: Jugend und Volk, 1987), 781.

48. Renate Feikes, "Exil der Wiener Medizin in Großbritannien," in *Immortal Austria? Austrians in Exile in Britain*, ed. Charmian Brinson, Richard Dove, and Jennifer Taylor (Amsterdam: Rodopi, 2007), 62.

49. Hubenstorf, "Vertriebene Medizin," 781.

50. Feikes, "Exil der Wiener Medizin in Großbritannien," 71.

51. Susanne Cohen-Weisz, *Jewish Life in Austria and Germany since 1945: Identity and Communal Reconstruction* (Budapest: Central European University Press, 2016), 64.

Dr. Felix Mandl returned to practice medicine in Vienna after living in exile in Palestine and serves as an example of a most successful reémigré doctor. Mandl was the head of the surgical department of the Canning-Child Hospital in Vienna and a lecturer at the University of Vienna's medical school when the Nazis came to power. After the Anschluss, the hospital was "Aryanized," and Mandl lost his position and was dismissed from the university. He emigrated to Switzerland in 1938 and then on to Palestine, where he assumed a position at Hadassah University Hospital in 1939 and was appointed professor a year later.[52] Although he enjoyed much success and appreciation in Palestine, Dr. Mandl returned to postwar Vienna to resume his career. In May 1947, he became the director of the surgical department of the Emperor Franz Josef Hospital in Vienna and resumed his role as a lecturer for surgery at the medical school.[53] Dr. Mandl's career continued at a brilliant pace. Among other positions, he served as the vice president of the International College of Surgeons, became a master of surgery in 1957, and in that same year received the city of Vienna's prize for natural sciences.[54]

JEWISH RETURNEES CONFRONTING THE PROBLEMS OF POSTWAR VIENNA

By the time most Jewish professionals returned to Vienna, the Austrian national identity as victim of the Germans had solidified. Many Jewish survivors reported hearing these self-conscious, even guilty, expressions of assumed blamelessness. In other cases, survivors witnessed antisemitism mixed with shame. Ernst Csillag worked at the post office, and on one occasion, his manager refused to honor a Jewish patron's *Amtsbescheinigung*

---

52. Karl Heinz Tragl, *Chronik der Wiener Krankenanstalten* (Vienna: Böhlau Verlag, 2007), 374.
53. "Felix Mandl, ao. Univ.-Prof. Dr.," 650 plus—History of the University of Vienna, accessed July 31, 2020, https://geschichte.univie.ac.at/en/persons/felix-mandl-ao-univ-prof-dr.
54. Judith Bauer-Merinsky, "Die Auswirkungen der Annexion Österreichs durch das Deutsche Reich auf die medizinische Fakultät der Universität Wien im Jahre 1938: Biographien entlassener Professoren und Dozenten" (PhD diss., University of Vienna, 1980), 150–52.

(official victim identification papers), which should have provided preferential treatment. "You won't give him anything!" she told Csillag and berated him in her office about giving money to a Jew. He finally spoke up and told her that he too was Jewish and fully aware of the rules of an *Amtsbescheinigung*. He watched as she immediately "got smaller and smaller," and then she apologized to him. From then on, the two got along very well, and Csillag believed that her guilty conscience actually made her protective of him. He claimed to have had no further such problems with coworkers and in fact specified that one inspection official, a former convinced and enthusiastic Nazi, had treated him particularly carefully.[55]

Csillag did encounter antisemitism with patrons. Once, he argued with a female customer who spoke with a thick Sudeten-German accent. Another customer mistook this for a Yiddish accent and took Csillag's side with the antisemitic comment, "Well, seems like she jumped from the grate," a reference to the ovens used for burning bodies in Nazi death camps.[56] Csillag's coworkers' shock and disapproval of the statement encouraged him. They supported him and admonished the customer. Although this particular situation also revealed the more positive of postwar Austrians' attitudes—in response to the more negative—it shows that Csillag's job nonetheless involved continuous contact with the general public and provided him ample opportunity to hear the unfiltered thoughts of everyday Austrians. Antisemitism remained an issue.

Practical matters, like housing, also continued to pose a challenge to returnees in 1946 and 1947. Following formal regulations and abiding by the city housing office's requirements often proved unproductive for reémigrés who sought permanent accommodations in Vienna. Many secured housing through chance encounters, personal and professional connections, and daring resourcefulness. As we have seen, actress and theater owner Stella Kadmon and her mother stayed first in a hotel upon their return from Palestine. Two weeks after Kadmon's arrival, a fan recognized her on the street. Pleased and relieved to see that she had survived, the fan offered to assist

---

55. Csillag interview.
56. Ibid.

her to secure housing, and his contact at the Wohnungsamt (government housing office) soon found her a two-room apartment that had belonged to a Nazi who was in the prisoner-of-war camp at Wolfsberg. The Nazi's wife had divorced her husband in an attempt to keep the apartment, but her efforts were in vain; she had been evicted that very morning. Kadmon had to move in immediately, before representatives of the housing office reassigned the dwelling. Kadmon and her mother bribed the building superintendent to say that they had been there a long time, and they moved into the empty two rooms. The following day, another man showed up at the apartment with a certificate issued by the housing office that indicated that he had been allocated the apartment. Kadmon and her mother remained firm and sat on the empty floor, insisting that it was theirs and that they had been in residence there for an extended period. The superintendent supported the women's story, and the parties commiserated about the "idiots working at the Wohnungsamt—how annoying!" After a bit more wrangling with the man and with the housing office officials, the women kept the apartment, and Kadmon stayed there permanently.[57]

This incident, one of many similar such accounts, shows the interplay and continued influence of all kinds of Austrian experiences before, during, and after Nazi oppression for all players involved. In another instance, a governmental housing authority with a mandate to serve the city's many homeless citizens in the postwar period might serve as an example of the rampant and institutional antisemitism permeating so much of Austrian society, especially after years of Nazi indoctrination. But someone with connections and celebrity could find ways to overcome or circumvent the discrimination that just months or years before had contributed to genocide. As prevalent as antisemitism was in postwar Vienna, so were perquisite and preferential treatment, even for Jews in some cases.

After Vienna's remaining Jews reemerged at war's end, after camp survivors returned home, and after politically active Austrian Jews returned

---

57. Kadmon interview.

from exile abroad, a fourth wave of Austrian Jews returned to Vienna to claim or reclaim their professional homes. They did so in the context of the physical rebuilding of a partially destroyed city and during the reconstruction of a national identity that attempted to define all Austrians as victims of the Nazis. They found the expectations and hopes that had sustained them through their years of exile dashed but still maintained the idea of Austria as their home even when their arrival proved neither joyful nor welcome.[58] The nation and city they fondly remembered from before the Anschluss no longer existed; rather, it was under construction in a new image. Nonetheless, many found a niche and reestablished themselves and their careers, albeit with an understood mutual silence while living among former Nazis.

As we shall see, rising Cold War tensions scotched hopes for denazification and much of the Allied enforcement of restitution, and both the Jewish community as a whole and individual Jews grappled to gain a foothold without much assistance or support. But many did reestablish professional lives or regain careers they had begun before the Anschluss, and those who stayed found or relearned ways to navigate a society that had always included latent and even outright antisemitism but was compounded by the experiences and resulting changed mentality of seven years of Nazi ideology.

Author Elisabeth Freundlich struggled desperately to reestablish herself in postwar Vienna. "If I had known the extent of the difficulties with which I would have to struggle after my return, perhaps I would not have been able to summon the courage to undertake that step," she admitted.[59] Although she arrived in her hometown with a completed novel, *Der Seelenvogel*, and two short stories, she received no recognition as an Austrian writer until 1986, when the novel finally was published—by the Paul Zsolnay Verlag. She never left, despite the difficulties. Similarly, Ernst Csillag, like so many others, never considered leaving. His family had not been religious. After

---

58. Reinprecht, "Jewish Identity in Postwar Austria," 208.
59. Elisabeth Freundlich, *Die fahrenden Jahre: Erinnerungen* (Salzburg: Otto Müller Verlag, 1992), 142.

the war, he married a gentile, and neither his children nor his grandchildren grew up with any religious observance. Nonetheless, he joined and maintained membership in the IKG and upheld that he felt connected to Judaism. And he identified as an Austrian, always comfortable in Vienna.[60]

---

60. Csillag interview.

6

EMERGING IDENTITIES AND ENDURING CHALLENGES

In the second week of February 1947, Franziska Tausig, the mother of Otto and mother-in-law of Hansi Tausig (who appears in chapter 4), sat on a train with 760 other Austrian Jews waiting to disembark in Vienna. They had survived the war in exile in Shanghai and were at the end of a two-month journey that had involved seven weeks of travel by sea from Shanghai to Naples and then another week by train to Vienna.[1] Franziska's husband had died in Shanghai from tuberculosis,[2] and so she traveled alone, eagerly anticipating her reunion with her son and her first meeting with his young wife. Although the train had arrived in the station, it took another half a day before it finally pulled up to the platform. Franziska recalled,

> The train had to wait an eternity to gain entry to the platform. It was cold and wet weather and we shivered miserably . . . sitting still in the same spot. They asked for our vaccination certificates. Then a doctor came to see if there were any sick people in the wagons. Finally we were given a piece of paper

---

1. "Heimkehr aus dem fernen Ost," *Der Mahnruf*, February 1947, 14.
2. Franziska Tausig, CM/1 file, 3.2.1.3/80854722/ITS Digital Archive, United States Holocaust Memorial Museum (USHMM), Washington, DC.

with an address of a hotel or a camp. And then in the biting cold came a man, bare-headed, with a white beard. We had no idea who this man was, who patiently climbed into each cattle car. Finally someone said, "That is our General Körner, the mayor of Vienna." He thanked us, that we in this time of distress and need, when every single person was needed to rebuild the city, that we were among the first to return. He said this so easily and naturally, that we enjoyed every word like a friendly welcome gift. As Mayor Körner reached the last car, the passengers in previous cars had already created a makeshift kitchen and made a goulash. I was already completely bereft of hope when a young man approached me and said, "Excuse me, Ma'am, but are you perhaps my mother?" This, my son's question, is the endpoint of my emigration and the beginning of a new phase of life at home [in der Heimat].³

Indeed, as Franziska Tausig recalled, Mayor Theodor Körner, along with a number of other governmental representatives, members of the Jewish Community Council, and representatives of the Joint and the United Nations Relief and Rehabilitation Administration (UNRRA) greeted the train (see the photograph on the cover of this book).⁴ Despite what seemed a big and formal welcome, they were met with a chaotic scene. The few cars and trucks on the road navigated snowy, winter streets with difficulty, but in any case, no transportation had been arranged for them or for their luggage. The IKG had organized accommodations for the new arrivals, but many did not reach their beds until late in the evening.⁵ Still, three days later, the Joint reported that all had settled down comfortably and had received Austrian ration cards, which the Joint was supplementing from its stocks.⁶

---

3. Franziska Tausig, *Shanghai Passage: Flucht und Exil einer Wienerin* (Vienna: Verlag für Gesellschaftskritik, 1987), 149–54.
4. "765 Jewish Refugees from Shanghai Return to Austria: Second Group to Arrive This Year," Jewish Telegraphic Agency, February, 14, 1947.
5. "Heimkehr aus dem fernen Ost," 14.
6. Percy Anders of the Friends Service Council to Kenneth Lee of the Friends Service Council, February 16, 1947, frame 0220, AR 45/54-146, Records of the New York Office of the American Jewish Joint Distribution Committee, 1945–1954, Archives of the American Jewish Joint Distribution Committee (JDC Archives), New York, NY.

These returning Jewish refugees were members of a larger group of German and Austrian Jews who had fled the Nazis to China when Shanghai emerged as an unlikely last resort. Neither visa nor medical exam had been required to travel there; one simply needed to pay the consul a fee of three dollars.[7] The Chinese consul general in Vienna, He Fengshan, issued visas to Austrian Jews seeking escape, as did many of his fellow consular officers across Europe.[8] After the November Pogrom (November 9–10, 1938), as many as two thousand German and Austrian Jews used such visas to obtain official release from Nazi concentration camps, exit visas from Greater Germany, and transit visas to third countries; indeed, most had gone to these third countries by the time war broke out in September 1939.[9] Many others, though, had managed to make their way to Shanghai to join a Jewish community that was at the time composed of some one thousand Sephardic Jewish families that had migrated there from Iraq in the nineteenth century, as well as a few thousand Ashkenazi Jews who had fled the Russian Revolution of 1917.[10]

The first Austrian Jews arrived in Shanghai in August 1938.[11] UNRRA documentation reveals that, of the 16,300 European Jews who finally found refuge there, 4,298 were Austrians.[12] Of those remaining at the end of

---

7. Debórah Dwork and Robert Jan van Pelt, *Flight from the Reich: Refugee Jews, 1933–1946* (New York: Norton, 2009), 137.

8. Historian Gao Bei persuasively challenges the long-held belief that He Fengshan issued such visas in defiance of Chinese foreign policy. She has shown rather that he and his colleagues explicitly followed the Chinese Foreign Ministry's instruction, and that policy included issuing visas to European Jews. See Gao Bei, *Shanghai Sanctuary: Chinese and Japanese Policy toward European Jewish Refugees during World War II* (New York: Oxford University Press, 2013), 50–55. Still, Yad Vashem, Israel's museum and memorial to the Holocaust, honored Ho Feng Shan with the title of Righteous Among the Nations for his humanitarian work assisting Viennese Jews by providing Chinese visas to enable their escape from Austria. For more information about Ho Feng Shan, see Yad Vashem, "Chinese Visas in Vienna: Feng-Shan Ho," Righteous Among the Nations, accessed May 15, 2015, http://www.yadvashem.org/yv/en/righteous/stories/ho.asp.

9. Dwork and van Pelt, *Flight from the Reich*, 411n44.

10. Avraham Altman and Irene Eber, "Flight to Shanghai, 1938–1940: The Larger Setting," *Yad Vashem Studies* 28 (2000): 11.

11. Elisabeth Buxbaum, *Transit Shanghai: Ein Leben im Exil* (Vienna: Edition Steinbauer, 2008), 15.

12. Dwork and van Pelt, *Flight from the Reich*, 318.

March 1946,[13] 1,400 had registered for repatriation.[14] The Joint office in Vienna, however, warned that the situation in the capital was untenable for Jews and cabled the New York main office (March 27) with the message, "Situation here totally negative," and requested an official order be given to Joint colleagues in Shanghai to do everything possible to discourage repatriation.[15] Further correspondence indicates disagreement between the Joint's New York City office and its branches in Paris and Vienna,[16] and finally Arthur Greenleigh (of the Paris office) wrote to Moses Leavitt in New York:

> I cannot stress too much the terrible destitution, poverty, struggle and anti-Semitism which now pervades Austria. In re[gard to] the continued residence of Jews in Austria, I should like to refer for your consideration a statement made by the representative of the Church before the Anglo-American Committee, which is as follows: "*Ich hasse nicht die Juden. Ich hasse das Judentum und das Judengeist.*" ["I do not hate the Jews. I hate Judaism and the Jewish spirit."] This statement of attitude from one of the chief representatives of the Church in Austria—Austria being a country in which the Church is one of the most dominant, if not the most dominant power—is of added significance in reflecting the atmosphere into which these people would be coming. I do not think it a function of the JDC to encourage people to return to Anti-Semitism.[17]

---

13. Report of the Committee of the Council for the Far East, May 28, 1946, cited in Buxbaum, *Transit Shanghai*, 180. The cited report stated that some 16,000 refugees were in China at the time and that 4,298 of them were Austrian Jews.

14. Moses A. Leavitt to Dr. Joseph Schwarz, AJDC Paris, March 28, 1946, frame 0240, AR 45/54-146, Records of the New York Office of the American Jewish Joint Distribution Committee, 1945–1954, JDC Archives.

15. Telegram from the Joint office in Vienna to the Joint main office in New York, March 27, 1946, frame 0241, AR 45/54-146, Records of the New York Office of the American Jewish Joint Distribution Committee, 1945–1954, JDC Archives.

16. Chain of correspondence following March 27, 1946, telegram from Joint office in Vienna to Joint main office in New York, frames 0232–0241, AR 45/54-146, Records of the New York Office of the American Jewish Joint Distribution Committee, 1945–1954, JDC Archives.

17. Arthur D. Greenleigh to Moses A Leavitt, May 22, 1946, AR194554/4/17/13/146, Records of the New York Office of the American Jewish Joint Distribution Committee, 1945–1954, JDC Archives.

Refugees in Shanghai realized that a Communist takeover was imminent and that Mao Zedong's troops would soon follow, and many decided to go home or to emigrate further.[18] The first group of a reported 34 Jewish repatriates from Shanghai arrived in Vienna on January 26, 1947, and found lodging with relatives or in housing provided by the Joint.[19] A couple of weeks later, on February 13, 1947, Franziska Tausig's train reached the city carrying some 760 more.[20]

Not everyone welcomed the Shanghai refugees' homecoming. A few days after Tausig and her fellow reémigrés arrived, the Jewish Community Council received an anonymous protest letter reiterating sentiments heard before with other waves of returnees. "Why must the Jews come back to Vienna to take our apartments?" the writer asked. "Far too few Jews were killed in the gas chambers, but we will complete the job."[21] Nonetheless, and despite the Joint's own official discouragement of repatriation, as of mid-February 1947, the Joint expected and was making plans to provide assistance to more returnees from Shanghai, Russia, and Palestine.[22]

In addition to the first two transports from Shanghai, another 1,300 men, women, and children still in China held Austrian visas.[23] Of the 796 Jewish repatriates from Shanghai in Vienna by May 25, 1947, 70 percent (560) were over the age of forty-five,[24] reflecting more mature survivors' desire to live in a familiar place and refusal to start over again in yet another foreign country. Many did not see a future anywhere else, especially those who sought to regain careers or employment. By 1950, 20 percent

---

18. Buxbaum, *Transit Shanghai*, 179.
19. "765 Jewish Refugees from Shanghai Return to Austria."
20. "Heimkehr aus dem fernen Ost," 14.
21. "Vienna Jewish Council Gets Letter Protesting Return of Repatriates from Shanghai," Jewish Telegraphic Agency, February 16, 1947.
22. JDC Archives, Records of the New York Office of the American Jewish Joint Distribution Committee, 1945–1954, AR 45/54 146, frame 0220, 16 Feb 1947 letter from Percy Anders of the Friends Service Council to Kenneth Lee of the Friends Service Council.
23. "First Group of Jewish Repatriates to Austria Arrives from Shanghai Refugee Colony," Jewish Telegraphic Agency, January 27, 1947.
24. List of repatriates from Shanghai in Vienna, May 25, 1947, 3.1.1.3/78805361/ITS Digital Archive, USHMM.

(about 850 of 4,298) of the Austrian Jews who had survived the war in Shanghai had returned.[25]

Austrian Jewish survivors from Shanghai did not arrive back in Vienna as early as other reémigrés who were motivated by personal reasons, but they too came seeking to regain their familial homes. Their movement and motivations serve as an illustration that, although distinct groups of returnees can be identified by their similar wartime experiences and in a rough chronology, such "waves" prove not so precisely divided. Motivations did not always fall into one tidy category of familial, political, and professional home, but rather intentions overlapped and timelines stretched. One family might have held more than one concept of "home," such as a couple of which the man sought to regain his professional home and his wife felt compelled to follow for reasons of familial home. And indeed, like the returnees from Shanghai, some exiles came back for reasons of family and did so a bit later in the postwar period.

Unlike so many others who took refuge in foreign countries, refugees who had survived the war in Shanghai had not found a sense of "home" there, nor a promise of one. Most elected not to stay, and many emigrated further to other countries. By the time Austrian Jews arrived in Vienna, they knew well that the Nazis had murdered many of their relatives and friends and had devastated their community. Nevertheless, they returned to the last place that they had been together with their families, their last home. And some, like Frau Tausig, did reunite with kin and found at least a part of the familial home that they sought. But even those who discovered that no one awaited them stayed and reclaimed at least the sentimental connection that contributed to their feeling of "home." Many simply failed to conceive of another place in which they might professionally or socially begin again due to challenges of age, language, or immigration restrictions.

---

25. Christoph Reinprecht, "Jewish Identity in Postwar Austria: Experiences and Dilemmas," in *Jewish Studies at the Central European University: Public Lectures, 1996–1999*, ed. András Kovács and Eszter Andor (Budapest: Central European University, 2000), 207.

Some 800 Shanghai reémigrés joined about 1,200 other Austrian Jews back in Vienna after living in exile abroad (around 700 from England, mostly *Kindertransport* survivors; 200 from Palestine; and 350 from Karaganda in the Soviet Union),[26] as well as the camp survivors who returned and those who had endured the war in the capital city. All had same ambition of rerooting in their hometown. After they had reconnected with surviving family members (if any), found a place to stay, and secured basic living necessities, and once they had cleared the immediate hurdles, the reestablishment of lives and livelihoods converged, and returnees' differing motivations and rationales mattered less. Their decisions made, for whatever reasons or combination thereof, they had arrived and formed a new, larger group of Austrian Jewish survivors in Vienna. They faced the same issues, despite the differing motivations or rationales that brought them there.

A poll conducted by the US occupation forces in 1947–48 revealed that 44 percent of Vienna's population agreed that "the Nazis exaggerated in their way of treating the Jews, but something had to happen in order to show them where they really belong."[27] This attitude shaped Austrian views on compensation and restitution, and throughout the unfolding post-Nazi years, heated debates surrounding these bitterly contested topics proved problematic and frustrating for Jews. Very few received prewar property and businesses that the Nazis and their supporters had stolen or otherwise obtained in dubious ways. And all of this took place in the context of a new and strengthening postwar Austrian national "first victim" identity and contributed to political action—and, often, inaction—that affected legislation and what semblance of denazification that took place. All bore down on returning Jews as they learned and relearned to navigate life in their hometown and as their Viennese Jewish identity both continued and was shaped anew in the postwar period.

---

26. Evelyn Adunka, *Die Vierte Gemeinde* (Berlin: Philo Verlag, 2000), 56.
27. Michael Schönberg, "Amerikanische Informations- und Medienpolitik in Österreich, 1945–50" (PhD diss., Vienna, 1975), cited in Reinprecht, "Jewish Identity in Postwar Austria," 205.

VICTIMS: MYTH AND REALITY

Immediately after the Red Army's conquest of Vienna, Austrian politicians rushed to assume roles in forming a new government and shaping a new postwar national identity. They did so with a determination to distance their country from Germany and what they claimed had been specifically *German* war crimes. As we have seen, they cunningly grabbed hold of and clung to the official language of the Allied powers' Moscow Declaration that served to solidify the myth of the country as the Nazis' "first victim," a guiding theme of both foreign and domestic Austrian policy that endured for decades. It was to this atmosphere that survivors returned. From the top levels of government to the people on the street, Austria and Austrians were victims.

"First Victim"

On April 27, 1945, Karl Renner, the leader of the provisional Austrian government under the Soviets, proclaimed the country's independence and autonomy. This statement nullified the Anschluss and included a list of Nazi Germany's violations of Austria, including a military occupation imposed on helpless and unwilling citizens, the degradation of Vienna to provincial city, and the plunder of the country's cultural and natural resources. This description of national pain and suffering did not, however, include the loss of some two hundred thousand Austrian Jews forcibly expelled or deported to their deaths. On November 25, 1945, the conservative Austrian People's Party won the first free national election, with the Socialist Party a close second. Under Chancellor Leopold Figl, the two parties established a coalition government that proved an enduring partnership for more than twenty years. The Nazis had persecuted Figl and most members of his cabinet—Figl himself suffered a total of more than five years in the Dachau and Mauthausen concentration camps—and with this the government presented itself with a strong "anti-fascist record,"[28] which emphasized the

---

28. Günter Bischof, "Allied Plans and Policies for the Occupation of Austria, 1938–1955," in *Austria in the Twentieth Century*, ed. Rolf Steininger, Günter Bischof, and Michael Gehler (New Brunswick, NJ: Transaction, 2002), 176.

desired anti-German "first victim" identity for an international audience. Leaders sought to highlight Austrian innocence to underscore Germany's sole responsibility for Nazi crimes and thus for reparations.

The "anti-fascist" characterization of government and leaders certainly did not mean freedom from antisemitism, nor did it permit perspective on or acknowledgment of the unique nature of the Nazi persecution of Jews. The Jewish community was disappointed that no Jews had gained official positions in the new government, despite the inclusion of three in Renner's provisional administration.[29] As previously mentioned, the electoral success of well-known antisemitic politicians like Leopold Kunschak and Julius Raab compounded Jews' distress and aroused fear that Austrian Jews still living abroad would choose not to repatriate.[30] In February 1947, Chancellor Figl assured Josef Silber of the Joint that there would be no "Jewish problem" under his government; Jews would be treated as Austrian nationals with all the rights and privileges of citizenship. Silber appeared to have been reassured by Figl's statement but also seemed to have read between the lines, as he went on to emphasize to his superiors that the Joint must maintain its operations in Vienna, even after Jewish displaced persons (DPs) emigrated onward, to help the remaining Austrian Jews rehabilitate.[31] Silber surely was aware that Figl was the same man who as chancellor in 1946 had publicly criticized exiles (so many of whom were Jews) for whom he thought "it certainly had been more comfortable ... to sit safely in their club-chairs than to suffer for Austria."[32] Just one month before Figl's statement, Karl Renner, who had assumed the role of federal president in the first government of the Second Republic, told a Jewish Telegraphic Agency (JTA)

---

29. "Austrian Provisional Government Includes Three Jews: Largest Number Ever Named to Cabinet," Jewish Telegraphic Agency, May 3, 1945.
30. "Anti-Semites Win Seats in Austrian National Council: Jewish Leaders Fearful," Jewish Telegraphic Agency, December 3, 1945.
31. J. S. Silber, Vienna, to AJDC, Paris—Mr. M. Beckelman, memo 913, February 27, 1947, frames 0855–0856, AR 45/54-143, Records of the New York Office of the American Jewish Joint Distribution Committee, 1945–1954, JDC Archives.
32. Martin Florian Herz, *Understanding Austria: The Political Reports and Analyses of Martin F. Herz, Political Officer of the U.S. Legation in Vienna, 1945–1948* (Salzburg: Reinhold Wagnleitner, 1984), 88.

reporter that as the Nazis had also stripped non-Jews of their possessions and had confined them to concentration camps, any special legislation for the restitution of confiscated property to Jews would be "un-democratic and [would] create new anti-Semitism."[33] The style and content of the language employed by both Figl and Renner represented the governmental attitude and indeed its policy and functioned to conceal antisemitism behind a rhetoric of democracy. It also reflected the political savvy of leaders who strove to satisfy their electorate; an appropriate and fair response to calls for reparations and restitution would have been economically crippling on a national and provincial level, as well as for those businesses and the individuals who had benefited from Nazi policies of "Aryanization" and forced and slave labor.

In addition, the reintegration of former Nazi Party members became a priority concern, and political parties came together in uncommon accord, all seeking the electoral support of former Nazis. The leading parties adopted a policy of silence about the past that both mirrored and strengthened the same in the lives of individuals, families, communities, and larger society.[34] This significant portion of the parties' constituency propelled what would evolve into a central theme in Austrian domestic postwar politics. Government leaders worked diligently on an international level to distance the country and its citizens from Nazi crimes, all the while working internally to restore former Nazis' professional and social statuses.

Allied policy and the practice of denazification during the occupation of Austria created the possibility to sidestep the actual and effective adjudication of former Nazis. The provisional government under the Allies was responsible for carrying out such processes but mainly exculpated former Nazis, who regained their professional positions and even collected compensation for material losses sustained *after* the war. That is, former Nazis

---

33. "Renner Says Special Restitution Laws for Jews Would Be 'Undemocratic,'" Jewish Telegraphic Agency, January 31, 1947. In the same statement, Renner went on to claim that no one could accuse him of being antisemitic because his son-in-law was Jewish.

34. Peter Pulzer, "Between Collectivism and Liberalism: The Political Evolution of Austria since 1945," in *Austria 1945–95: Fifty Years of the Second Republic*, ed. Kurt Richard Luther and Peter Pulzer (Aldershot, UK: Ashgate, 1998), 229.

received compensation from the Austrian government for sanctions and penalties placed on them by the Allies. Newly restructured political parties assumed the position that few Austrians had been truly committed and resolute Nazi Party members, and Renner himself provided the explanation that most had only given in to financial and social pressures.[35]

Other politicians gave confusing and conflicting messages about their impressions of Viennese society and the situation for returning Jews. Vienna's Socialist mayor Theodor Körner, who greeted Franziska Tausig and 760 other Jews returning to Vienna in February 1947, wrote in a 1947 *Wiener Zeitung* article that press reports of antisemitism in Vienna consisted of deliberate lies: "The Viennese [person] is a cosmopolitan and thus from the start not anti-Semitic. Anti-Jewish tendencies are now still alien to them."[36] Not long after, however, Socialist interior minister Oskar Helmer warned of the danger of "Jewish dissemination."[37] Austrian leaders also opposed benefits and budget lines for the Jewish community. As previously mentioned, agriculture minister Josef Kraus argued against a proposed advance of funds to the IKG from a pool of heirless Jewish assets stolen by the Nazis, as he thought it gave one group preferential treatment. Helmer concurred; it could only add to "a perpetuation of distinctions," he said, with which they wanted nothing to do.[38]

The presence of Jewish DPs from other parts of Europe and a national responsibility for their welfare added to politicians' irritation. They might reluctantly recognize Austrian Jews as citizens and promise to uphold their associated rights, but the some one hundred thousand eastern European

---

35. Heidemarie Uhl, "From Victim Myth to Co-responsibility Thesis: Nazi Rule, World War II, and the Holocaust in Austrian Memory," in *The Politics of Memory in Postwar Europe*, ed. Richard Ned Lebow, Wulf Kansteiner, and Claudio Fogu (Durham, NC: Duke University Press, 2006), 71.

36. Reinprecht, "Jewish Identity in Postwar Austria," 206.

37. Robert Knight, *"Ich bin dafür, die Sache in die Länge zu ziehen": Wortprotokolle der österreichischen Bundesregierung von 1945–52 über die Entschädigung der Juden* (Frankfurt am Main: Athenäum Verlag, 1988), 197.

38. Robert Knight, "'Neutrality,' Not Sympathy: Jews in Post-war Austria," in *Austrians and Jews in the Twentieth Century: From Franz Joseph to Waldheim*, ed. Robert S. Wistrich (New York: St. Martin's, 1992), 222.

Jews migrating through or temporarily residing in the country posed another problem to a government set on distancing itself from responsibility for Nazi crimes. More socially acceptable and enduring prejudices against Jews from the east allowed Socialist president Karl Renner to remark, "I do not think that Austria in its current state should allow the establishment of a new Jewish community from Eastern Europe while our own people need jobs."[39] It may have been possible to find a way to see Austrian Jews' place in the newly forming Second Republic, even if only to appease the Allies, but eastern European Jews were another story. Plus, from their point of view as Austrian politicians, *they* were victims of the Germans.

Renner and his provisional government worked assiduously to frame the Germans as the sole responsible perpetrators of Nazi crimes during World War II and the Holocaust in order to shirk responsibility for compensation and reparations payments. Austrian leaders took advantage of Cold War tensions to pit the Western powers against the Soviets for financial benefit and to secure acceptance by all four Allied occupiers of the narrative of the country as the Nazis' first victim. They characterized the end of the Nazi regime in Austria as "liberation" by the Soviet Army and Austrian resistance fighters.[40] The logic of evolving postwar national identity involved the acceptance that the Anschluss had been a forced military invasion and occupation, after which there was no "Austria" but rather the Ostmark, a province of Nazi Germany. Residents had had no choice about joining Greater Germany, and thus they and their reconstructed postwar nation bore no burden and responsibility for Nazi crimes or for restitution claims.[41] Further, they asserted, the German military occupiers had forced the country and its citizens into war that "no Austrian ever wanted."[42] Therefore, they were all victims, from returning soldier to bystander to "minor" Nazi Party members.

---

39. Knight, "Ich bin dafür," 61.
40. Uhl, "From Victim Myth to Co-responsibility Thesis," 66.
41. Knight, "Ich bin dafür," 105.
42. Bundesministerium für Unterricht, *Freiheit für Österreich: Dokumente* (Vienna: Österreichischer Bundesverlag, 1955), 11–14.

Excluding Jews

Cloaked in a bombast of democracy and democratic values, the postwar government officially refused to differentiate between any subgroup of victims. In doing so, the cultural and political atmosphere steeped in antisemitism fostered the alienation of the most vulnerable and oppressed victims—Jews. The Renner government appointed *Fürsorgekommissionen* (welfare commissions) in May 1945 and tasked them with providing relief for Austrian war victims and concentration camp survivors who had returned.[43] The passage of the Opferfürsorgegesetz (Victims' Welfare Act) followed on July 17, 1945, and provided victims' pensions, assistance finding housing and work (through issued *Opferausweise*, victim identification papers),[44] food, and clothing to "victims of fascism." It also clearly defined "victims" as concentration camp survivors who had been persecuted on political grounds and resistance fighters; excluded were those who had been oppressed on the basis of race, religion, and nationality. The KZ-Verband (concentration camp survivor association), established in 1945, also initially omitted Jews from its membership, as well as Roma and Sinti and homosexuals. It also did not admit those who had been punished for helping slave laborers,[45] which reveals more about the Austrian understanding of "resistance" that developed in the context of the postwar victim mentality. These people had not defended their victim homeland with "gun in hand," as those who were deemed active resisters had done. Rather, they had tried to help individual victims persecuted within Austrian borders (by Austrians!) and had been caught and were penalized with a similar persecution. Such resistance did not count. The group finally took on a representative from the Viennese Jewish community in 1946 and began

---

43. "Zeittafel," in *Wieder gut machen? Enteignung, Zwangsarbeit, Entschädigung, Restitution: Österreich 1938–1945/1945–1999*, ed. Gertraud Diendorfer (Innsbruck: Sonderband der Informationen zur Politischen Bildung, 1999), 178–79.

44. "Rückerstattung und Entschädigung: Leistungen Österreichs nach 1945," Austrian Reconciliation Fund, accessed March 4, 2015, http://www.reconciliationfund.at.

45. Helga Embacher, *Neubeginn ohne Illusionen: Juden in Österreich nach 1945* (Vienna: Picus Verlag, 1995), 196–98.

to provide *Opferausweise* to Jews, thus making victims' benefits available to them.[46]

A new version of the Victims' Welfare Law in 1947 defined two groups of victims. The first consisted of Austrian resistance fighters who, because they had taken "gun in hand," held official certification of victim status as having been active resisters between March 6, 1933, and May 9, 1945.[47] All were entitled to immediate financial support and later to a pension as victims of either the Nazis or the preceding Austrofascist regime. This pension was later reduced to the level of *Kriegsopferrenten* (war victim's pension). Those who were entitled also received health-care coverage, and surviving family members had the right to claim benefits in the name of dead resistance fighters. The second group of victims defined by the law comprised those who were persecuted on grounds of race, religion, or nationality in the same time period.[48] They became eligible for victim identification papers but had no claim to a pension. Both groups were to receive help in the form of money to rebuild their lives and a modest annual tax credit.[49] Victims of either category also had to hold Austrian citizenship.

Victims' welfare legislation was strategically worded and included loopholes and complicated language that excluded Jews and some other particularly defenseless victim groups. Roma and Sinti victims of the Nazis received no compensation until a 1988 amendment to the law included them,[50] and only in 2005 did a further adjustment finally include homosexual and so-called asocial victims, as well as those who had been sterilized

---

46. Brigitte, Bailer, Florian Freund, Elisabeth Klamper, Wolfgang Neugebauer, Gerhard Ungar, and Brigitte Ungar-Klein, *Erzählte Geschichte: Berichte von Widerstandskämpfern und Verfolgten*, vol. 3, *Jüdische Schicksale* (Vienna: Österreichischer Bundesverlag, 1992), 672.

47. Bundesgesetz vom 4. Juli 1947 über die Fürsorge für die Opfer des Kampfes um ein freies, demokratisches Österreich und die Opfer politischer Verfolgung (Opferfürsorgegesetz), BGBl. Nr. 183/1947, *Bundesgesetzblatt für die Republik Österreich*, September 1, 1947, 821. The law specifies that this group "actively took weapons in hand" for the fight to free Austria.

48. Ibid., 821.

49. Bailer et al., *Erzählte Geschichte*, 672.

50. Erika Thurner, "Nazi and Postwar Policy against Roma and Sinti in Austria," in *The Roma—a Minority in Europe*, ed. Roni Stauber and Raphael Vago (Budapest: Central European University Press, 2007), 55–67.

and the subjects of other medical experiments.[51] The practical reality of these policies meant that, between veterans' benefits paid to former Wehrmacht soldiers and the recognition of political "resistance fighters," everyone in Austria was receiving governmental support *except* some of the most powerless yet most victimized groups under the Nazis.

Jews received no significant monetary support or tax relief until 1949. To obtain that, they had to be Austrian citizens at the time of application; but the Nazi regime had stripped Jews of their nationality, and the postwar government had not automatically restored it. In fact, the government required that one be a permanent resident of the country to apply to regain citizenship, and therefore one had to reside in Austria to claim assistance as a victim. This clearly excluded the majority of Austrian Jews—more than one hundred thousand—who had fled the Nazis to other countries, stayed abroad, and never planned to return. It also excluded camp survivors who chose not to go back after the war to make a home in Austria. The Austrian government finally granted Austrian Jews who retained their adopted citizenship the possibility to apply for compensation under the Opferfürsorgegesetz in 1953, but only after Allied intervention and that of the United States and Great Britain in particular.[52] The minuscule number of Jews who did receive the status of "freedom fighters" got that designation only because they were validated as Austrians persecuted for political reasons, such as the later chancellor (1970–83) Bruno Kreisky.

Austrian Jews could be victims as *Austrians* but not as Jews. Government leaders were specific that any relief they received was not a form of compensation.[53] To add insult to betrayal, the government assumed the responsibility to compensate former Nazi Party members for losses they incurred through the Allies' anti-Nazi sanctions. By the government's logic, Austrians

---

51. Nicole L. Immler, "Restitution and Dynamics of Memory: A Neglected Trans-generational Perspective," in *Mediation, Remediation, and the Dynamics of Cultural Memory*, ed. Astrid Erll and Ann Rigney (Berlin: Walter de Gruyter, 2009), 207.

52. Brigitte Bailer, "They Were All Victims: The Selective Treatment of the Consequences of National Socialism," in *Austrian Historical Memory and National Identity*, ed. Gunter Bischof and Anton Pelinka (New Brunswick, NJ: Transaction, 1997), 108.

53. Bailer et al., *Erzählte Geschichte*, 673.

had been victimized by both a German prewar and wartime occupation *and* a postwar Allied one. Appealing to this much-larger group of "victims" proved politically advantageous as political parties reestablished themselves. Gaining votes from the tiny remaining Jewish community would have advanced political goals and agendas very little or not at all.

In addition to not providing aid to returning and remaining Austrian Jews, politicians also castigated them for having abandoned their country during crisis. This sentiment started from the top levels of government and society and seeped into the mentality of individual gentiles. Political leaders accused exiles of having enjoyed comfort and safety abroad while Austrian soldiers were forced to fight and die in the Wehrmacht, and others echoed a sentiment of additional blame placed on world Jewry for not coming to Austria's rescue at the time of the Anschluss.[54]

Under Allied Occupation

The Austrian government's pursuit of a postwar national identity continued in the context of the country's physical reconstruction and its challenges. A "double speak," as historian Heidemarie Uhl dubbed this discourse, endured as leaders portrayed their nation as a victim of the Nazis to an international audience, while at home they celebrated heroic Wehrmacht soldiers who sacrificed for their "fatherland."[55] All this played out under the quadripartite Allied occupation. As the 1940s came to an end, a new Austrian national identity solidified, including the crucial components of the country's neutrality and its status as the first victim of the Nazis. As tensions escalated among the Allies (especially between the United States and the Soviet Union), no one cared about pursuing Austrian responsibility as a perpetrator country. Any façade of denazification dropped, and Western Allies' leaders were satisfied so long as little Austria remained in the "West."

---

54. Knight, "Neutrality," 226.
55. Heidemarie Uhl, "Das österreichische Gedächtnis," in: *Die Lebendigkeit der Geschichte— (Dis)Kontinuitäten in Diskursen über den Nationalsozialismus*, ed. Eleonore Lappin and Bernhard Schneider (St. Ingbert: Röhrig, 2001), 38.

The original occupation agreement for Austria called for "total control," but on June 28, 1946, the Allies relaxed that condition with a second agreement that loosened the Allied Council's direct oversight of the Austrian government. Only a unanimous negative veto from all four powers could stop legislation, and this rarely occurred. With Cold War tensions on the rise, the Soviets frequently opposed lawmaking and decrees that the Western powers had approved. By the spring of 1946, the Soviets had taken advantage of their zone of occupation and, through the auspices of the USIA (Administration for Soviet Property in Austria) holding company, seized "German assets," broadly defined. As permitted by the Western Allies, the Soviet Union pursued reparations owed to them through profits gained in plundering property and exploiting the geographic areas of their control. It has been estimated that Austria paid more than $1 billion through such reparations claimed by the USIA.[56] Both the Western Allies' tolerance of this form of compensation and the Soviets' assumption of it reveal a tacit lack of acceptance of the victim myth, or at least a less codified mode of forcing Austria to assume some responsibility for its role in World War II. A second, lesser-known passage of the Moscow Declaration had stated that Austria had responsibility for having allied itself with Nazi Germany and that this would be considered, as well as Austria's contribution "to her liberation," in a final postwar settlement. Leaders effectively buried this piece, and by the time of the 1955 Staatsvertrag (Austrian State Treaty), the preamble of which was largely based on the Moscow Declaration, Figl convinced the Allies to drop it from the text altogether.[57]

All Viennese, gentiles and Jews, found ways to conceal or not reveal intentions, plans, and even their pasts in order to live more easily and uneventfully under Allied occupation and among neighbors, colleagues, and even friends who had conflicting or oppositional wartime experiences. As Jewish returnees reestablished themselves, however, components of this concealment posed a particular set of obstacles in both the social and professional

---

56. Bischof, "Allied Plans and Policies for the Occupation of Austria," 177.
57. David Art, *The Politics of the Nazi Past in Germany and Austria* (New York: Cambridge University Press, 2006), 105.

realms. US military authorities in particular tried to help the struggling Jewish community, as we shall see, but as Cold War tensions mounted toward the end of the 1940s, they paid less attention to reparations and the restitution of property. Individuals turned for assistance to the IKG and to foreign Jewish organizations to help with the difficulties, hurdles, and outright obstacles in these processes.

RESTITUTION OF "ARYANIZED" PROPERTY

Issues surrounding the restitution—or not—of property stolen, both outright and that "Aryanized" under Nazi policy, endures to this day as an ongoing legacy of the persecution of Jews in Austria. Only a rare few claims on such property were recognized, and many returnees gave up without filing one. According to Christoph Reinprecht's sociological survey of Austrian Jews who returned to Austria, 60 percent of his interviewees never even tried to go back to former apartments that theoretically they could have claimed as lost property. Of those who could prove their legal claim to capital or land, just two-thirds received restitution compensation, and even then, it amounted to a small proportion of the property's original value.[58]

For survivors returning to Vienna in 1945, securing shelter was a priority, and thus the recovery of homes stood as an immediate concern. The first to try to reclaim their families' residences were those who had endured the Nazis and the war in the city (see chapter 2) and concentration camp survivors who arrived back in the first months after their liberation (see chapter 3). Some found it startlingly easy to secure new apartments among those standing empty after Nazi residents had abandoned them as they fled the approaching Soviet Army. The Red Army and the Austrian provisional government also assigned to returnees the dwellings vacated by Nazis. Others found their original apartments empty or took over abandoned dwellings in the same or nearby apartment houses, circumstances that occurred more often in the chaos and confusion of immediate postwar Vienna and before

---

58. Reinprecht, "Jewish Identity in Postwar Austria," 208.

laws about reparations and restitution went into effect. On May 8, 1945, for example, Elisabeth Welt Trahan and her father found their family's apartment occupied,[59] but they were able simply to move into another one a floor below. As mentioned in chapter 2, there Elisabeth found evidence of the previous tenants' political leanings, including a copy of *Mein Kampf*.[60] Once the government established a *Wohnungsamt* (housing office) to serve all people without shelter, homeless Jews became dependent on municipal bureaucrats for housing and encountered the official and unofficial discrimination inherent in postwar Vienna. Many concentration camp survivors reported that they met an attitude of incredulity from civil servants who claimed not to believe their stories of the camps and the details of their persecution. If it all had really been so bad, they reasoned—and let the survivors know—they would not have been able to survive to return at all.[61]

The month of May 1945 saw the establishment of the Bundesministeriums für Vermögenssicherung und Wirtschaftsplanung (Federal Ministry of Property Protection and Economic Planning).[62] And on May 10, 1945, just two days after the war's official end, the fifth Kabinettsratssitzung: "Arisiertes" Vermögen (Cabinet Council Meeting on "Aryanized" Assets) took place.[63] From this meeting came the 1945 Anmeldegesetz (Registration Act), which mandated a June 1945 deadline for property holders to register assets acquired through "Aryanization" or otherwise taken by the Nazi regime after the Anschluss.[64] This was to include both owners who had

---

59. In 1946, Elisabeth Welt and her father were registered as living at Strudlhofgasse 12/14 in Vienna's ninth district. See Liste der in Wien lebenden Glaubensjuden, 1946, 3.1.1.3/78805460/ ITS Digital Archive, USHMM.

60. Elizabeth Welt Trahan, *Walking with Ghosts: A Jewish Childhood in Wartime Vienna* (New York: Peter Lang, 1998), 214.

61. Helga Embacher, "Unwelcome in Austria: Returnees and Concentration Camp Survivors," in *When the War Was Over: Women, War and Peace in Europe, 1940–1956*, ed. Claire Duchen and Irene Bandhauer-Schöffmann (London: Leicester University Press, 2000), 197.

62. "Zeittafel," 178–79.

63. Knight, *"Ich bin dafür,"* 82.

64. 10. Gesetz über die Erfassung arisierter und anderer im Zusammenhange mit der nationalsozialistische Machtübernahme entzogenen Vermögenschaften vom 10 Mai 1945, BGBl. Nr. 10/1945, *Bundesgesetzblatt für die Republik Österreich*, May 28, 1945, 3. Stück, 16.

been the direct expropriators under "Aryanization" laws and subsequent owners of such property. Registration was incomplete, and the language of the decree had included nothing specific about the *return* of property. To top it off, as mentioned previously, this cabinet meeting concentrated on the return of SPÖ property and that of associated groups that had lost assets under the Austrofascist dictatorship in the mid-1930s. And it was during this gathering that Renner made his shameful and insensitive—to say the least—statement on the impossibility of compensating every "small Jewish merchant or peddler for his loss."[65] Renner knew that this statement represented the SPÖ's broad base, estimated to have been 47 percent of the Austrian population at the time, and included many "owners" of Jews' former property who had no interest in giving it back. Jews constituted less than one-tenth of 1 percent of the postwar population and made little impact on the views and actions of the leadership.

On VE Day, May 8, 1945, the provisional government had passed a Verbotsgesetz, a constitutional law banning the Nazi Party and its affiliate army and organizations and making recidivism illegal. With this legislation, all Nazi-held property officially changed to Austrian ownership.[66] A little over one month later, on June 26, 1945, the Kriegsverbrechergesetz, a constitutional law on war crimes and other National Socialist misdeeds, outlined that the punishment for conviction for crimes against humanity, war crimes, and international law would be the confiscation of all assets.[67] However, neither piece of legislation meant much until the Western occupation powers recognized the provisional government at the end of October 1945, and the Allied Council did not begin to approve the laws until early November of that year.

By August 1945, the Austrian provisional government took responsibility for the assignment of property, and with that shift, tensions and difficulties increased. The central office created to deal with housing concerns overturned initial decisions that had been made under Soviet supervision

---

65. Knight, "Ich bin dafür," 83.
66. Klaus Eisterer, "Austria under Allied Occupation," in Steininger, Bischof, and Gehler, *Austria in the Twentieth Century*, 207.
67. Ibid.

and declared them "not yet legal," thereby benefiting "Aryanizers" holding Jews' possessions. Some sixty thousand apartments in Vienna had been "Aryanized," and those who were in custody of Jews' former homes and businesses feared losing them to the rightful owners.[68] In addition, the Soviets had named former Jewish owners as "temporary administrators" of their old businesses, but the Renner government reinstated "Aryanizers" into management positions. Jewish businesspeople lost or rightfully feared losing their enterprises once again.[69] In fact, IKG president David Brill asserted that the government specifically prevented former Jewish owners from remaining or serving in such positions, claiming that "public administrators" had been installed to protect "Aryanizers." In a September 7, 1947, interview with a JTA reporter, Brill related the story of a cardboard-factory owner who returned from exile in Shanghai. The "Austrian collaborationist" in possession of the facility refused him entry to his own plant and retained the enterprise worth some $100,000. And among the Jewish administrators appointed by the Soviets to head businesses formerly owned by Jews was Franz Fuerth, who in the postwar ran a carpet factory. The new Austrian government dismissed him and replaced him with a man who had been imprisoned for three months as a Nazi war criminal. These abuses were only a few among many, Brill maintained.[70]

The chaos of postwar housing assignments coupled with anti-Jewish discrimination combined for bizarre outcomes. Frieda Fraenkel and her husband arrived in Vienna in 1950 after years of exile and internment in Italy and attempted to regain their old apartment. They were unsuccessful in that effort, but the former Nazi living in their home was forced to give them back their furniture.[71] On the other hand, Gertrude Putschin's family had

---

68. Embacher, "Unwelcome in Austria," 198.
69. "Vienna Jews Appeal to U.S. Authorities for Aid in Obtaining Their Confiscated Property," Jewish Telegraphic Agency, November 5, 1945; "Confusion in Austria Makes It Difficult for Jews to Regain Their Former Dwellings," Jewish Telegraphic Agency, August 30, 1945.
70. "President of Vienna Jewish Community Charges Govt. Sabotaging Restitution Law," Jewish Telegraphic Agency, September 8, 1947.
71. Frieda Fraenkel interview, 412, Dokumentationsarchiv des österreichischen Widerstandes (DÖW), Vienna, Austria. Frau Fraenkel had not wanted to return to Vienna after the war and would have preferred to remain in Italy. Her only complaint about the Italians was their lack of

to return furniture and home goods that they had received "on loan," as the Nazi who had abandoned them came back and took advantage of his legal right to demand them.[72] In cases where officials assigned dispossessed Jews to vacant apartments in which Nazis had lived—many of them "Aryanized" or otherwise stolen from Jewish families—they required that the Jews agree to relinquish the property to the "rightful" owners if they returned. And as we have seen with Kurt Fräser, the protection and advantage of having served in an Allied military only helped while one still wore the uniform. Fräser's hopes of regaining his family home were dashed with his discharge (see chapter 5). Antisemitic discrimination encountered during the housing-application process prompted a 1946 agreement between the IKG and the city of Vienna to work together to provide IKG members with dwellings that had been abandoned by Nazis who had left or fled the city.[73] Overall, however, the Austrian courts restored many homes to Nazis. In 1946, some 8,400 victims occupied Nazis' former dwellings; in 1950, only 730 still lived in them.[74]

Although the Allies' policy proved permissive and lax with regard to denazification, they did try to assist Jews with regaining their property. Soon after occupying the city, the Allies began to enforce the return of IKG medical facilities, for example. At war's end, the Ältestenrat controlled and ran one Jewish hospital in Vienna; by October 1945, it operated five homes for concentration camp survivors who required housing, medical services, and food.[75] In November of the same year, leaders of

---

punctuality. Her husband had insisted they go back to their hometown for his professional reasons and, in making his case, appealed to her intolerance of Italians' lateness. He told her, "Wir können mit den Italienern nicht Schritt halten, die sind so unpünktlich, sind wunderbar, aber geschäftlich kann ich nicht mit ihnen arbeiten" (We can't work with the Italian pace. They are so unpunctual. They are wonderful [people], but I can't work with them professionally.).

72. Bailer et al., *Erzählte Geschichte*, 687–88.

73. *Bericht des Präsidiums der Israelitischen Kultusgemeinde Wien über die Tätigkeit in den Jahren 1945 bis 1948* (Vienna: Israelitische Kultusgemeinde Wien, 1948), 25.

74. Bailer et al., *Erzählte Geschichte*, 269 n26.

75. Memo from Major Judah Nadich, US Army, to Commanding General, USFA, APO 777, US Army, October 23, 1945, Folder 104 through 105, Box 16, DP Section, Int. Affairs/DP Div., RG 260, General Records 1945–50, United States National Archives and Records Administration (NARA), College Park, MD.

the IKG officially requested assistance from the US Army to secure the restitution of Jews' former property, as well as some one hundred IKG-owned buildings. The formal request to General Mark Clark, the US representative of the Allied control commission for Austria, highlighted the inaction of the provisional government toward the compensation of Jews and described the antisemitic discrimination that public officials directed at returning camp survivors. Further, the Austrian government still held ownership of more than one hundred of the Jewish community's former real estate assets.[76]

After the first postwar Austrian government took office, a series of laws began to go into effect dealing with restitution issues, but those instituted in 1946 proved to be of little or no significant help to Jews' claims. The May 15, 1946, Bundesgesetz über die Nichtigerklärung von Rechtsgeschäften und sonstigen Rechtshandlungen, die während der deutschen Besetzung Österreichs erfolgt sind (federal law invalidating legal transactions and other legal actions that took place during the German occupation of Austria) had nullified legal acts and transactions, including contracts, that concerned the seizure of property under Nazi authorities but was never properly enforced.[77] Had the government applied this law properly and by its terms, there would have been no need for subsequent decades of restitution and compensation negotiations and amendments and addenda.

Between July 1946 and July 1949, the Austrian government passed seven pieces of legislation regarding the restitution of property stolen by the Nazis or under Nazi law (see table 6.1). The laws required the state and individuals to restore properties, companies, patents, brands, design copyrights, and employment contracts to the original owners or holders.[78] However, carefully and loosely worded terms offered loopholes and interpretations that permitted further injustices. In early January 1947, the Jewish Telegraphic Agency reported that Jews in Vienna had enjoyed little success in regaining

---

76. "Vienna Jews Appeal to U.S. Authorities," Jewish Telegraphic Agency, November 5, 1945.
77. Knight, "Ich bin dafür," 264.
78. Jewish Community Vienna Department of Restitution Affairs, "Measures Taken between 1945–1995," accessed August 17, 2020, http://www.restitution.or.at/historischer-hintergrund/hh-zwischen_e.html.

TABLE 6.1. AUSTRIAN RESTITUTION LEGISLATION

Legislation	Description
First Restitution Act, July 26, 1946[a]	Concerned with the restitution of property directly expropriated by the Nazis (not by private citizens or companies) and held and administered by the Republic of Austria or one of its federal states as successor and beneficiary of the Nazi regime.
Second Restitution Act, February 6, 1947[b]	Supplemented the first law to deal with property in the hands of the Austrian government because of owners' postwar forfeiture due to war crimes convictions or proven involvement with a National Socialist organization.
Third Restitution Act, February 6, 1947[c]	Dealt with property wrongfully taken and transferred to private individuals or businesses. This act outlined dealings regarding Jews' and other victims' property claims for assets taken for racial, national, or political reasons.
Fourth Restitution Act, May 21, 1947[d]	Pertaining to businesses and entities transformed or dissolved under Nazi law. This applied to companies' names, property, commercial patents, and private employment contracts.
Fifth Restitution Act, June 22, 1949[e]	Dealt with the restitution of shareholders' rights and interests, the status of partners in business, and members of trade organizations and other business entities that were confiscated and that subsequently ceased to exist under Nazi law.
Sixth Restitution Act, June 30, 1949[f]	Concerned with the restitution of confiscated trademarks, patents, and pattern rights.
Seventh Restitution Act, July 14, 1949[g]	Addressed outstanding claims on employment contracts in the private sector, including wages, severance payments, and pensions.

[a] Bundesgesetz vom 26. Juli 1946 über die Rückstellung entzogener Vermögen, die sich in Verwaltung des Bundes oder der Bundesländer befinden (Erstes Rückstellungsgesetz), RIS—*Bundesgesetzblatt von 1945–2003*, 156/1946.

[b] Bundesgesetz vom 6. Februar 1947 über die Rückstellung entzogener Vermögen, die sich im Eigentum der Republik Österreich befinden (Zweites Rückstellungsgesetz), RIS—*Bundesgesetzblatt von 1945–2003*, 53/1947.

[c] Bundesgesetz vom 6. Februar 1947 über die Nichtigkeit von Vermögensentziehungen (Drittes Rückstellungsgesetz), RIS—*Bundesgesetzblatt von 1945–2003*, 54/1947.

[d] Bundesgestz vom 21. Mai 1947, betreffend die unter nationalsozialistischem Zwang geänderten oder gelöschten Firmennamen (Viertes Rückstellungsgesetz), RIS—*Bundesgesetzblatt von 1945–2003*, 143/1947.

[e] Bundesgesetz vom 22. Juni 1949 über die Rückstellung entzogenen Vermögens juristischer Personen des Wirtschaftslebens, die ihre Rechtspersönlichkeit unter nationalsozialistischem Zwang verloren haben (Fünftes Rückstellungsgesetz), RIS—*Bundesgesetzblatt von 1945–2003*, 164/1949.

[f] Bundesgesetz vom 30. Juni 1949 über die Rückstellung gewerblicher Schutzrechte (Sechstes Rückstellungsgesetz), RIS—*Bundesgesetzblatt von 1945–2003*, 199/149.

[g] Bundesgesetz vom 14. Juli 1949 über die Geltendmachung entzogener oder nicht erfüllter Ansprüche aus Dienstverhältnissen in der Privatwirtschaft (Siebentes Rückstellungsgesetz), RIS—*Bundesgesetzblatt von 1945–2003*, 207/1949.

their homes and that six hundred either lived in institutions or were homeless. In addition, the same article stated that the Viennese Jewish community and international Jewish organizations working in the city also worried about the imminent arrival of an expected fifteen hundred repatriates from Shanghai: "no one has any idea where they are to be lodged."[79] Two months later, a Joint report described property restitution as dire and related that more than twenty-five hundred dwellings of Austrian Jews and several hundred IKG-owned buildings had yet to be returned.[80]

Despite the prospects created by such legislation aimed at remedying the ownership of illegally attained property and assets, subsequent legal interpretations and rulings favored former Nazis and "Aryanizers." In September 1947, IKG president David Brill characterized the first four laws as "a public scandal." Brill accused the Ministry of Property and Custody of sabotaging the restitution of Jewish property. At that time, an estimated eight thousand Austrian Jews lived in Vienna, and IKG leaders portrayed the unfair and ineffective restitution laws as a main cause for many of them seeking to emigrate abroad. In addition, by that date, the Jewish community reportedly controlled only ten units of its 216 prewar properties. All were hospitals, nursing homes, or administration buildings, and six of the ten had been in Jewish hands throughout the war and were thus easily retained. Only four had been returned to the community after the Nazi defeat.[81]

This all played out under the quadripartite Allied occupation and in the context of increasing Cold War tensions. As the 1940s closed, the development of an Austrian national identity as a neutral country and the first victim of the Nazis continued. And as friction between the Western Allies (and in particular the United States) and the Soviet Union escalated, attention to Austria as a perpetrator country faded. The Western Allies' leaders

---

79. "Renner Says Special Restitution Laws for Jews Would Be 'Undemocratic,'" Jewish Telegraphic Agency, January 31, 1947.

80. "European Research, Blanche Bernstein," confidential JDC report, March 24, 1947, frame 0844, AR 45/54-143, Records of the New York Office of the American Jewish Joint Distribution Committee, 1945–1954, JDC Archives.

81. "President of Vienna Jewish Community Charges Govt. Sabotaging Restitution Law," Jewish Telegraphic Agency, September 8, 1947.

were satisfied as long as Austria remained neutral and not under Soviet domination, and any energy for denazification and restitution waned.

POSTWAR IDENTITIES AND RESTITUTION PROBLEMS

With the Austrian government's official endorsement and promotion from the end of the war through the late 1940s, the victim myth took a foundational role in the postwar development of Austrian national identity. At the same time, however, political leaders successfully reintegrated former Nazis into society and, most importantly, into their supportive electorate. About 90 percent of former Nazi Party members in Austria were amnestied in 1946; they were reinstated to their jobs and paid compensation for material and financial losses they had suffered even after 1945.[82] "Less incriminated" former party members regained voting rights in time for the 1949 elections, and the competition for their support occasioned a new political strategy of distancing resistance fighters and victims of fascism in domestic politics.[83] West Germany stands in contrast to Austria on the issue of restitution. Although leaders of both countries avoided bringing justice to the majority of former Nazis and war criminals and while the reintegration of Nazis into postwar society served as a common goal in both former perpetrator nations, West Germany did negotiate for and pay substantial restitution to the (mostly Jewish) victims and to the State of Israel.[84]

A continued spotlight on the small percentage of Austrians who had been in opposition to the Nazis could have served to alienate the more significant part of the body of citizens who willingly took part at all levels

---

82. Heidemarie Uhl, "The Politics of Memory: Austria's Perception of the Second World War and the National Socialist Period," in *Austrian Historical Memory and National Identity*, Contemporary Austrian Studies 5, ed. Günter Bischof and Anton Pelinka (New Brunswick, NJ: Transaction, 1997), 71–72. Such pardons led to the creation of the Federation of Independents (*Verband der Unabhängigen*, or VdU), the predecessor party to Austria's current-day Freedom Party (*Freiheitliche Partei Österreich*, or FPÖ).

83. Uhl, "From Victim Myth to Co-responsibility Thesis," 50.

84. See Jeffrey Herf, *Divided Memory: The Nazi Past in the Two Germanys* (Cambridge, MA: Harvard University Press, 1997), 267–333.

of the Nazi regime and who retained Nazi political leanings. In order for politicians to benefit from goodwill abroad and to earn support at home, continued "double speak" prevailed.[85] While leaders courted former Nazis' votes, they presented their nation internationally as the Nazis' first victim and as distinctly non-German, and they continued to use the evidence of the Austrian resistance movement as proof of antifascism.

By the early 1950s, citizens pressed for war memorials to honor Austrians killed while "doing their duty" as Wehrmacht soldiers serving the "fatherland." Veterans' organizations gained strength and established such memorials with the full support of Austrian politicians who emphasized the rehabilitation of soldiers. They were no longer "double victims"—that is, citizens forced to live under an unwanted military occupation *and* soldiers pressed unwillingly into service. On the domestic level, talk of Austrian resistance minimized as Nazi crimes became marginalized, and politicians paid public tribute to former Wehrmacht soldiers, praising them as heroes who had sacrificed for their country.[86]

Even before the end of the 1940s, however, former Nazis and "Aryanizers" had begun to loom large in the minds of their leaders seeking a wide base of voters. As they continued on in postwar society, they learned that their significance permitted them to enjoy not only the rights of protection from the government but also what amounted to a pardon for wartime activities and in many cases "Aryanization" benefits. An extreme but representative example of the victimhood mentality in postwar Austria can be seen in the creation of government-sanctioned advocacy and protective associations created by "Aryanizers" in reaction to the 1947 restitution laws. These groups organized and advocated on behalf of "Aryanizers" who portrayed themselves as victimized by Austrian Jews who came back and filed restitution claims on their former properties. These organizations provide a case study of the collision of postwar national identity with the reality of survivors' return and rerooting experiences. These associations' work and their political success as a lobbying organ sponsoring the defense of the

---

85. Uhl, "Das österreichische Gedächtnis," 38.
86. Uhl, "From Victim Myth to Co-responsibility Thesis," 51.

beneficiaries of "Aryanization" and "their" property also reveal the public nature of domestic Austrian postwar politics and the open and accepted interest of those who had participated and profited from the Nazi regime.

OPPOSITION TO RESTITUTION: DER SCHUTZVERBAND DER RÜCKSTELLUNGSBETROFFENEN

With the institution of restitution laws, dissatisfaction grew among the Austrian possessors of "Aryanized" property. The third of these restitution laws, which went into effect on February 6, 1947, dealt specifically with belongings taken for "racial, national, or political reasons" and aroused resistance among the beneficiaries' of Nazi "Aryanization" policies. Those who were concerned with maintaining their neighbors' possessions formed an advocacy group, the Schutzverband der Rückstellungsbetroffenen (Protective Association for Parties Affected by Restitution), which united them in a campaign for protection from Jews' claims on their former properties. Discussions about the restitution of assets acquired under Nazi appropriation policies and in the hands of public entities postwar had begun immediately after the establishment of the provisional government.[87] However, this third law proved much more controversial than either of the first two, as in theory it regulated the return of private property that had mostly been owned by Jews and had been acquired through "Aryanization."

At the time of the Anschluss, which ushered in the Nazis' immediate and violent persecution of Austrian Jews, the dire circumstances of the Jews were clear to all. Purchasers took advantage of the situation to pay less than fair market value to acquire apartments, houses, businesses, and even small material goods such as furniture and carpeting. The Nazi system provided for buyers to deposit funds directly into sellers' bank accounts, but then the

---

87. Brigitte Bailer-Galanda and Eva Blimlinger, "Restitution and Compensation of Property in Austria, 1945–2007," in *New Perspectives on Austrians and World War II*, ed. Günter Bischof, Fritz Plasser, and Barbara Stelzl-Marx (New Brunswick, NJ: Transaction, 2009), 309.

government froze Jews' accounts in order to take much of their assets for taxes that they forced Jews to pay, including the Reichsfluchtsteuer, literally, Reich Flight Tax, which was levied on Jews who sought to emigrate. Once their accounts were frozen, Jewish holders had access neither to the already below-market-value payment nor to their preexisting funds. Although it was clear to the purchaser that prices for this property sat far below those for the assets of non-Jews, the system of transfer allowed "Aryanizers" to consider themselves participants in a fair transaction and later to feel relieved of responsibility for the subsequent action of the state. With their dealings legal under Nazi legislation, individuals could claim that they never saw these transactions as theft, although they most likely knew what the Nazi apparatus planned and carried out against their neighbors' finances. "Aryanizers" willingly took part through their opportunistic agreement to underpay people in extraordinarily stressful, life-or-death situations.

After the war, as Austrians painted the picture of an aggressive Nazi invasion and occupation of their country, they reasoned that the Germans carried the responsibility for robbing the Jews. The state asserted its innocence in the face of all the crimes of the "German occupiers," upholding that neither Austria nor the Austrian government had existed between 1938 and 1945, and therefore the postwar German government carried the responsibility for reparations and restitution. Austrian laws regulating restitution processes stirred irritation among owners who desired to retain assets. The strict enforcement of such legislation threatened to contradict the victim narrative of the postwar government, and over time the government showed its official and unofficial support of property owners' complaints and thereby permitted avenues that allowed them to organize themselves to advocate for the retention of belongings. Despite the Allies' interest in the restoration of property, persistent and shrewd Austrian politicians found ways to more or less stall or avoid reparations and compensation. With good reason, historian Robert Knight chose Minister of the Interior Oskar Helmer's words for the title of his book, "*Ich bin dafür, die Sache in die Länge zu ziehen*" (I am in favor of letting the matter drag on), to represent the postwar government's sentiments toward Jewish Austrians and their return home. This quote certainly represented citizens from all levels of society who were interested in drawing out the processes of restitution.

When the third restitution law went into effect, Austrians in possession of property that formerly belonged to Jews watched with trepidation, realizing the precarious status of their assets. Some quickly organized themselves and applied to the Wahlen und verschiedene Rechtsangelegenheiten or Magistratsabteilung 62 (MA 62), the Vienna city government's department for matters of electoral and related legal affairs. They sought official permission to form advocacy groups to protect and retain ownership of assets received through transactions that took place after the Anschluss. The Schutzverband der Rückstellungsverpflichteten (literally, Protective Organization of Parties Involved in Restitution) submitted its goals, mission statement, and statutes for review on April 30, 1947. The group outlined its intentions to hold meetings, distribute petitions, publish news about regulatory decisions related to restitution and other relevant literature, and arrange legal advice and help for its members. The state's decision—signed by Interior Minister Helmer—denied the official formation of the association, stating that the organizers clearly sought to perpetuate National Socialist sentiment in Austria.[88]

The organizers appealed, explaining that some of the group's members had endured political persecution during the war, and claimed that this experience proved their lack of interest in Nazi ideology. They also offered possible instances in which holders of property formerly owned by Jews might be harmed by the restitution laws. For example, they claimed that the owner of a carpet stolen from a Jewish household should not be responsible for returning it if he or she was the second or third owner. That is, the appellants acknowledged that its group's members indeed held unfairly obtained items but took the view that either that person's own suffering under the Nazis or the fact that he or she had not taken the property himself or herself meant that he or she had enjoyed no benefit from "Aryanization."[89] Organizers repeatedly stated that their members had been party to fair and voluntary transactions, but in this case, the state finally upheld its

---

88. Decision by Bundesminister Helmer, October 14, 1947, G 203-15/43-48: A32/1 (prov.)-575, 1.3.2.119.A32.1947.6107/1947–6107/1947, Wiener Stadt- und Landesarchiv (WStLA), Vienna, Austria.

89. Appeal by Dr. Hans Gutmann, G 203-15/43-48: A32/1 (prov.)-575, 1.3.2.119.A32.1947.6107/1947–6107/1947, WStLA. Attorney Dr. Hans Gutmann represented the applicants—Gisela

ruling and denied the appeal of the Schutzverband der Rückstellungsverpflichteten. Interior Minister Helmer also signed this decision.[90]

Two additional hopeful organizations attempted similar applications but met the same fate as the earlier groups. The Vereinigung der Rückstellungsbetroffenen (Association for Parties Concerned with Restitution) applied in March 1948. The Sicherheitsdirektion (Security Directorate) of MA 62 initially rejected its request, but the group appealed, stating that the organization sought to represent only buyers who had taken part in voluntary transactions with Jews and argued that it was unfair that they suffer punishment because of others' improper dealings. The group claimed to support the requirement compelling "Aryanizers" to restitute property but contended that its members were different and warned the government and the Allies against considering all post-Anschluss sales as belonging to the same category. At first, the group's appeal was unsuccessful, but a memo dated August 3, 1948, directed reconsideration and reopening the investigation.[91] On April 6, 1948, the Union Rückstellungsverpflichteter (Union of Parties Involved in Restitution) also tried to gain approval to form an association, but again Helmer signed a negative response, charging the organization with promoting National Socialist sentiment.[92]

The Schutzverband der Rückstellungsbetroffenen submitted its application in early May 1948. By presenting more harmless-seeming statutes, this organization showed clear signs of having learned from the failed attempts of the prior groups. The main signatory of the application, Hans Oberhammer, had also been a party in the earlier group's unsuccessful proposals. This group's application met with approval, and an added note from the Bundesministeriums für Vermögenssicherung und Wirtschaftsplanung (Federal Ministry for the Security of Property and Economic Planning) stated that it saw an advantage to having a partner with which

---

Gertrude Beck, Irma Gutmann, and Ludwig Bucsanyi. Presumably married, Dr. and Ms. Gutmann shared the same address.
  90. 1.3.2.119.A32.1947.6107/1947–6107/1947, WStLA.
  91. 1.3.2.119.A32.1948.5097/1948–5097/1948, WStLA.
  92. 1.3.2.119.A32.1948.7194/1948–7194/1948, WStLA.

to work in case of negotiations during the implementation of the restitution laws.[93]

The change in governmental response to the applications over this short period of time represented a strengthening facet of the postwar victim myth that involved the perceived further victimization of Austrian citizens inflicted by returning Jews. It also showed Austrian politicians' realization of how much latitude they enjoyed under the Allied occupying powers in the context of rapidly developing Cold War politics, and their actions regarding the Schutzverband legitimized the organization and its work. The government had recognized its electorate and found the leeway to represent it. Understanding the Allies' desire to maintain a neutral Austria and to limit Soviet expansion served to foster the desired national narrative of guiltlessness. The country and its citizens eagerly settled into this story line, feeling relieved of both economic and moral responsibility.

The first public meeting of the Schutzverband, held in September 1948 in the Hotel Wimberger, began with a presentation about the third restitution act, which, the speaker declared, represented a "setback in the reconstruction of our constitutional state." The speaker went on to uphold the innocence of the group's members, predicting that with this law, "ordinary honest and respectable citizens, mostly members of the working class [would be crucified] without the protection of law [and would] lose their property, sometimes their life-savings . . . , while restitution applicants enrich themselves unjustifiably." Concentration camp survivors and antifascist demonstrators disrupted the meeting, and the police broke it up.[94] News of the Schutzverband also reached the United States and sparked criticism that led the Austrian general consul in New York to request information and advice in anticipation of Austrian émigrés in the United States who, he thought, would protest and initiate violent attacks as word of the organization and its activities became better known. The consul also expected restitution claims. The Foreign Ministry inquired about the dissolution

---

93. Brigitte Bailer-Galanda, *Die Entstehung der Rückstellungs- und Entschädigungsgesetzgebung: Die Republik Österreich und das in der NS-Zeit entzogene Vermögen* (Vienna: Oldenbourg, 2003), 169–70.

94. Ibid., 170–71.

of the Schutzverband; but Interior Minister Helmer upheld the decision to approve it, and the consul in New York was advised simply to take the position that the Schutzverband had been created legitimately under the Austrian legal framework.[95]

THE VOICE OF THE SCHUTZVERBAND: *UNSER RECHT*

The first issue of the Schutzverband's newspaper, *Unser Recht: Offizielles Organ des Schutzverbandes Rückstellungsbetroffener* (Our right: The official newspaper of the Protective Association for Parties Affected by Restitution), introduced central themes that would recur over the course of its publication from September 1948 to December 1960.[96] For the first few years, it published one issue per month, distributed free of charge, but toward the end of the publication period, it printed only one or two per year. Most issues included copies of recent restitution-relevant news articles with editorial commentary and reports about parliamentary activity and decisions. Letters outlining members' experiences as "victims" of the Jewish former owners of their property were also included. The content and the language used throughout the nearly twelve-year print run illuminate the attitudes and feelings of victimhood among members.

From the start, the Schutzverband used *Unser Recht* to stress the organization's guiding principles, even if only to its membership. First and foremost, it claimed to represent fair and honest buyers.[97] The group complained that the third restitution law invalidated any and all sales contracts made with Jewish sellers after the Anschluss, regardless of how that contract

---

95. Ibid., 171.
96. *Unser Recht*, September 1948, 1. It is worth noting another trace of lingering victim myth sentiment in Vienna: as of the time of publication of this book, the Austrian National Library has cataloged *Unser Recht*, the official newspaper of the Schutzverband, under the keywords "Österreich, Nationalsozialismus, Opfer, Zeitschrift" (Austria, National Socialism, victim, periodical).
97. "Wiedergutmachung," *Unser Recht*, September 1948, 2–3.

came about.⁹⁸ It urged the government to review restitution claims as individual cases in order to exonerate those who participated in voluntary sales and to apply the laws only to unjust or improper transactions that had come about for "racial, national, or political reasons."⁹⁹ The editors of the newspaper left unsaid that official documentation of forcible sales simply did not exist and that no other objective facts pointed to the actual intentions of each party. Despite the inability to determine a seller's reason, *Unser Recht* writers repeatedly upheld that their organization's members had purchased property that Jews sold voluntarily.

Another recurrent and predictable theme consisted of characterizing Austria and all Austrian citizens as victims. According to the Schutzverband—as well as the narrative under construction at the time—all Austrians had suffered under Nazi oppression, and accordingly no hierarchy could be created in which Jews' experiences and losses took priority over others. The author of one article printed in the December 1948 issue expressed this viewpoint with a threat: if a certain group were to gain a privileged status above others, "who knows how quickly this supposed advantage could turn into a serious disadvantage." Another writer portrayed Schutzverband members as heroes who actually *saved* lives by buying drastically undervalued property to enable Jews' flight from Nazi Vienna.¹⁰⁰ And yet another likened the refusal to buy Jews' assets during times of "Aryanization" to an act of the Gestapo, while a colleague asserted that to decline a "begging" Jew's attempt to sell possessions would have set him or her on the road to Auschwitz.¹⁰¹

In the pages of *Unser Recht*, Schutzverband members expressed frustration about restitution legislation that they believed harmed the Austrian nation. Challenged on a philosophical and moral level, they claimed that the Allies' and Austrian politicians' discussion of the need for restitution as fair and constitutional implied that Austrian citizens did not understand

---

98. *Unser Recht*, October 1948, 7.
99. "Motivenbericht und Vorschlag zum Fünften Rückstellungsgesetz," *Unser Recht*, December 1948, 8.
100. "Demokratie und Drittes Rückstellungsgesetz," *Unser Recht*, December 1948, 7–8.
101. "Gerechtigkeit... wir rufen Dich!," *Unser Recht*, November 1948, 1–3.

right from wrong. Schutzverband members expressed shock at such talk; they asserted that the population held a deep-rooted, innate sense of justice that rendered them incapable of wrongdoing. Demonizing law-abiding citizens by portraying them as morally dubious profiteers of "Aryanization" led only to a hostile environment for democracy and freedom, a writer argued in *Unser Recht*.[102] Similarly, other newsletter contributors explained that Austrians living in the countryside led deeply religious and righteous lives and that, therefore, committing impropriety was simply impossible.[103] They reasoned that by nature Austrians simply did not take improper action. Such subjective, biased sentiment reinforced *Unser Recht* readers' feelings of victimhood at the hands of the occupying powers, political enemies, and Jews with malevolent and even vengeful intentions.

Schutzverband articles also posited that restitution laws harmed the economy by removing money from the country and sending it to former owners or their families now living abroad, assuming that none intended to live again in Austria.[104] Many survivors did initiate restitution claims with hopes of returning home, but protracted court cases and official harassment prompted them to abandon ideas of regaining a place to live or a business to run.[105] During such long and drawn-out processes, the original owners often died, and their relatives continued the petition for restitution. Indeed, their heirs rarely planned to live in Austria, which particularly bothered the Schutzverband members. For them, the attempts of survivors' relatives to regain property proved Jews' greed and desire for revenge. Vengeance, however, implied an awareness of original wrongdoing; such inconsistencies recurred in the pages of *Unser Recht* throughout its period of publication. A similar contradiction to the constant contention of Schutzverband members' good natures and intentions, a September 1948 article urged both sides

---

102. "Wiedergutmachung," *Unser Recht*, September 1948, 3.

103. "Quer durch Restitutionsfälle des Dritten Rückstellungsgesetzes," *Unser Recht*, August 1949, 8.

104. "Unser Vorschlag zur Novellierung des Dritten Rückstellungsgesetzes," *Unser Recht*, December 1948, 3–5; as reprinted from *Neues Österreich*, 28 September 1948, 3.

105. Ursula Schwarz, "Das Wiener Verlagswesen der Nachkriegszeit: Eine Untersuchung der Rolle der öffentlichen Verwalter bei der Entnazifizierung und bei der Rückstellung arisierter Verlage und Buchhandlungen" (Diplomarbeit, Universität Wien, 2003), 86.

to "carry the burden of the past together" and rejected a "biblical eye-for-an-eye" situation.¹⁰⁶

Unser Recht writers fought accusations that theirs was a club for disgruntled, defeated Nazis, often pointing out the persecution of Schutzverband members under the Third Reich, but with only vague details of their suffering. Some complained that the Nazis had driven them out of business, without indication of how or why. Many described the "heroic" assistance they and their colleagues had lent to Jews after the Anschluss, as well as "persecution" they suffered by the claims of returning property owners after the war.¹⁰⁷ The repeated statement that the Schutzverband officially denied membership to staunch Nazis went unchallenged. In other issues, authors stressed the advanced age of many of the groups' members to emphasize their innocence and helplessness, as well as the alleged impossibility of their former membership in the Nazi Party.¹⁰⁸ Unsurprisingly, contradictions and denial pervaded Schutzverband logic.

In most cases, *Unser Recht* did not print overt antisemitic statements, but at times Schutzverband members revealed their true sentiments. In December 1948, the Editorial Department replied threateningly to someone it called "Anonymous Foreigner." The editor essentially directed him to mind his own business and stated that the unidentified writer's "daitsch" (*Deutsch*, or German, but with a spelling that signified a Yiddish accent) reveals his obvious heritage.¹⁰⁹ When referring to those who were seeking restitution, writers resorted to antisemitic stereotypes of untrustworthy Jewish sellers who simply waited for the first moment to regain assets from a "just buyer."¹¹⁰ The Schutzverband also tried to use any relatively positive statement made by a Jewish Austrian to its advantage. When a camp survivor reflected on the injustice he observed in the restitution policy, for

---

106. "Was rechtfertigt das Begehren nach Novellierung des dritten Rückstellungsgesetzes und was ist anzustreben?," *Unser Recht*, September 1948, 6–7.

107. "Gründung und Organisation des Schutzverbandes Rückstellungs-Betroffener," *Unser Recht*, October 1948, 1–3.

108. "Die Tragik des Greisenehepaares," *Unser Recht*, November 1948, 5; and "Tragödie auf Tragödie," *Unser Recht*, November 1948, 7.

109. "Briefkasten der Redaktion," *Unser Recht*, December 1948, 16.

110. "Um die Novelle zum Dritten Rückstellungsgesetz," *Unser Recht*, November 1948, 2–3.

example, he found himself profiled in *Unser Recht* as proof that even Jews saw unfairness in the laws.[111] The organization also identified examples of so-called Mischlinge who somehow had fallen victim to restitution laws and exploited them for its purposes.[112]

As the government worked to institute Austria's and Austrians' victim status as actual domestic and foreign policy, its support of the activities of such individuals and organizations made sense. As *Unser Recht* reminded politicians in its May 1949 issue, the government could ill afford experimenting with restitution laws at election time, especially with the organization's estimated representation of two hundred thousand members.[113] In fact, that same year, the support of the Schutzverband proved crucial to the electoral success of the newly formed party the Verband der Unabhängigen (VdU, Federation of Independents, renamed the Freiheitliche Partei Österreichs, or Freedom Party, in 1956). VdU membership included many former Nazi Party members.[114] The government and populace were in agreement that all Austrians had suffered under Nazi persecution and that no subgroup of the populace should be prioritized or favored. The Schutzverband argued not only that its members were victims but also—and therefore—that they were not Nazis. For the Schutzverband, this straightforward yet unrelated fact justified retaining the stolen homes, businesses, and goods of their Jewish neighbors. And indeed, the Schutzverband found support and active membership through the late 1960s.[115]

Decades later, the Austrian Historical Commission determined that a number of factors had hindered the restitution process, including not only the design of the third restitution law but also the resistance of individual "Aryanizers" and the activities of the Schutzverband der Rückstellungs-

---

111. "Quer durch Restitutionsfälle des dritten Rückstellungsgesetzes," *Unser Recht*, December 1948, 13–14.

112. "Der Kauf des Judenhauses immer das Verhängnis" and "Aus der Spruchpraxis," *Unser Recht*, December 1948, 8.

113. *Unser Recht*, May 1949, 6.

114. Brigitte Bailer, "'Ohne den Staat weiter damit zu belasten . . .': Bemerkungen zur österreichischen Rückstellungsgesetzgebung," *Zeitgeschichte* 11/12 (1993): 372.

115. Bailer, "Ohne den Staat weiter damit zu belasten," 59.

betroffenen.¹¹⁶ In the immediate phase of restitution processes following the 1947 legislation, some applicants had met with the successful recovery of assets. But by the early 1950s, in the context of a political climate warmed to the reintegration of former Nazis, antirestitution sentiment had been roused, and attempts were made to amend the third restitution law. The tides turned, and increasing numbers of "Aryanizers" retained their ill-gotten property.¹¹⁷

VIENNESE JEWISH IDENTITY: PREWAR AND POSTWAR

Jews returned to reclaim a place in a society in which they recalled their community's firm roots and successful establishment before the war. Even with Vienna's virulent antisemitism, particularly after World War I, Jews had deftly maneuvered discrimination to live and work among reluctant or even hostile neighbors. A quadripartite identity not only functioned but also served them well. Loyal to the monarchy, they considered themselves politically Austrian but also culturally German, ethnically Jewish, and, above all, Viennese. After World War I and Austria's reduction to a rump state, Viennese Jews clung to this constellation and hoped to retain it.¹¹⁸ Austrian national identity, however, had not changed with the end of World War I, and many Austrians considered themselves German and yearned for union with Germany (Anschluss). The strong antisemitic component

---

116. Franz-Stefan Meissel, Thomas Olechowski, and Cristoph Gnant, *Untersuchungen zur Praxis der Verfahren vor den Rückstellungskommissionen* (Vienna: Oldenbourg Verlag, 2004), 22. The Republic of Austria's Historikerkommission (Historical Commission) was established by the Austrian Cabinet on October 1, 1998, to investigate and report on the whole complex of expropriations that took place in Austria during the Nazi era and on the nation's restitution and compensation activity (including other financial or social benefits) after 1945. For more information, see the Historikerkommission's website at http://www.historikerkommission.gv.at/deutsch_home.html.

117. Brigitte Bailer-Galanda, "Aspects of Austria's Dealing with Her National Socialist Past" (lecture at the Documentation Centre of Austrian Resistance in Vienna, Vienna, February 11, 2009), 6.

118. Marsha Rozenblit, *Reconstructing a National Identity: The Jews of Habsburg Austria during World War I* (New York: Oxford University Press, 2001), 161.

of this German national identity, however, made it impossible for Jews to conceive of themselves as nationally "German."

Defense stratagems cultivated through years of the particular brand of Viennese Jewish acculturation helped protect Viennese Jews and validate their continued existence.[119] They had adopted the tastes and styles of the society around them, but Viennese Jews had acculturated as a group and thereby developed new ways and behaviors that continued to signify their Jewishness, both to themselves and to those around them. Viennese Jews lived together in the same neighborhoods, attended the same schools, and socialized and even married among one another, all of which ensured Jewish group survival in Vienna. That ended with the Anschluss and the ensuing systematic destruction of the community, including the forced emigration of some 135,000 Austrian Jews and the mass murder of another 65,000.

Jews returning to postwar Vienna continued the long trajectory of acculturation and accommodation, again seeking to find the best ways to reestablish themselves in a society changed by seven years of Nazi rule and more unfriendly and averse to Jewish citizens than it had been before the Anschluss. For returnees, this meant employing a certain level of discretion about their Jewish identity, perhaps even more cautiously than they had before the Nazi years. But it meant, too, a resumption of their identification as Austrians who also kept a connection to German culture and their Jewish ethnic identity. They consciously and willingly chose to live again among gentile Austrians, many of whom had at least sympathized with Nazi ideology, while others had benefited from the robbery and expulsion of the Jewish community or even taken an active part in the genocide perpetrated on Europe's Jews. Returnees did not live in hiding, and they upheld their rights and commitment to the country as Austrians; but they also realized that a quieter approach to their Jewish identification and affiliation would serve them well.

Austrian Jews' motivations for return had focused largely on questions of personal identity that centered on Vienna. Many sought instinctively to

---

119. Marsha Rozenblit, *The Jews of Vienna, 1867–1914* (Albany: State University of New York Press, 1983), 195.

go back to a familial home. Camp survivors went back to their hometown and joined those who had reemerged after hiding or surviving under protected circumstances, but neither group may have considered much beyond a hopeful reunion with family and situating oneself in a familiar—and a familial—place. Even after confronting the challenges of post-Nazi Vienna, many remained, having taken a measured decision to do so. Politically affiliated reémigrés identified as specifically Austrian Social Democrats and Communists and arrived with idealistic expectations of doing their duty as dictated by these beliefs. Although they may have been quickly disabused of these notions, many stayed to take part in rebuilding and reshaping "their" Austria. Their identity as politically active (Jewish) Austrians meant that despite—or even because of—the remnants of Nazi ideology, they would remain to combat and change its legacies. And Austrian Jewish professionals—mostly men—maintained a specific identification with their country through training and language; for them, Vienna was the only possible option for renewed professional life. This group of survivors often took their decision later than those who returned more immediately for family and political reasons. The promise of denazification might have reinforced their decisions to attempt to resume professions, despite knowing that the government and professional organizations deterred their homecoming. Arriving later also permitted Jewish professionals the possibility of some awareness of the difficulties of return and a clearer picture of what to expect when they went back. Nonetheless, many of them did so and soon realized that taking part in the national silence on the issue of responsibility and guilt for Nazi crimes served as their best way to get along in postwar Vienna.

As we have seen with the example of Friedrich Torberg and his work (chapter 5), Jews who rejoined professional life in their hometown felt compelled to background their Jewish identity. Torberg wrote extensively about the "lost" Jewish element of Viennese society but never explicitly about what Austria and Austrians had taken and destroyed. Without placing blame, no discussion about responsibility could ensue, and without discussion, no confrontation. Carefully chosen and indirect language permitted gentiles to avoid considering their Jewish neighbors' experiences. It also allowed Austrian Jews to live among former Nazis without thinking about their neighbors' wartime activities. Indeed, their successful reintegration meant reestablishing a Jewish identity within the context of a nation reconstructing its national identity.

Jacqueline Vansant writes in *Reclaiming Heimat* that, despite all that had transpired, many survivors returned because they felt Austrian and wanted to reconnect to an Austrian "we."[120] I would more specifically argue that, in fact, they sought to resume their position and part in the professional, cultural, and social life they recalled and had sorely missed *in Vienna*. They wanted to be Viennese again. They wanted to reengage with a *Viennese* "we." Anthropologist Matti Bunzl writes that many Austrian Jews readily disavow their Austrian identity, reporting that they feel Viennese but not Austrian. Their everyday language reflects this—their use of the term "Austrian" is understood to be in reference to non-Jews.[121] Their city can still be associated with culture and beauty, while the whole of Austria connotes Holocaust, Hitler, and a modern-day right-wing government. "Viennese Jews" enjoy a higher status than "Austrian Jews"; therefore, within Austria, they are Viennese, and outside the country, they would emphasize the specifically Viennese and Viennese-Jewish elements of their identity.[122]

Writer Ernst Lothar defended his decision to return to Vienna with reference to the whole of Austria and specified, "I'm not returning to people, but rather, you'll forgive the pompous expression, to a landscape that I need in order to live."[123] Like Lothar, some survivors also relate different feelings for the place versus the people and break it down to identification with city rather than country. Some share different versions of "I love Vienna; I just don't like the Austrians."[124] Others say, "I love Vienna; it's the Viennese

---

120. Jacqueline Vansant, *Reclaiming Heimat: Trauma and Mourning in Memoirs by Jewish Austrian Reémigrés* (Detroit: Wayne State University Press, 2001), 15.

121. Matti Bunzl, "Austrian Zionism and the Jews of the New Europe," *Jewish Social Studies* 9, no. 2 (2003): 163.

122. Susanne Cohen-Weisz, "From Bare Survival to European Jewish Vision: Jewish Life and Identity in Vienna" (working paper, European Forum at the Hebrew University, Center for Austrian Studies, Jerusalem, 2008), 32–33.

123. Quoted in Vansant, *Reclaiming Heimat*, 111.

124. For example, Trude Berger specified that her love of the country does not include the people. "Aber gross ist mein Liebe vielleicht zu dem *Land*; nicht zu dem Menschen." See Trude

I can do without!"[125] Nonetheless, those who remained chose to live in a place with which they identified but among a people about whom they felt, at best, ambivalent. Many returnees found that the welcoming and friendly circles within which they operated often led to their effective insulation from antisemitic hostilities, which enabled them to live with some safeguard against the legacies of the past. Erich Lessing found none of his prewar Jewish friends alive in Vienna, and many of his non-Jewish friends had perished as well. He remembered, however, no particularly bad experiences with gentiles. "Rather," he said, "nonexperience."[126] Lessing found a different city upon his return, and non-Jewish circles that had been closed to him in 1938 were oddly open. Before the war, his group of friends and those of his family had largely comprised Jews and Social Democrats; but after, "it was a completely different society and a different approach to life and to the society." Lessing found postwar Austrian culture "mixed," in a way he had not experienced before 1938. On the one hand, the more liberal and open-minded enjoyed a new openness to this mixing. On the other, as Lessing said, "People who had been Nazis had either changed color or said that they never really were in the party. This is an Austrian specialty."[127]

Lessing acknowledged a "subterranean" postwar antisemitism but recognized that he and his family had lived in a closed circle of left-wing acquaintances that he said he might even have categorized as "philosemitic." Nonetheless, he also described a time that he heard an acquaintance catch himself just before making an antisemitic remark. Lessing spoke up and told the man that he would like to hear the rest of his statement. Everyone present went silent. They all knew what he had been about to say. As Lessing pointed out, his perception of an integrated Vienna may also have

---

Berger, interview 47865, Visual History Archive (VHA), USC Shoah Foundation, Los Angeles, CA, accessed online at the Strassler Center, Clark University, May 2, 2010.
125. Dr. Ruth Schauder, conversation with author, Vienna, Austria, October 23, 2012.
126. Erich Lessing, interview with author, Vienna, Austria, January 27, 2011.
127. Ibid. In our interview, Lessing told the following story to illustrate his point: They used to say that, during denazification, when you asked people in Berlin if they had been party members, they said, "Yes." When you asked someone in Munich, they said, "The party? What was the party? Me, oh, no, never heard of it." And when you asked someone in Vienna, they said, "Me? No . . . but him!"

been a product of the circles in which he lived and socialized. He married a non-Jewish Austrian woman in 1949 and enjoyed warm and loving relationships with members of her family. In fact, the young couple lived with her parents for about three years, as they found housing hard to secure in the city. They overcame their different experiences of the preceding years. Erich's wife had been a member of the Bund Deutscher Mädel (BDM; League of German Girls, the female branch of the Hitler Youth) in Nazi Vienna and had enjoyed some prominence. A recording of her voice played during Allied air raids to warn residents to seek shelter from bombs. Membership in the BDM and associated activities did not necessarily signify a convinced Nazi; Lessing, his wife, and his in-law family acknowledged that reality, and they openly welcomed him. The young couple's happy marriage, good family relationships, and the acceptance Erich felt among his wife's relatives and in their enmeshed group of friends speak to the complicated nature of postwar Austrian gentile *and* Jewish identities, as well as Jews' assimilation in a postgenocidal society.[128]

Maria Dorothea Simon also reestablished herself in her hometown after surviving the war in exile in the United Kingdom. After her return, she invited some former classmates to her apartment and noted that, although pleased to see her again, they acted subservient. "And none of them had been Nazis or had wanted me murdered with the rest," she wrote with distinct sarcasm. Simon was well aware that many of her schoolmates had been enthusiastic Nazis and in an interview admitted ulterior motives behind her invitation. "Just look," she thought, "I'm still alive and I have two lovely children. You weren't able to kill me!" Despite her bitter feelings toward these acquaintances, Simon upheld later that she had not suffered from antisemitism in postwar Vienna.[129] Her testimony reveals an awareness of

---

128. Ibid. Lessing exhibited one element of the complicated nature of postwar life and identities—from the start of our interview, he repeated that all was much simpler than one (I) might like to make it. He remained emphatic that the Vienna to which he had returned and in which he lived in the current day had been changed for the better, stressing the differences between prewar and postwar social circles and the interreligious mixing that involved actual interaction after the war.

129. Maria Dorothea Simon, "Selbstzeugnis," in *Soziale Arbeit in Selbstzeugnissen*, vol. 2, ed. Hermann Heitkamp and Alfred Plewa (Freiburg im Breisgan: Lambertus, 2002), 246–47.

such discrimination as a general problem but also suggests that she, like many other survivors who returned, employed self-defense mechanisms that included ignoring subtle or covert discrimination in order to adjust psychologically to life among former Nazis and bystanders to genocide. Simon did not report confronting her former schoolmates but rather made it clear that although they all chose to live together again, she knew the truth. Her survival and return served as a victory, even if she never openly reveled in it. She and so many others realized that they could resume much of the life they had previously enjoyed if only they participated in the national silence on the Nazi years. If Jews did not talk with Austrian gentiles about where they had been and what had happened to them and their families, then Austrian gentiles in turn would not confront returnees with the reality of their wartime activities and loyalties.

A distinct drawback to this approach was fantasy about the wartime doings of neighbors, coworkers, and friends. With no exchange or discussion, one could only imagine. Alternatively, if this "don't ask, don't tell" policy proved effective in hiding the truths of the past for a time, it could be blown apart quite suddenly. Frieda Fraenkel's return and reconnection with prewar friends had gone quite well in her estimation. She reported that for decades they lived together quite nicely—until the Waldheim Affair. In 1986, the former general secretary to the United Nations Kurt Waldheim ran as a candidate for the office of the president of the Austrian Federal Republic. With the help of documentation provided by the World Jewish Congress, the *New York Times* reported on Waldheim's wartime activities and criticized Austria for permitting such a candidate. He had been a member of the SA-Cavalry Corps and the Nazi Student League and had been in a position to be well aware of the genocide of the Jews of Saloniki. The ensuing campaign against him and against Austria enflamed antisemitism and sparked vocal and public blame of world Jewry for Waldheim's and the nation's troubles. The discussion of wartime activities became public and hostile, and in the end, antisemitism helped Waldheim get elected. With the sudden openness and aggression, Frau Fraenkel's comfortable, quiet existence in Vienna changed. Indignant that the Waldheim Affair had become a "Jewish thing," she first spoke out among friends. When they reacted defensively, however, she reverted to holding herself back in silence to avoid any falling out with them. "I was afraid of my friends. I was afraid of people . . . a bad feeling because I always think that they are on the other side."[130] For years, Frau Fraenkel and her friends lived in silence about such topics, but with the debate forced into the public sphere, she could not avoid hearing her friends' and neighbors' antisemitic opinions and had to consider their positions and their pasts. The antisemitic sentiment fomented under years of Nazi ideology had not gone away; it had, as Erich Lessing said, only gone "subterranean."

And so Austrian Jews returned to Vienna and chose to stay to reestablish their homes with their families, with political parties, and in their chosen professions. Once these survivors from different wartime locations and experiences had rerooted, they faced shared and similar challenges and obstacles moving forward. Their return constituted an attempt to reconnect to their sense of belonging as specifically "Viennese." Their reentry, however, quickly brought them face-to-face with the reality that their Austrian neighbors' attitudes and mind-set had not changed much after the Nazi defeat. Many Austrian Jews returned to Vienna with ideas that their return was expected and desired but were quickly disabused of such notions.

As a new postwar Austrian national identity took shape and solidified, returning Jews recognized the necessity of employing discretion about their Jewish identity. Survivors learned instead to take part in a national silence. An unspoken agreement kept both gentile Austrians and returning Jews from discussing their locations and activities during the Nazi years. Returnees recognized that they could avoid confrontation and uncomfortable conversation by carefully avoiding certain topics or at least speaking vaguely and with care not to place direct blame on Austria or individual Austrians. With these safety mechanisms in place, the political and social circles to which returning Austrian Jews belonged permitted most to report an insulation from day-to-day discrimination in a highly antisemitic city.

---

130. Fraenkel interview.

Returning Jews did, however, encounter clear discrimination and a lack of political representation on a community and governmental level. With the victim myth cemented soon after the end of the war, government leaders and elected officials knew their constituencies and realized that strict adherence to restitution laws and participation in reparations payment would cause their careers to suffer and their parties to lose support. Politicians took care to appeal to the large portion of the electorate that had been members of the Nazi Party, as well as to those who had benefited from Nazi "Aryanization" policies. Satisfying the tiny Jewish fraction of the population made no political sense, and postwar politics and emerging Cold War tensions between the Allied powers provided a perfect setting in which to eagerly assume a victim identity and to avoid blame for Austrian participation in Nazi crimes.

This hostile atmosphere notwithstanding, survivors' motivations for return and for remaining had everything to do with their individual and group identification as Austrian—and, in particular, as Viennese. Their familial, political, and professional affiliations tied them to the city, and even if much had changed drastically, they willingly reestablished their lives and learned new ways to maneuver in their *home*, Vienna.

CONCLUSION

Born in Vienna to an assimilated, nonobservant Jewish family, Bruno Kreisky was active in Austria's Social Democratic movement as a student. He suffered imprisonment under the Austrofascist regime and was also incarcerated briefly by the Nazis. They released him dependent on his immediate emigration from the country, and he fled to Sweden, where he continued his political engagement, working with the international Social Democrats. He returned to Vienna in May 1946 and resumed political activities on behalf of the Austrian government, which immediately assigned him to its foreign office in Stockholm. He went home permanently at the end of 1950, and his political climb peaked when he became chancellor in 1970. Just twenty-five years after the end of World War II and the attempted annihilation of European Jewry, the head of state of a former Nazi country was a Viennese Jewish returnee, a Holocaust survivor.

Kreisky accomplished a great deal for his country. Before his chancellorship, he had a key role in drafting the Staatsvertrag (Austrian State Treaty, ratified in 1955 at the end of the Allies' occupation of the country). While he was in office, the economy came to near full employment, the social welfare system (which remains Austria's pride today) grew and strengthened, and the official workweek was shortened to forty hours. But some of Kreisky's actions proved controversial and did nothing to gain him favor with Jewish leaders. He maintained good relationships with Egyptian president Anwar Sadat and Libyan prime minister Muammar Gadaffi, and during the Kreisky administration, the Palestine Liberation Organization (PLO) established an official office in Vienna. At the same time, Austria under

Kreisky became a transit country for Jews fleeing the Soviet Union to Israel and the United States.

Kreisky strategically identified mainly as a political and not as a Jewish persecutee of the Nazis. In many situations, he strove to highlight and heighten his Austrianness by foregrounding his antifascist and resistance past and ignored the fact that being Jewish in Nazi Austria had been a death sentence. A self-proclaimed agnostic, he claimed no identification with the Jewish community and regarded Judaism as a religion and neither a culture nor a nation. But Kreisky also never denied his Jewish family background. Rather, he assumed and wielded it when it was of political advantage. He acted specifically as a Jew, for example, when he showed willingness to form a coalition with former Waffen SS officer Friedrich Peter and the far-right Freedom Party, although fortunately no such partnership became necessary.[1] Kreisky's foreign policy in the Middle East and his forgiveness and tacit pardon of former Nazis appealed to gentile Austrians, and in such cases, his Jewish identity served to validate him as an Austrian leader.

Kreisky's implausible insistence that he had suffered no antisemitism in his Viennese youth was one of many claims that also enhanced his popularity among gentile Austrians and served to position him as a Jew who could provide absolution from guilt for the Holocaust. As historian Robert Wistrich has written, "Kreisky was destined to become the *Entlastungsjude* (exonerating Jew) freeing Austrians of the burdens of complicity in the German mass murder."[2] Opinion polls conducted in the 1980s by the Paul Lazarsfeld Society showed that Kreisky was singled out as "possessing in even greater measure the attributes that summed up the meaning and characteristics of Austria," even more so than the celebrated skier Annemarie Moser-Pröll and the well-known actor Heinz Conrads.[3] He remains

---

1. Anton Pelinka, "Mainstreaming der jüdischen Identität? Wie der Antisemitismus einen logischen Mix an Identitäten verhindert—am Beispiel Bruno Kreisky," *Das Jüdische Echo* 57 (2008–9): 122.

2. Robert S. Wistrich, *From Ambivalence to Betrayal: The Left, the Jews, and Israel* (Lincoln: University of Nebraska Press, 2012), 479.

3. Cited in Ernst Bruckmüller, "The National Identity of the Austrians," in *The National Question in Europe in Historical Context*, ed. Mikulas Teich and Roy Porter (Cambridge: Cambridge University Press, 1993), 204.

one of the country's most beloved politicians, second only to the Emperor Franz Josef.

Kreisky's example, albeit extreme and public, demonstrates the ambiguous and careful way a Jewish returnee could successfully handle family heritage and experiences of persecution under the Nazis in order to manage in postwar Austria. In many ways, he embodies both the conundrum of postwar Austrian national identity *and* the complexity of the Viennese Jewish identity developing within that context. A Jewish Austrian and a Social Democrat, he survived the Nazis in exile abroad and returned to Vienna to reclaim a political home. Once reengaged, he rose through the ranks to serve the country in its highest office, and in the shadow of the Holocaust, he helped to solidify a positive Austrian identity for his country's citizens, gentiles and Jews alike. The enigma of Austria's beloved Kreisky may be better understood when viewed through the lens of *The Compromise of Return*. Indeed, his case elucidates many aspects of this book's main themes.

A small fraction of the prewar Jewish population reclaimed their home through the reestablishment of lives, families, and careers in Vienna after the Holocaust. The majority of those who fled from the Nazis to locations around the globe remained in their adopted countries or emigrated further, where many re-created or found "home" anew—or at least trusted that it lay in store for them there. But those who went back still conceived only of the Danubian capital as home, and they stayed when they recovered at least some version of the memory and feeling they held dear. They arrived back in waves, the timing of which largely depended on their location and experiences during the war and their motivations and expectations for remigration. Each sought to regain a *familial home*, *political home*, or *professional home*—or some combination of the three; their wartime whereabouts and all that they had encountered, as well as the fellow (Jewish and gentile) Austrians with whom they had lived and socialized, frequently determined the time and means of their journeys and the conditions they faced upon arrival.

Those who had managed to live out the war in the city itself constituted the first group to (at least figuratively) return. They reemerged and reengaged in the chaos of immediate postwar Vienna almost instantly upon the Red Army's capture and occupation of the capital. They made no conscious decision about "return" but rather instinctively resumed daily life in their partially destroyed and traumatized city. Some had survived in hiding (*U-Boote*), while others had lived under a protected status as a spouse in a mixed marriage, as the child of such a union, or as an employee of the Jewish community. They resurfaced into life in their familial home, a place they had never physically left but from which they had been thrust and excluded.

Concentration camp survivors followed the Jews who had remained in the city by weeks or months. They made their ways to Vienna as soon after liberation as possible, some by their own means and others with repatriation assistance from the Allies. They wanted to go back to the place they had last been with family, although most were disappointed in their quest to locate surviving relatives. Nonetheless, the desire to reconnect with their familial home drove them there.

Austrian Jews who had lived out the war abroad and engaged with their political parties in exile formed the next wave of reémigrés, some as early as the end of 1945. Many returned under the auspices of their organizations and with fellow members. While in exile, their leaders had told them that Austria and Austrians awaited them and would welcome them. They reinforced the myth of Austria as "first victim" of the Nazis and gave merit to the idea that the Anschluss had been an unwanted military invasion and occupation by Germany. With this in mind, Jewish Communists and Socialists sought to regain their political home and arrived in Vienna with idealistic expectations of taking part in the reconstruction of an autonomous and democratic Austria. They were soon disabused of any notion that their fellow Austrians desired their homecoming, but most stayed and indeed took part in the rebuilding of what would become the Second Republic of Austria.

A fourth cohort trailed the politically affiliated reémigrés and included those who sought to reattach to a professional home. Writers, lawyers, and doctors, for example, could conceive of working only in Vienna and felt bound to the city by language, training, and certification. Conditions in their lands of exile had been such that many had been unable to work in their chosen fields or to keep their standard of living to the level to which they had been accustomed. These professionals, most of them men, decided that resuming their chosen career paths was worth the challenges of living among former Nazis and their supporters.

The majority of Jews who would return to Vienna had done so by the end of 1947. With differing expectations and motivations before their arrival, their experiences converged once back in their hometown and as the reestablishment of lives, families, and the larger community commenced. They met with discrimination in various forms in public and in the workplace, but Viennese Jews retained the ability to navigate the long-standing and endemic antisemitism that had long marked the city's history. A series of restitution laws went into effect that same year and aroused the appearance of more outspoken and public antisemitic sentiment. Property owners who had benefited from Nazi "Aryanization" policies formed advocacy organizations to help them in their fight to retain "their" property. Few Jews regained their former residences and businesses. But still, most stayed.

On May 15, 1955, Austria's Foreign Minister Figl and the four Allies' representatives signed the Austrian State Treaty at the Belvedere Palace in Vienna, and with it the Second Republic of Austria was founded. The goal of establishing a free and independent nation had been achieved ten years after the end of the war. The phrasing of the State Treaty included the entrenched language of victimhood and omitted reference to responsibility as a perpetrator nation.[4] The Austrian Parliament passed a constitutional law proclaiming the country's permanent neutrality on October 26, 1955, immediately after the last occupation soldiers had departed.[5]

During the ten years of occupation, the Allies had tacitly condoned Austria's identification as victim and thereby fostered this important facet of a developing postwar national identity. A lack of denazification practice in the country, viewed alongside the Soviets' practice of pursuit of reparations

---

4. David Art, *The Politics of the Nazi Past in Germany and Austria* (New York: Cambridge University Press, 2006), 105.

5. Bruno Kreisky, Matthew Paul Berg, Jill Lewis, and Oliver Rathkolb, *The Struggle for a Democratic Austria: Bruno Kreisky on Peace and Social Justice* (New York: Berghahn Books, 2000), 275.

through plunder and exploitation of regions under their control, suggests the Allies' implicit understanding of Austria's responsibility for Nazi war crimes and intentional silence: eliding Austria's culpability suited everyone.[6] Both neutrality and victimhood stood as pillars of an Austrian national identity that developed in the postwar years and framed the context into which Austrian Jews rerooted.

Both some degree of acceptance of the victim myth and previous experience traversing the city's inherent antisemitism served the returnees. They reentered a society that had retained all the ambiguities with which they had been socialized and to which they were accustomed. As Viennese, in fact, they returned *because* such ambiguity was a part of their identity, resulting from the history of the multinational, multiethnic empire. Marsha Rozenblit's description of a tripartite Austrian Jewish identity—the possibility of feeling German, Austrian, and Jewish, all at once—was a trait derived from a larger and particular Viennese cultural characteristic, one that also dictates the recognition of a fourth facet; even with all of these identifications, Viennese Jews were, above all, *Viennese*. Their multiple identities revealed an immersion into and acceptance of a multifaceted, at times contradictory, culture. Even after the Holocaust, returnees believed they could resume lives as Viennese *and* Jewish.

Friedrich Torberg's work exemplifies the discretion employed to live and work comfortably as a Jew in postwar Vienna. Although much of his writing focuses on a Jewish element of Viennese society that had been lost, he never explicitly states who had taken it away. Without direct attribution of blame, no dialogue or confrontation could ensue, and such careful handling and indirect language permitted gentile neighbors to remain willfully ignorant of their Jewish neighbors' experiences. A mutual silence also allowed survivors to live among former Nazis and to suppress thought about their possible involvement in war crimes. The development of postwar Viennese Jewish identity occurred within the context of the reformulation of a larger

---

6. Günter Bischof, "Allied Plans and Policies for the Occupation of Austria, 1938–1955," in *Austria in the Twentieth Century*, ed. Rolf Steininger, Günter Bischof, and Michael Gehler (New Brunswick, NJ: Transaction, 2009), 177.

national identity characterized by victimhood and neutrality. Wishing to resume life in Vienna, Jews left this characterization largely unchallenged.

Important to returning Jews was that they felt thoroughly *Viennese*. They wanted to again be part of *that* city and *that* society, defining themselves and operating within the boundaries it required. Reémigrés recommenced the delicate navigation of antisemitism with the assumption that they could handle the challenges of such discrimination. Presuming it would pose no more of a problem than they had encountered before, they considered Austrians' embrace or tolerance of the Nazis' eliminationist antisemitism to have derived from opportunism rather than from principled, deeply held conviction. This acceptance of some level of the postwar victim myth enabled Jews to cohabitate with former Nazis: with the Germans gone, they expected Austrian antisemitism would revert to the "simple" prewar bias that they well knew. They quickly realized, however, that seven years of Nazi indoctrination had left its mark on the population. They adapted and learned to overcome and to avoid the obstacles that confronted them in their return. Home after all had motivated and enticed them back, and once there, the majority of them indeed made it home again, even if that home was neither the same as before nor exactly as they expected.

BIBLIOGRAPHY

MANUSCRIPT ARCHIVES

Archives of the American Jewish Joint Distribution Committee. New York, NY.
Central Archives for the History of the Jewish People. Jerusalem, Israel.
Centropa. Vienna, Austria.
Das Archiv der Israelitischen Kultusgemeinde Wien (Archive of the Jewish Community of Vienna). Vienna, Austria.
Dokumentationsarchiv des österreichischen Widerstandes (DÖW; Documentation Centre of Austrian Resistance). Vienna, Austria.
Kintaert, Barbara. Private collection. Vienna, Austria.
Leo Baeck Institute. New York, NY.
   Austrian Heritage Collection.
National Archives of the United Kingdom. London, UK.
Österreichisches Staatsarchiv (Austrian National Archives). Vienna, Austria.
United States Holocaust Memorial Museum Library and Archive. Washington, DC.
   International Tracing Service (ITS) Digital Archive.
   Steven Spielberg Film and Video Archive.
United States National Archives and Records Administration. College Park, MD.
Visual History Archive (VHA). USC Shoah Foundation Institute. Los Angeles, CA.
Wiener Library for the Study of the Holocaust & Genocide. London, UK.
Wiener Stadt- und Landesarchiv MA 8 (Vienna City and Provincial Archive). Vienna, Austria.

OTHER SOURCES

Adunka, Evelyn. *Die Vierte Gemeinde: Die Geschichte der Wiener Juden von 1945 bis heute.* Berlin: Philo Verlag, 2000.
Allen, William. *The Nazi Seizure of Power: The Experiences of a Single German Town, 1922–1945.* New York: Franklin Watts, 1984.

Altman, Avraham, and Irene Eber. "Flight to Shanghai, 1938–1940: The Larger Setting." *Yad Vashem Studies* 28 (2000): 41–71.

Améry, Jean. *Jenseits von Schuld und Sühne: Bewältigungsversuche eines Überwältigten.* Stuttgart: Klett-Cotta Verlag, 1977.

Anderl, Gabriele, and Dirk Rupnow. *Die Zentralstelle für jüdische Auswanderung als Beraubungsinstitution.* Munich: Veröffentlichungen der Historikerkommission der Republic Österreich 20/1, 2004.

Anthony, Elizabeth, and Dirk Rupnow. "Wien IX, Seegasse 9: Ein österreichisch-jüdischer Geschichtsort." In *Nurinst Jahrbuch 2010, Beiträge zur deutschen und jüdischen Geschichte, Schwerpunktthema: Leben danach—Jüdischer Neubeginn im Land der Täter,* edited by Jim G. Tobias and Peter Zinke, 98–113. Nuremberg: Antogo Verlag, 2010.

Arendt, Hannah. *Eichmann in Jerusalem: A Report on the Banality of Evil.* New York: Penguin Books, 1994.

Art, David. *The Politics of the Nazi Past in Germany and Austria.* New York: Cambridge University Press, 2006.

Austrian Centre. *This Is Austria.* London: Austrian Centre, 1943.

Bailer, Brigitte. "'Ohne den Staat weiter damit zu belasten . . .': Bemerkungen zur österreichischen Rückstellungsgesetzgebung." *Zeitgeschichte* 11/12 (1993): 367–81.

———. "They Were All Victims: The Selective Treatment of the Consequences of National Socialism." In *Austrian Historical Memory and National Identity,* edited by Gunter Bischof and Anton Pelinka, 103–15. New Brunswick, NJ: Transaction, 1997.

———. *Wiedergutmachung kein Thema: Österreich und die Opfer des Nationalsozialismus.* Vienna: Löcker Verlag, 1993.

Bailer, Brigitte, Florian Freund, Elisabeth Klamper, Wolfgang Neugebauer, Gerhard Ungar, and Brigitte Ungar-Klein. *Erzählte Geschichte: Berichte von Widerstandskämpfern und Verfolgten,* vol. 3, *Jüdische Schicksale.* Vienna: Österreichischer Bundesverlag, 1992.

Bailer-Galanda, Brigitte. "Aspects of Austria's Dealing with her National Socialist Past." Lecture at the Documentation Centre of Austrian Resistance in Vienna, Vienna, February 11, 2009.

———. *Die Entstehung der Rückstellungs- und Entschädigungsgesetzgebung: Die Republik Österreich und das in der NS-Zeit entzogene Vermögen.* Vienna: Oldenbourg, 2003.

Bailer-Galanda, Brigitte, and Eva Blimlinger. "Restitution and Compensation of Property in Austria, 1945–2007." In *New Perspectives on Austrians and World War II,* edited by Günter Bischof, Fritz Plasser, and Barbara Stelzl-Marx, 306–24. New Brunswick, NJ: Transaction, 2009.

Bandhauer-Schöffmann, Irene, and Ela Hornung. "War and Gender Identity: The Experience of Austrian Women, 1945–1950." In *Austrian Women in the Nineteenth and Twentieth Centuries: Cross-Disciplinary Perspectives,* edited by David F. Good, Margarete Grandner, and Mary Jo Maynes, 213–34. Providence, RI: Berghahn Books, 1996.

Bankier, David, ed. *The Jews Are Coming Back: The Return of the Jews to Their Countries of Origin after WWII.* New York: Berghahn Books, 2005.

Bauer, Yehuda. *American Jewry and the Holocaust: The American Jewish Joint Distribution Committee, 1939–1945.* Detroit: Wayne State University Press, 1981.

———. *My Brother's Keeper: A History of the American Jewish Joint Distribution Committee, 1929–1939*. Philadelphia: Jewish Publication Society of America, 1974.
———. *Out of the Ashes: The Impact of American Jews on Post-Holocaust European Jewry*. New York: Pergamon, 1989.
Bauer-Merinsky, Judith. "Die Auswirkungen der Annexion Österreichs durch das Deutsche Reich auf die medizinische Fakultät der Universität Wien im Jahre 1938: Biographien entlassener Professoren und Dozenten." PhD diss., University of Vienna, 1980.
Bearman, Marietta. "'Austria Tomorrow?' Planning for a Post-war Austria." In *Out of Austria: The Austrian Centre in London in World War II*, edited by Marietta Bearman, Charmian Brinson, Richard Dove, Anthony Grenville, and Jennifer Taylor, 210–37. London: Tauris Academic Studies, 2008.
Bearman, Marietta, and Charmian Brinson. "'No Easy Matter': Closure and After." In *Out of Austria: The Austrian Centre in London in World War II*, edited by Marietta Bearman, Charmian Brinson, Richard Dove, Anthony Grenville, and Jennifer Taylor, 238–53. London: Tauris Academic Studies, 2008.
Bearman, Marietta, Charmian Brinson, Richard Dove, Anthony Grenville, and Jennifer Taylor, eds. *Out of Austria: The Austrian Centre in London in World War II*. London: Tauris Academic Studies, 2008.
Beckerman, Ruth. *Jenseits des Krieges*. Vienna: Löcker Verlag, 1998.
Bei, Gao. *Shanghai Sanctuary: Chinese and Japanese Policy toward European Jewish Refugees during World War II*. New York: Oxford University Press, 2013.
Bendersky, Joseph W. *The "Jewish Threat": Anti-Semitic Politics of the U.S. Army*. New York: Basic Books, 2000.
Bericht des Präsidiums der Israelitischen Kultusgemeinde Wien über die Tätigkeit in den Jahren 1945 bis 1948. Vienna: Israelitische Kultusgemeinde Wien, 1948.
Berkeley, George. *Hitler's Gift: The Story of Theresienstadt*. Boston: Branden Books, 1993.
Binder, Dieter A. "The Christian Corporatist State: Austria from 1934 to 1938." In *Austria in the Twentieth Century*, edited by Rolf Steininger, Günter Bischof, and Michael Gehler, 72–84. New Brunswick, NJ: Transaction, 2002.
Bischof, Günter. "Allied Plans and Policies for the Occupation of Austria, 1938–1955." In *Austria in the Twentieth Century*, edited by Rolf Steininger, Günter Bischof, and Michael Gehler, 162–89. New Brunswick, NJ: Transaction, 2009.
———. *Austria in the First Cold War, 1945–55: The Leverage of the Weak*. New York: St. Martin's, 1999.
———. "Between East and West: The Origins of Post–World War II Austrian Diplomacy during the Early Occupation Period." In *Austrian Foreign Policy in Historical Context*, edited by Günter Bischof, Anton Pelinka, and Michael Gehler, 113–42. New Brunswick, NJ: Transaction, 2006.
———. "Founding Myths and Compartmentalized Past: New Literature on the Construction, Hibernation, and Deconstruction of World War II Memory in Postwar Austria." In *Austrian Historical Memory and National Identity*, edited by Günter Bischof and Anton Pelinka, Contemporary Austrian Studies 5, 302–41. New Brunswick, NJ: Transaction, 1997.

Bloch, Joseph. *Der nationale Zwist und die Juden in Österreich*. Vienna: Gottlieb, 1886.
Bollauf, Traude. *Dienstmädchen—Emigration: Die Flucht jüdischer Frauen aus Österreich und Deutschland nach England 1938/39*. Vienna: LIT Verlag, 2011.
Botz, Gerhard. "The Dynamics of Persecution in Austria, 1938–1945." In *Austrians and Jews in the Twentieth Century: From Franz Josef to Waldheim*, edited by Robert Wistrich, 199–219. New York: St. Martin's, 1992.
Boyer, John W. *Political Radicalism in Late Imperial Vienna: Origins of the Christian Social Movement, 1848–1897*. Chicago: University of Chicago Press, 1981.
Brenner, Michael. *After the Holocaust: Rebuilding Jewish Lives in Postwar Germany*. Princeton, NJ: Princeton University Press, 1997.
———. "East European and German Jews in Postwar Germany, 1945–50." In *Jews, Germans, Memory: Reconstructions of Jewish Life in Germany*, edited by Y. Michal Bodemann, 49–63. Ann Arbor: University of Michigan Press, 1996.
Brinson, Charmian. "'A Very Ambitious Plan': The Early Days of the Austrian Centre." In *Out of Austria: The Austrian Centre in London in World War II*, edited by Marietta Bearman, Charmian Brinson, Richard Dove, Anthony Grenville, and Jennifer Taylor, 6–21. London: Tauris Academic Studies, 2008.
Bruckmüller, Ernst. "The National Identity of the Austrians." In *The National Question in Europe in Historical Context*, edited by Mikulas Teich and Roy Porter, 196–227. Cambridge: Cambridge University Press, 1993.
Büchler, Yehoshua R. "Reconstruction Efforts in Hostile Surroundings—Slovaks and Jews after World War II." In *The Jews Are Coming Back: The Return of the Jews to Their Countries of Origin after WWII*. Edited by David Bankier, 257–76. New York: Berghahn Books, 2005.
Bukey, Evan Burr. *Hitler's Austria: Popular Sentiment in the Nazi Era, 1938–1945*. Chapel Hill: North Carolina University Press, 2000.
———. *Jews and Intermarriage in Nazi Austria*. New York: Cambridge University Press, 2011.
Bundesministerium für Unterricht. *Freiheit für Österreich: Dokumente*. Vienna: Österreichischer Bundesverlag, 1955.
Bunzl, Matti. "Austrian Zionism and the Jews of the New Europe." *Jewish Social Studies* 9, no. 2 (2003): 154–73.
Buxbaum, Elisabeth. *Transit Shanghai: Ein Leben im Exil*. Vienna: Edition Steinbauer, 2008.
Cesarani, David. *Becoming Eichmann: Rethinking the Life, Crimes, and Trial of a "Desk Murderer."* Cambridge, MA: Da Capo, 2006.
Cesarani, David, and Tony Kushner, eds. *The Internment of Aliens in Twentieth Century Britain*. London: Frank Cass, 1993.
Clare, George. *Before the Wall: Berlin Days, 1946–1948*. New York: Dutton, Penguin, 1990.
———. *Last Waltz in Vienna: The Rise and Destruction of a Family, 1842–1942*. New York: Holt, Rinehart, and Winston, 1980.
Cohen, Beth B. *Case Closed: Holocaust Survivors in Postwar America*. Piscataway, NJ: Rutgers University Press, 2007.

Cohen-Weisz, Susanne. "From Bare Survival to European Jewish Vision: Jewish Life and Identity in Vienna." Working paper, European Forum at the Hebrew University, Center for Austrian Studies, Jerusalem, 2008.

———. *Jewish Life in Austria and Germany since 1945: Identity and Communal Reconstruction*. Budapest: Central European University Press, 2016.

Cohn, Carla. *My Nine Lives*. Buckinghamshire, UK: Shield Crest, 2010.

de Haan, Ido. "The Construction of a National Trauma: The Memory of the Persecution of the Jews in the Netherlands." *Netherlands' Journal of Social Sciences* 34, no. 2 (1998): 196–217.

Der Lebensbaum: Der Wiener Israelitischen Kultusgemeine, 1960–1964. Vienna: Israelitishche Kultusgemeinde Wien, Fritz Molden Grossdruckerei und Verlag Gesellschaft m.b.H., 1964.

Diendorfer, Gertraud, ed. *Wieder gut machen? Enteignung, Zwangsarbeit, Entschädigung, Restitution: Österreich 1938–1945/1945–1999*. Innsbruck: Sonderband der Informationen zur Politischen Bildung, 1999.

Dinnerstein, Leonard. *America and the Survivors of the Holocaust*. New York: Columbia University Press, 1982.

Dobroszycki, Lucjan. *Survivors of the Holocaust in Poland: A Portrait Based on Jewish Community Records, 1944–1947*. New York: M. E. Sharpe, 1994.

Dove, Richard. Introduction to *Out of Austria: The Austrian Centre in London in World War II*, edited by Marietta Bearman, Charmian Brinson, Richard Dove, Anthony Grenville, and Jennifer Taylor, 1–5. London: Tauris Academic Studies, 2008.

Dreier, Werner. "Doppelte Wahrheit: Ein Beitrag zur Geschichte der Tausendmarksperre." *Montfort* 37, no. 1 (1985): 63–71.

Duizend-Jensen, Angelika Shoshana. *Jüdische Gemeinden, Vereine, Stiftungen und Fonds: "Arisierung" und Restitution*. Vienna: Historikerkommission, 2002.

Dwork, Debórah, and Robert Jan van Pelt. *Flight from the Reich: Refugee Jews, 1933–1946*. New York: Norton, 2009.

———. *Holocaust: A History*. New York: Norton, 2002.

Eckstein, Tanja, and Julia Kaldori, eds. *Wie wir gelebt haben: Wiener Juden erinnern sich an ihr 20. Jahrhundert*. Vienna: Mandelbaum Verlag, 2008.

Eisterer, Klaus. "Austria under Allied Occupation." In *Austria in the Twentieth Century*, edited by Rolf Steininger, Günter Bischof, and Michael Gehler, 190–211. New Brunswick, NJ: Transaction, 2002.

Embacher, Helga. *Neubeginn ohne Illusionen: Juden in Österreich nach 1945*. Vienna: Picus Verlag, 1995.

———. "Unwelcome in Austria: Returnees and Concentration Camp Survivors." In *When the War Was Over: Women, War and Peace in Europe, 1940–1956*, edited by Claire Duchen and Irene Bandhauer-Schöffmann, 194–206. London: Leicester University Press, 2000.

———. "Viennese Jewish Functionaries on Trial: Accusations, Defense Strategies and Hidden Agendas." In *Jewish Honor Courts: Revenge, Retribution, and Reconciliation in Europe and Israel after the Holocaust*, edited by Laura Jockusch and Gabriel N. Finder, 165–96. Detroit: Wayne State University Press, 2015.

Erickson, John. *The Road to Berlin: Stalin's War with Germany*. New Haven, CT: Yale University Press, 1983.
Etzersdorfer, Irene, and Hans Schafranek, eds. *Erzählte Geschichte: Der Februar 1934 in Wien*. Vienna: Autorenkollektiv, 1984.
Evans, Richard J. *The Coming of the Third Reich*. New York: Penguin, 2004.
———. *The Third Reich in Power*. New York: Penguin, 2005.
Feikes, Renate. "Exil der Wiener Medizin in Großbritannien." In *Immortal Austria? Austrians in Exile in Britain*, edited by Charmian Brinson, Richard Dove, and Jennifer Taylor, 61–74. Amsterdam: Rodopi, 2007.
Fiala, Josef. *Die Februarkämpfe 1934 in Wien Meidling und Liesung: Ein Bürgerkrieg, der keiner war*. Hamburg: disserta Verlag, 2013.
Forster, David, "Café Sindelar Revisited: Verlauf und Folgen der Sindelar-Debatte." In *Fußball unterm Hakenkreuz in der "Ostmark,"* edited by David Forster, Jakob Rosenberg, Georg Spitaler, 314–30. Göttingen: Verlag die Werkstatt, 2014.
Fox, John P. "German and Austrian Jewish Volunteers in Britain's Armed Forces, 1939–1945." *Leo Baeck Institute Yearbook* 1995:21–50.
Fraller, Elisabeth, and George Langnas, eds. *Mignon: Tagebücher und Briefe einer jüdischen Krankenschwester in Wien, 1938–1949*. Innsbruck: Studien Verlag, 2010.
Frank, Sonja. Introduction to *Young Austria: Österreicherinnen im Britischen Exil, 1938–1947; Für ein freies, demokratisches und unabhängiges Österreich*, edited by Sonja Frank, 17–26. Vienna: ÖGB Verlag, 2012.
———, ed. *Young Austria: Österreicherinnen im Britischen Exil, 1938–1947; Für ein freies, demokratisches und unabhängiges Österreich*. Vienna: ÖGB Verlag, 2012.
Free Austrian Movement. *The Case of Austria*. London: New Europe, 1942.
Freidenreich, Harriet Pass. *Jewish Politics in Vienna, 1918–1938*. Bloomington: Indiana University Press, 1991.
Freundlich, Elisabeth. *Die fahrenden Jahre: Erinnerungen*. Salzburg: Otto Müller Verlag, 1992.
Friedjung, Prive. *"Wir wollten nur das Paradies auf Erden": Die Erinnerungen einer jüdischen Kommunisten aus der Bukowina*. Vienna: Böhlau Verlag, 1995.
Friedman, Towiah. *Dr. Josef Löwenherz, Direktor der Kultusgemeinde Wien war Schützling Adolf Eichmanns und Brunners, 1938–45: Somit überlebte er den Krieg und das Nazi-Regimes*. Haifa: Institute of Documentation, 1995.
———. *The Hunter*. Translated and edited by David C. Gross. Garden City, NY: Doubleday, 1961.
Gay, Ruth. *Safe among the Germans: Liberated Jews after World War II*. New Haven, CT: Yale University Press, 2002.
Geiss, Imanuel. *The Question of German Unification, 1806–1996*. London: Routledge, 1997.
Geller, Jay Howard. *Jews in Post-Holocaust Germany, 1945–1953*. Cambridge: Cambridge University Press, 2005.
Ginsberg, Benjamin. *How the Jews Defeated Hitler: Exploding the Myth of Jewish Passivity in the Face of Nazism*. Lanham, MD: Rowman and Littlefield, 2013.

Gold, Hugo. *Geschichte der Juden in Wien: Ein Gedenkbuch*. Tel Aviv: Olamenu, 1966.
Golsan, Richard J. "The Legacy of World War II in France: Mapping the Discourses of Memory." In *The Politics of Memory in Postwar Europe*, edited by Richard Ned Lebow, Wulf Kansteiner, and Claudio Fogu, 73–101. Durham, NC: Duke University Press, 2006.
Göpfert, Rebekka. *Der jüdische Kindertransport von Deutschland nach England, 1938/39*. Frankfurt: Campus Verlag, 1999.
Graf, Roland. "Anachronism or Sting in the Flesh? The Remarkable Success of Austria's Regional Communist Newspapers (1948–2000)." Paper presented at the Postgraduate Conference, St. Antony's College, Oxford, UK, May 24–26, 2002.
Granville, Johanna. "Neutral Encounters of the Paranoid Kind: Austria's Reactions to the Hungarian Crisis of 1956." In *Austrian Foreign Policy in Historical Context*, edited by Günter Bischof, Anton Pelinka, and Michael Gehler, 143–69. New Brunswick, NJ: Transaction, 2006.
Gregor, Diana. *heim.at.home*. Vienna: Metroverlag, 2012.
Grenville, Anthony. *Jewish Refugees from Germany and Austria in Britain, 1933–1970: Their Image in AJR Information*. Edgware, UK: Valentine Mitchell, 2010.
———. "The Politics of the Austrian Centre." In *Out of Austria: The Austrian Centre in London in World War II*, edited by Marietta Bearman, Charmian Brinson, Richard Dove, Anthony Grenville, and Jennifer Taylor, 22–52. London: Tauris Academic Studies, 2008.
Grenville, Anthony, and Andrea Reiter, eds. *"I Didn't Want to Float; I Wanted to Belong to Something": Refugee Organizations in Britain, 1933–1945*. Yearbook of the Research Centre for German and Austrian Exile Studies 10. Amsterdam: Rodopi, 2008.
———. *Political Exile and Exile Politics in Britain after 1933*. Amsterdam: Rodopi, 2011.
Gross, Jan T. *Fear: Anti-Semitism in Poland after Auschwitz*. New York: Random House, 2006.
Grossmann, Atina. *Jews, Germans, and Allies: Close Encounters in Occupied Germany*. Princeton, NJ: Princeton University Press, 2007.
Gruber, Helmut. *Red Vienna: Experiment in Working-Class Culture, 1919–1934*. Oxford: Oxford University Press, 1991.
Gutterman, Bella. *A Narrow Bridge to Life: Jewish Forced Labor and Survival in the Gross-Rosen Camp System, 1940–1945*. Jerusalem: Yad Vashem Jerusalem, 2008.
Hagen, William W. *German History in Modern Times: Four Lives of the Nation*. New York: Cambridge University Press, 2012.
Hall, Murray G. "Publishers and Institutions in Austria, 1918–45." In *A History of Austrian Literature, 1918–2000*, edited by Katrin Maria Kohl and Ritchie Robertson, 75–86. Rochester, NY: Camden House, 2006.
Hamann, Brigitte. *Hitler's Vienna: A Portrait of the Tyrant as a Young Man*. New York: I. B. Tauris, 2010.
Hammel, Andrea, and Bea Lewkowicz, eds., *The Kindertransport to Britain, 1938/39: New Perspectives*. Yearbook of the Research Centre for German and Austrian Exile Studies 13. Amsterdam: Rodopi, 2012.

Hausner, Gideon. *Justice in Jerusalem*. New York: Schocken, 1968.
Hecht, Dieter J., Eleonore Lappin-Eppel, and Michaela Raggam-Blesch. *Topographie der Shoah: Gedächnisorte das zerstörten jüdischen Wien*. Vienna: Mandelbaum Verlag, 2015.
Heineman, Elizabeth D. *What Difference Does a Husband Make? Women and Marital Status in Nazi and Postwar Germany*. Berkeley: University of California Press, 1999.
Herf, Jeffrey. *Divided Memory: The Nazi Past in the Two Germanys*. Cambridge, MA: Harvard University Press, 1997.
Herz, Martin Florian. *Understanding Austria: The Political Reports and Analyses of Martin F. Herz, Political Officer of the U.S. Legation in Vienna, 1945–1948*. Salzburg: Reinhold Wagnleitner, 1984.
Herzog, Hillary Hope. *"Vienna Is Different": Jewish Writers in Austria from the Fin-de-Siècle to the Present*. New York: Berghahn Books, 2013.
Hoffmann, Christhard. "The Contribution of German-Speaking Jewish Immigrants to British Historiography." In *Second Chance: Two Centuries of German-speaking Jews in the United Kingdom*, edited by Werner E. Mosse, Julius Carlebach, and Gerhard Hirschfeld, 153–75. Tübingen: J. C. B. Mohr, 1991.
Hondius, Dienke. *Return: Holocaust Survivors and Dutch Anti-Semitism*. Westport, CT: Praeger, 2003.
Hubenstorf, Michael. "Vertriebene Medizin—Finale des Niedergangs der Wiener Medizinischen Schule." In *Vertriebene Vernunft: Emigration und Exil der österreichischen Wissenschaft*, vol. 2, edited by Friedrich Stadler, 766–93. Vienna: Jugend und Volk, 1987.
Hughes, Michael. *Nationalism and Society: Germany, 1800–1945*. London: E. Arnold, 1988.
Ich rege mich noch heute auf, wenn ich es erzähle: Frauen berichten über ihr Leben in der Zeit von 1934 bis 1945. AUF-Eine Frauenzeitschrift: Sonderheft zum Bedenkjahr 1988. Vienna: Frauenzentrum, 1988.
Immler, Nicole L. "Restitution and Dynamics of Memory: A Neglected Trans-generational Perspective." In *Mediation, Remediation, and the Dynamics of Cultural Memory*, edited by Astrid Erll and Ann Rigney, 205–28. Berlin: Walter de Gruyter, 2009.
Into the Arms of Strangers: Stories of the Kindertransport. Written and directed by Mark Jonathan Harris. Warner Brothers Pictures, 2001. DVD.
Jah, Akim. *Die Deportation der Juden aus Berlin: Die nationalsozialistische Vernichtungspolitik und das Sammellager Große Hamburger Straße*. Berlin: Be.Bra Wissenschaft Verlag, 2013.
Jelavich, Barbara. *Modern Austria: Empire and Republic, 1815–1986*. Cambridge: Cambridge University Press, 1987.
Jenseits des Krieges. Written and directed by Ruth Beckerman. Hoanzl Vertrieb, 1996. DVD.
Jockusch, Laura. *Collect and Record! Jewish Holocaust Documentation in Early Postwar Europe*. Oxford: Oxford University Press, 2012.
Kaplan, Marion. *Between Dignity and Despair*. New York: Oxford University Press, 1998.
Kauders, Anthony. *Unmögliche Heimat: Eine deutsch-jüdische Geschichte der Bundesrepublik*. Munich: Deutsche Verlags-Anstalt, 2007.
Kleindel, Walter. *Die Chronik Österreichs*. Dortmund: Chronik Verlag, 1984.
Klein-Löw, Stella. *Erinnerungen: Erlebtes und Gedachtes*. Vienna: Jugend und Volk, 1980.

Knight, Robert. *"Ich bin dafür, die Sache in die Länge zu ziehen"*: Wortprotokolle der österreichischen Bundesregierung von 1945–52 über die Entschädigung der Juden. Frankfurt am Main: Athenäum Verlag, 1988.

———. "'Neutrality,' Not Sympathy: Jews in Post-war Austria." In *Austrians and Jews in the Twentieth Century: From Franz Joseph to Waldheim*, edited by Robert S. Wistrich, 220–33. New York: St. Martin's, 1992.

Kochan, Miriam. "Women's Experiences of Internment." In *The Internment of Aliens in Twentieth Century Britain*, edited by David Cesarani and Tony Kushner, 147–66. London: Frank Cass, 1993.

Konrad, Helmut. "The Significance of February 1934 in Austria in Both National and International Context." In *Routes into Abyss: Coping with the Crises in the 1930s*, edited by Helmut Konrad and Wolfgang Maderthaner, 20–32. New York: Berghahn Books, 2013.

Koonz, Claudia. *Mothers in the Fatherland: Women, the Family, and Nazi Politics*. New York: St. Martin's, 1987.

Kotvytska, Olena. "Exilerfahrung und die Heimkehr österreichischer Autoren jüdischer Herkunft am Beispiel von Friedrich Torberg und Ernst Lothar." *Linguae Mundi* 5 (2010): 39–53.

Kraus, Marita. *Heimkehr in ein Fremdesland: Geschichte der Remigration nach 1945*. Munich: Beck, 2001.

Kreisky, Bruno. *Zwischen den Zeiten*. Berlin: Siedler, 1986.

Kreisky, Bruno, Matthew Paul Berg, Jill Lewis, and Oliver Rathkolb. *The Struggle for a Democratic Austria: Bruno Kreisky on Peace and Social Justice*. New York: Berghahn Books, 2000.

Kushner, Tony. "An Alien Occupation—Jewish Refugees and Domestic Service in Britain, 1933–1948." In *Second Chance: Two Centuries of German-speaking Jews in the United Kingdom*, edited by Werner E. Mosse, 553–78. Tübingen: J. C. B. Mohr, 1991.

———. *The Persistence of Prejudice*. Manchester: Manchester University Press, 1989.

Lachs, Minna. *Zwischen zwei Welten*. Vienna: Löcker Verlag, 1992.

Lagrou, Pieter. *The Legacy of Nazi Occupation: Patriotic Memory and National Recovery in Western Europe, 1945–1965*. Cambridge: Cambridge University Press, 1999.

Laqueur, Walter. *Generation Exodus: The Fate of Young Jewish Refugees from Nazi Germany*. Hanover, NH: Brandeis University Press, 2001.

Lavsky, Hagit. *New Beginnings: Holocaust Survivors in Bergen-Belsen and the British Zone in Germany, 1945–1950*. Detroit: Wayne State University Press, 2002.

Levenkron, Nomi. "'Prostitution,' Rape, and Sexual Slavery during World War II." In *Sexual Violence against Jewish Women during the Holocaust*, edited by Sonja Maria Hedgepeth and Rochelle G. Saidel, 13–28. Lebanon, NH: University Press of New England, 2010.

Lewis, Jill. "Dancing on a Tight Rope: The Beginning of the Marshall Plan." In *The Marshall Plan in Austria*, edited by Günter Bischof, Anton Pelinka, and Dieter Stiefel, 138–55. New Brunswick, NJ: Transaction, 2000.

London, Louise. *Whitehall and the Jews, 1933–1948*. New York: Cambridge University Press, 2000.

Lotteraner, Max. *Österreicher im Exil, 1934–1945*. Linz: Kammer für Arbeiter und Angestellte für Oberösterreich, 1977.

Lühe, Irmela von der, Axel Schildt, and Stefanie Schüler-Springorum. *"Auch in Deutschland waren wir nicht wirklich zu Hause": Jüdische Remigration nach 1945*. Göttingen: Wallstein, 2008.

MacDonogh, Giles. *1938: Hitler's Gamble*. New York: Basic Books, 2009.

Maderthamer, Wolfgang. "12 February 1934: Social Democracy and Civil War." In *Austria in the Twentieth Century*, edited by Rolf Steininger, Günter Bischof, and Michael Gehler, 45–71. New Brunswick, NJ: Transaction, 2002.

McCagg, William O. *A History of Habsburg Jews, 1670–1918*. Bloomington: Indiana University Press, 1989.

Meissel, Franz-Stefan, Thomas Olechowski, and Cristoph Gnant. *Untersuchungen zur Praxis der Verfahren vor den Rückstellungskommissionen*. Vienna: Oldenbourg Verlag, 2004.

Meyer, Beate. "Between Self-Assertion and Forced Collaboration: The Reich Association of Jews in Germany, 1939–1945." In *Jewish Life in Nazi Germany: Dilemmas and Responses*, edited by Francis R. Nicosia and David Scrase, 149–69. New York: Berghahn Books, 2012.

———. *"Jüdische Mischlinge": Rassenpolitik und Verfolgungserfahrung, 1933–1945*. Munich: Dölling und Galitz Verlag, 1999.

Michman, Dan. *The Emergence of Jewish Ghettos during the Holocaust*. Cambridge: Cambridge University Press, 2011.

Moser, C. Gwyn. "Jewish *U-Boote* in Austria, 1938–1945." *Simon Wiesenthal Center Annual* 2 (1985): 52–61.

Moser, Jonny. *Demographie der jüdischen Bevölkerung Österreichs, 1938–1945*. Vienna: Dokumentationsarchiv des österreichischen Widerstandes, 1999.

———. "Der Verfolgung der Juden." In *Widerstand und Verfolgung in Wien 1934–1945: Eine Dokumentation*, edited by Wolfgang Neugebauer, 335–40. Vienna: Österreichischer Bundesverlag für Unterricht, Wissenschaft und Kunst, 1975.

———. *Wallenbergs Laufbursche: Jugenderinnerungen, 1938–1945*. Vienna: Picus Verlag, 2006.

Muchitsch, Wolfgang. *Österreicher im Exil: Großbritannien, 1938–1945; Eine Dokumentation*. Edited by Dokumentationsarchiv des österreichischen Widerstandes. Vienna: Österreicher Bundesverlag, 1992.

My Knees Were Jumping: Remembering the Kindertransports. Directed by Melissa Hacker. Docurama, 2003. DVD.

Nationalsozialistische Deutsche Arbeiter-Partei and Robert Ley. *Organisationsbuch der NSDAP*. Munich: Zentralverlag der NSDAP, 1940.

Neck, Rudolf, Adam Wandruszka, Kurt Peball, and Isabella Ackerl. *Protokolle des Ministerrates der Ersten Republik, 1918–1938*. Vienna: Verlag der Österreichischen Staatsdruckerei, 1980.

Neugebauer, Wolfgang. *Widerstand und Verfolgung in Wien, 1934–1945: Eine Dokumentation*. Vol. 3. Vienna: Österreichischer Bundesverlag für Unterricht, Wissenschaft und Kunst, 1975.

Niederland, Doron. "Die Immigration." In *Vertreibung und Neubeginn: Israelische Bürger österreichischer Herkunft*, edited by Erika Weinzierl and Otto D. Kulka, 339–444. Vienna: Böhlau Verlag, 1992.
Niklas, Martin. ". . . *Die schönste Stadt der Welt": Österreichische Jüdinnen und Juden in Theresienstadt*. Vienna: Dokumentationsarchiv des Österreichischen Widerstandes, 2009.
Offenberger, Ilana. *The Jews of Nazi Vienna, 1938–1945: Rescue and Destruction*. New York: Palgrave Macmillan, 2017.
Pauley, Bruce F. "Austria." In *The World Reacts to the Holocaust*, edited by David S. Wyman, 473–513. Baltimore: Johns Hopkins University Press, 1996.
———. *From Prejudice to Persecution: A History of Austrian Antisemitism*. Chapel Hill: University of North Carolina Press, 1992.
———. "Political Antisemitism in Interwar Vienna." In *Jews, Antisemitism and Culture in Vienna*, edited by Ivar Oxaal, Michael Pollak, and Gerhard Botz, 152–73. London: Routledge and Kegan Paul, 1987.
Pelinka, Anton. "Mainstreaming der jüdischen Identität? Wie der Antisemitismus einen logischen Mix an Identitäten verhindert—am Beispiel Bruno Kreisky." *Das Jüdische Echo* 57 (2008–9): 119–23.
Pick, Hella. *Guilty Victim: Austria from the Holocaust to Haider*. New York: I. B. Tauris, 2000.
Pulzer, Peter. "Between Collectivism and Liberalism: The Political Evolution of Austria since 1945." In *Austria 1945–95: Fifty Years of the Second Republic*, edited by Kurt Richard Luther and Peter Pulzer, 227–34. Aldershot, UK: Ashgate, 1998.
Rabinbach, Anson. *The Crisis of Austrian Socialism: From Red Vienna to Civil War, 1927–1934*. Chicago: University of Chicago Press, 1983.
Rabinovici, Doron. *Instanzen der Ohnmacht: Wien 1938–1945, der Weg zum Judenrat*. Frankfurt am Main: Jüdischer Verlag, 2000.
Rathkolb, Oliver. *Die paradoxe Republik: Österreich 1945 bis 2005*. Vienna: Zsolnay, 2005.
Rattner, Anna, and Lola Blonder. *1938—Zuflucht Palästina: Zwei Frauen berichten*. Vienna: Geyer, 1989.
Red-White-Red Book: Justice for Austria; Descriptions, Documents and Proofs to the Antecedents and History of the Occupation of Austria, from Official Sources. Vienna: Austrian State Printing House, 1947.
Reilly, Joanne. *Belsen: The Liberation of a Concentration Camp*. London: Routledge, 1998.
Reinprecht, Christoph. "Jewish Identity in Postwar Austria: Experiences and Dilemmas." In *Jewish Studies at the Central European University: Public Lectures, 1996–1999*, edited by András Kovács and Eszter Andor, 203–15. Budapest: Central European University, 2000.
———. *Zurückgekehrt: Identität und Bruch in der Biographie österreichischer Juden*. Vienna: Braumüller, 1992.
Reiter, Andrea. "Political Exile and Exile Politics in Britain: Introduction." In *Political Exile and Exile Politics in Britain after 1933*, edited by Anthony Grenville and Andrea Reiter, xi–xxvii Amsterdam: Rodopi, 2011.
Rosenkranz, Herbert. *Verfolgung und Selbstbehauptung: Die Juden in Österreich, 1938–1945*. Vienna: Herold Verlag, 1978.

Rot-Weiss-Rot Buch: Gerechtigkeit für Österreich! Darstellungen, Dokumente und Nachweise zur Vorgeschichte und Geschichte der Okkupation Österreichs (nach amtlichen Quellen). Vienna: Druck und Verlag der österreichischen Staatsdruckerei, 1946.

Rousso, Henry. *The Vichy Syndrome: History and Memory in France since 1944.* Cambridge, MA: Harvard University Press, 2006.

Rozenblit, Marsha. *The Jews of Vienna, 1867–1914.* Albany: State University of New York Press, 1983.

———. *Reconstructing a National Identity: The Jews of Habsburg Austria during World War I.* New York: Oxford University Press, 2001.

Safrian, Hans. *Eichmann's Men.* Cambridge: Cambridge University Press, 2010.

Safrian, Hans, and Hans Witek. *Und keiner war dabei: Dokumente des alltäglichen Antisemitismus in Wien 1938.* Vienna: Picus Verlag, 1988.

Sagi, Nana. *German Reparations: A History of Negotiations.* Jerusalem: Magnes, Hebrew University, 1986.

Sauer, Barbara, and Ilse Reiter-Zatloukal. *Advokaten 1938: Das Schicksal der in den Jahren 1938 bis 1945 verfolgten österreichischen Rechtsanwältinnen und Rechtsanwälte.* Vienna: Manz, 2010.

Schefbeck, Günther. *Österreich 1934: Vorgeschichte—Ereignisse—Wirkungen.* Vienna: Verlag für Geschichte und Politik, 2004.

Schneider, Gertrude. *Exile and Destruction: The Fate of Austrian Jews, 1938–1945.* Westport, CT: Praeger, 1995.

Scholz, Wilhelm. *Ein Weg ins Leben: Das neue Österreich und die Judenfrage.* London: Free Austrian Books, 1943.

Schorske, Carl E. *Fin-de-Siècle Vienna: Politics and Culture.* New York: Knopf, 1980.

Schwarz, Ursula. "Das Wiener Verlagswesen der Nachkriegszeit: Eine Untersuchung der Rolle der öffentlichen Verwalter bei der Entnazifizierung und bei der Rückstellung arisierter Verlage und Buchhandlungen." Diplomarbeit, Universität Wien, 2003.

Segalman, Ralph. "Letters to My Grandchildren." Unpublished memoir, Northridge, CA, 2001.

Segev, Tom. *Simon Wiesenthal: The Life and Legends.* New York: Doubleday, 2010.

Sekules, Edith. *Surviving the Nazis, Exile, and Siberia.* Portland, OR: Vallentine Mitchell, 2000.

Sherman, A. J. *Island Refuge: Britain and the Refugees from the Third Reich, 1933–1939.* Berkeley: University of California Press, 1973.

Silverman, Lisa. *Becoming Austrians: Jews and Culture between the World Wars.* Oxford: Oxford University Press, 2012.

———. "Repossessing the Past? Property, Memory and Austrian Jewish Narrative Histories." *Austrian Studies* 11 (2003): 138–53.

Simon, Maria Dorothea. "Selbstzeugnis." In *Soziale Arbeit in Selbstzeugnissen*, vol. 2, edited by Hermann Heitkamp and Alfred Plewa, 225–72. Freiburg in Breisgau: Lambertus, 2002.

Spiel, Hilde. *Rückkehr nach Wien: Ein Tagebuch.* Vienna: Milena Verlag, 2009.

Steininger, Rolf. *Austria, Germany, and the Cold War: From the Anschluss to the State Treaty.* New York: Berghahn Books, 2008.

———. "12 November 1918–2 March 1938: The Road to the Anschluß." In *Austria in the Twentieth Century*, edited by Rolf Steininger, Günter Bischof, and Michael Gehler, 85–114. New Brunswick, NJ: Transaction, 2002.
Stent, Ronald. *A Bespattered Page? The Internment of "His Majesty's Most Loyal Enemy Aliens."* London: Andre Deutsch, 1980.
Stibbe, Matthew. *Women in the Third Reich*. London: Arnold, 2003.
Stone, Dan. *The Liberation of the Camps: The End of the Holocaust and Its Aftermath*. New Haven, CT: Yale University Press, 2015.
Szymanski, Tekla. "Der *Aufbau*—'Unser Aller Tagebuch.'" In *Die Jeckes*, edited by Gisela Dachs, 108–18. Frankfurt am Main: Jüdischer Verlag im Suhrkamp-Verlag, 2005.
Tausig, Franziska. *Shanghai Passage: Flucht und Exil einer Wienerin*. Vienna: Verlag für Gesellschaftskritik, 1987.
Taylor, Frederick. *Exorcising Hitler: The Occupation and Denazification of Germany*. London: Bloomsbury, 2011.
Teschner, Gerhard J. "Saar Region." In *The Greater German Reich and the Jews: Nazi Persecution Policies in the Annexed Territories, 1935–1945*, edited by Wolf Gruner and Jörg Osterloh, 13–38. New York: Berghahn Books, 2015.
Thalberg, Hans. *Von der Kunst, Österreicher zu sein: Erinnerungen und Tagebuchnotizen*. Vienna: Böhlau Verlag, 1984.
Thomas, Hugh. *The Spanish Civil War*. London: Penguin, 2001.
Thurner, Erika. "Nazi and Postwar Policy against Roma and Sinti in Austria." In *The Roma—a Minority in Europe*, edited by Roni Stauber and Raphael Vago, 55–67. Budapest: Central European University Press, 2007.
Torberg, Friedrich. *Die Tante Jolesch oder der Untergang des Abendlandes in Anekdoten*. Munich: Georg Müller Verlag, 1975.
Tragl, Karl Heinz. *Chronik der Wiener Krankenanstalten*. Vienna: Böhlau Verlag, 2007.
Trahan, Elizabeth Welt. *Walking with Ghosts: A Jewish Childhood in Wartime Vienna*. New York: Peter Lang, 1998.
Uhl, Heidemarie. "Das österreichische Gedächtnis." In *Die Lebendigkeit der Geschichte—(Dis-)Kontinuitäten in Diskursen über den Nationalsozialismus*, edited by Eleonore Lappin and Bernhard Schneider, 30–46. St. Ingbert: Röhrig, 2001.
———. "From Victim Myth to Co-responsibility Thesis: Nazi Rule, World War II, and the Holocaust in Austrian Memory." In *The Politics of Memory in Postwar Europe*, edited by Richard Ned Lebow, Wulf Kansteiner, and Claudio Fogu, 40–72. Durham, NC: Duke University Press, 2006.
———. "The Politics of Memory: Austria's Perception of the Second World War and the National Socialist Period." In *Austrian Historical Memory and National Identity*, Contemporary Austrian Studies 5, edited by Günter Bischof and Anton Pelinka, 64–94. New Brunswick, NJ: Transaction, 1997.
Ungar-Klein, Brigitte. "Bei Freunden untergetaucht—U-Boot in Wien." In *Der Pogrom 1938: Judenverfolgung in Österreich und Deutschland; Dokumentation eines Symposiums der Volkshochschule Brigittenau*, edited by Kurt Schmid and Robert Streibel, 87–92. Vienna: Picus Verlag, 1990.

Ungar-Klein, Brigitte. "Überleben im Versteck—Rückkehr in die Normalität?" In *Überleben der Shoah—und danach*, edited by Alexander Friedmann, Elvira Glück, and David Vyssoki, 31–57. Vienna: Picus Verlag, 1999.

US Congress, Senate Committee on Foreign Relations, and US Department of State. *A Decade of American Foreign Policy: Basic Documents, 1941–49*. Washington, DC: Government Printing Office, 1950.

Utgaard, Peter. *Remembering and Forgetting Nazism: Education, National Identity, and the Victim Myth in Postwar Austria*. New York: Berghahn Books, 2003.

Vansant, Jacqueline. *Reclaiming Heimat: Trauma and Mourning in Memoirs by Jewish Austrian Reémigrés*. Detroit: Wayne State University Press, 2001.

Wahrhaftig, Zorach. *Uprooted: Jewish Refugees and Displaced Persons after Liberation*. New York: Institute of Jewish Affairs of the American Jewish Congress and World Jewish Congress, 1946.

Warren, John. "'Weiße Strümpfe oder neue Kutten': Cultural Decline in Vienna in the 1930s." In *Interwar Vienna: Culture Between Tradition and Modernity*, edited by Deborah Holmes and Lisa Silverman, 32–55. Rochester, NY: Camden House, 2009.

Wasserstein, Bernard. *Britain and the Jews of Europe, 1939–1945*. Oxford: Oxford University Press, 1988.

Weindling, Paul. "The Contribution of Central European Jews to Medical Science and Practice in Britain in the 1930s–1950s." In *Second Chance: Two Centuries of German-Speaking Jews in the United Kingdom*, edited by Werner E. Mosse, Julius Carlebach, and Gerhard Hirschfeld, 243–54. Tübingen: J. C. B. Mohr, 1991.

Weinzierl, Erika. *Zu wenig Gerechte: Österreicher und Judenverfolgung in 1938–1945*. Graz: Verlag Styria, 1969.

Weinzierl, Erika, and Otto D. Kulka, eds. *Vertreibung und Neubeginn: Israelische Bürger österreichischer Herkunft*. Vienna: Böhlau Verlag, 1992.

Welcome in Vienna: Wohin und Zurück. Written by Georg Stefan Troller. Directed by Axel Corti. Austria, 1986.

West, Franz Carl. *Zurück oder nicht zurück?* London: Free Austrian Movement / Austrian Centre, 1942.

Westphal, Uwe. "German, Czech and Austrian Jews in English Publishing." In *Second Chance: Two Centuries of German-Speaking Jews in the United Kingdom*, edited by Werner E. Mosse, Julius Carlebach, and Gerhard Hirschfeld, 195–208. Tübingen: J. C. B. Mohr, 1991.

Wexberg-Kubesch, Anna. *Vergiss nie, dass Du ein jüdisches Kind bist: Der Kindertransport nach England, 1938/39*. Vienna: Mandelbaum Verlag, 2013.

Whiteside, Andrew Gladding. *The Socialism of Fools: Georg Ritter von Schönerer and Austrian Pan-Germanism*. Berkeley: University of California Press, 1975.

Wiesmüller, Wolfgang. *Eine Schwierige Heimkehr: Österreichischen Literatur im Exil, 1938–1945*. Innsbruck: Institut für Germanistik, 1991.

Wilder-Okladek, F. *The Return Movement of Jews to Austria after the Second World War*. The Hague: Martinus Nijhoff, 1969.

Wilsford, David. *Political Leaders of Contemporary Western Europe: A Biographical Dictionary*. Westport, CT: Greenwood, 1995.
Wistrich, Robert S. *From Ambivalence to Betrayal: The Left, the Jews, and Israel*. Lincoln: University of Nebraska Press, 2012.
———. *A Lethal Obsession: Antisemitism from Antiquity to the Global Jihad*. New York: Random House, 2010.
Wyman, Mark. *DP: Europe's Displaced Persons*. Ithaca, NY: Cornell University Press, 1998.
Yablonka, Hanna. *Survivors of the Holocaust: Israel after the War*. New York: NYU Press, 1999.
Zangl, Veronika. "Remigration and Lost Time: Resuming Life after the Holocaust." In *Memory and Migration: Multidisciplinary Approaches to Memory*, edited by Julia Creet and Andreas Kitzmann, 52–67. Toronto: University of Toronto Press, 2011.
Zöllner, Erich. *Geschichte Österreichs: Von den Anfängen bis zur Gegenwart*. 8th ed. Munich: Verlag für Geschichte und Politik Wien, R. Oldenbourg Verlag, 1990.
Zelman, Leon. "Wiener jüdische Gemeinde nach 1945." *Mitteilungsblatt der Aktion gegen den Antisemitismus* 120 (November 1990).
Zubok, Vladislav M. *Failed Empire: The Soviet Union in the Cold War from Stalin to Gorbachev*. Chapel Hill: University of North Carolina Press, 2009.

INDEX

Page numbers in italics refer to tables and illustrations.

air raids, 53, 55, 93n28, 100, 151–52, 232
Allied Council, 66, 206, 209
Allied occupation, 3–4, 10, 11, 42, 143; Austrian government and, 104–6, 205–7; Austrian identity and, 206–8, 214–15; on "denazification," 199–200, 205; employment with, 150, 172–73; rebuilding Vienna and, 66–67, 82; reparations and, 206, 211–12, 218; Soviet Union and, 61, 66, 207, 214; victim myth and, 67, 156, 205–7
Alpinists, 46, 46n15
Ältestenrat, 45–46, 49, 51, 70, 115, 211; leaders, 40, 41n87, 43, 45, 70, 88; surviving officials and families, 48–49; war crimes and trials of, 76–81
American Jewish Joint Distribution Committee (Joint or JDC), 35, 73, 74, 75–76, 80, 94–95, 98, 113, 114, 121, 145–46, 159, 169, 170, 171, 173, 191, 192–95, 198, 214
Améry, Jean, 128–29
Anschluss: antisemitism and, 18–19; Austria becoming Greater Germany, 24–27; Austrian Communist Party before, 130–32; Austrian Communist Party on, 24–25; Austrian government and, 107, 197–98; concept of, 8, 18–19; "first victim" argument and nullification of, 197–98; gender roles after, 35–37; history of, 8–9, 11, 18–19; Italy and, 24–25; Nazis and, 25–26, 127–28, 131–32; opposition to, 23–25; politics before, 130–32; politics of, 21–26, 127–30;
post-Anschluss realities, 26–29; Social Democratic Party before, 130–32; Social Democratic Party on, 24–25; violence after, 27–28, 34–35
antifascism, 68, 106, 155–56, 198, 216, 221, 237
antisemitism, 1, 3, 59, 99–103, 151–54, 177–78, 185–86, 211; Anschluss and, 18–19; in Austrian government, 198–205; Austrian nationalism and, 17–18, 142; Catholic, 68; in employment, 185–86; German nationalism and, 18, 142; for Jewish returnees, 111, 130, 144–47, 151–54, 212; in legislation, 22, 209–15, 217–22; postwar, 10, 59–60, 67–69, 97, 98, 99–103, 151–54, 177–78, 185–86, 198–99, 211, 231–35; property ownership and, 198–99; racism and, 18; after World War I, 7–8. *See also* persecution of Jews; violence
AP (Associated Press), 182
"Aryanization," 10; concentration camps and, 28–29; Jewish persecution and, 27–29, 33, 57, 99, 109–10, 152; property ownership and, 27–28, 29, 33, 57, 97, 100, 109–12, 207–12, 214–18; Reich Flight Tax and, 217–18; "wild Aryanization," 27–28, 33
Asch, Alexander, 96–97
Asch, Lili, 96–97, 96nn39–42
Asch, Sholem, 97
Assets Transfer Agency, 33
Associated Press (AP), 182
Association of Jewish Refugees (UK), 105

259

Aufbau (publication), 72–73, 76, 82, 164
Ausgleich, 17–18, 19
Austria: 1848 Revolution in, 17; Cold War and, 10–11; economy in, 22–23, 56, 113, 224–25; German departure from, 9; history of Jews in, 15–26; map of, 1933, 24. *See also under specific topics*
Austrian Centre, 133–38, 135, 141–42; closure of, 143
Austrian citizenship: for Jews, 17, 19, 51, 65–66, 67, 204–5; victim status and, 107, 203; after World War II, 65–66, 198
Austrian Communist Party (KPÖ), 1, 69, 73, 134–38, 161; before Anschluss, 23–25, 130–32; on Anschluss, 24–25; in exile, 132–43; FAM and, 138–41; postwar realities and, 154–60; preparing communists for return to political home, 9, 141–43; victim myth and, 127–30, 137, 138–41, 143–44, 146, 162–63, 239; after World War II, 104, 143–54; during World War II, 125–33
Austrian government: Allied occupation and, 104–6, 205–7; Anschluss and, 107, 197–98; antisemitism in, 198–205; Austrian elections after war, 67–69, 154, 155–59, 198–99, 215, 233–34; coalition government and new Austrian identity, 155–59; concentration camp survivor benefits from, 107–9; concentration camp survivors' reception by, 104–12; IKG, KPÖ, and SPÖ in postwar reconstruction, 159–60; Jewish exclusion from victim assistance by, 202–5; on Nazi war crimes, 104–7; postwar political parties, 10, 105, 106, 156–57, 199–200, 215–16, 226, 235; postwar reintegration of Nazis by, 105, 112, 156–57, 199–200, 204–5, 214, 215, 227, 237; on property, 57–58, 64, 97, 109–12, 157, 199, 201, 207–15; during Renner government, 62–66, 67, 68, 93, 104–6, 111, 155, 197–205, 210; victim myth and, 62, 66, 68, 104–9, 138–41, 146–47, 155–59, 162, 197–201, 202–5, 215–17; victim status and, 106–9, 156–58, 159, 203–5, 226–27. *See also* politics
Austrian Historical Commission, 226–27, 227n116

Austrian independence, 1, 25, 63, 197, 240
Austrian Labour Club, 137–38
Austrian national identity, 13, 68, 105–9; Allied occupation and, 206–8, 214–15; Austrian collective and, 4, 230; coalition government and new, 155–59; after Habsburg Empire, 21–22; postwar struggle for, 152–53, 214–17; restitution and, 214–17
Austrian News (publication), 141
Austrian Social Democratic Party (SPÖ), 68n85, 154, 163, 183, 236–38; before Anschluss, 21–23, 130–32; on Anschluss, 24–25; in exile, 9, 126–30, 132–43; FAM and, 140–41; London Bureau of the Austrian Socialists and, 140–41; political home and, 128; SPÖ, 110, 153–60; victim myth and, 127–30, 138–41, 143–44, 155–56, 162–63, 239; after World War II, 68–69, 110, 143–54; during World War II, 126–30
Austrian State Treaty (1955), 206, 236, 240
Austrian War Criminal Law (1945), 80–81
Austrofascism, 8, 24–25, 127, 130, 236

Baeck, Leo, 74
Baltic states, 38–39, 170
basic needs: for concentration camp survivors, 86, 113–15; provisions and communication through Kultusgemeinde, 113–15; securing, 56–58, 61, 72–73, 86, 113–15; for survivors of Soviet labor camps, 171
Bauer, Otto, 69
BDM (Bund Deutscher Mädel), 232
Beckerman, Ruth, 172n21
Bei, Gao, 192n8
belonging, 3–5, 129–30, 234
Benedikt, Heinrich, 176
Berger, Trude, 53, 53n43, 55, 56, 58–59, 83, 230n124
Between Dignity and Despair (Kaplan), 36
Binder, Trude, 95, 100–101
Bischoff, Karl H., 181
black market, 20, 56, 61, 113
Bloch, Joseph Samuel, 17
books, 125–26; banned, 164
Brill, David, 71, 159–60, 210, 214

British Labour Party, 138
Brod, Max, 165–66
Brück, Gizela, 16
Bund Deutscher Mädel (BDM), 232
Bürckel, Josef, 30–31
Burgenland, 60, 61

Caro, Gabriele (Jella), 120, 120n133
Case of Austria, The (publication), 139–40
Catholic antisemitism, 68
Catholic fascism, 8, 24–25
Catholicism, 19, 23, 29
censorship, 125–26
Central Powers, World War I, 7–8
Chandler, Gertrude, 123
Chanukah celebrations, 114, 121
children, 32, 34–35, 39, 72, 148; education for, 121
Christian Social Party, 18, 23–24, 154
Churchill, Winston, 10
civil war of 1934, 23–24, 130–31
Clare, George, 81, 152
Clark, General Mark, 66, 72, 75, 110–11, 118–19, 212
clothing, 152–53
coalition government, 68, 154, 154–59
Cold War, 62, 104, 144, 163, 188, 201, 206–7, 214, 221, 235; Austria and, 10–11; communism and, 66–67
communication, 113–45
communism, 66–67, 69; disillusionment with, 160–63. *See also* Austrian Communist Party
concentration camps, 25–26, 36, 38–39, 127, 175, 192, 197; death marches and, 84, 87, 90
concentration camp survivors, 2, 7, 9, 12, 42, 64, 71, 72–73, 84–124, 202, 221; arriving home, 93–103, 123–24, 239; Austrian government and reception of, 104–12; basic needs for, 86–87, 113–15; elderly, 91–93, 119–20; familial home for, 86, 95, 123–24; gentiles' interactions with, 99–103, 208; government benefits for, 107–9; IKG and, 95, 98, 112–23; repatriation transports for, 87–90; return journeys, 86–93; searching for family and friends, 94–97; in Terezín, 87–90, 93, 93n27
Conrads, Heinz, 237
Corti, Axel, 171n19
Csillag, Ernst, 170–71, 170n12, 185–86, 188–89
Czechoslovakia, 107; Austrian political parties' activity in, 131; Soviet Union in, 154–55, 161
Czuczka, Charlotte, 36–37

Danneberg-Löw, Franzi, 49
Danube Canal, 44–45, 53–54, 54
death marches, 84, 87, 90, 123
denazification, 177–79, 184, 196, 211, 215, 224, 231n127; Allied occupation and, 67, 156, 199–200, 205, 240; of IKG and Jewish community, 76–81; politics and, 199–200; reparations and, 106, 199–200
deportations, Nazi: 8, 25, 28, 39, 40, 46, 48, 49–50, 51, 65, 76–81, 87, 88, 93, 96n39, 98n48, 101, 108, 116, 120n133, 162, 172, 175, 177
displaced persons (DPs), 3, 96, 99, 103, 113, 118, 120–22, 164, 171, 198, 200–201. *See also* emigration; exile; Jewish returnees
doctors, 9, 76, 80, 108, 168, 176, 177, 184–85, 239
Dollfuss, Engelbert, 23–24, 131
DPs. *See* displaced persons
Dutch Jews, 6, 6n11
Dwork, Debórah, 38

Eckstein, Tanja, 15n1
economy: in Austria, 22–23, 67, 184, 224–25, 236; black market and, 56, 113; restitution and, 224–25
education: for children, 121; after exile, 148, 149–50
Ehrlich, Aaron, 67–68, 111
Eichmann, Adolf, 29–31, 77, 79
elderly: from concentration camps, 91–93, 116; KZ Rückkehrerheim at Seegasse 9 and, 115–23; survivors, 98, 114; in Terezín, 87–88, 93; Viennese Jews, 31, 32, 87
Embacher, Helga, 40, 73, 77, 169

emigration, 2, 13, 36, 69, 82, 90, 194–95; Emigration Department and management of, 30–35, 31n55, 77; fees and taxes, 32, 34; forced, 4–5, 7, 8, 13, 31–35, 70, 116, 228, 236; IKG and, 30–35, 39, 133; Jewish persecution and, 33–35, 40–41; of Jewish survivors, 5–6, 81–82, 236; passports and, 33; plan for expulsion and, 30–31; property ownership and, 33–34; refugees and, 34–35, 134–36, 164–67, 191–95; requirements and clearance for, 31–34; totals, 37–38, 39, 39n80, 133, 228; to United Kingdom, 1–2, 32, 34–35, 37, 39, 125, 133–34, 168, 176, 179, 181, 184, 232–33; to United States, 13, 26n35, 37–38, 39, 74, 76, 79, 82n138, 97, 158–59, 164–65, 168, 174, 179, 184; for women, 32, 36–37, 39. *See also* exile; Jewish returnees

employment, 35, 52; with Allied occupation, 150, 172–73; antisemitism in, 185–86; for bankers, 182; with Communist Party, 148, 150; for doctors, 176, 177, 184–85; after exile, 147–50, 171–74; finding, 97–99; identity and, 229–30; with IKG, 2, 8, 40, 49, 76–77, 88, 99, 239; for journalists and publishing, 169, 181–82; by KZ Rückkehrerheim at Seegasse 9, 120; for lawyers, 169, 182–84; postwar issues in, 180–89; professional returnees and, 164–74; professionals in postwar Vienna, 180–82; reestablishing, 164–68, 171–74; victim myth and, 172

energy utilities, 56, 61

entertainment, 114, 121–22; at the Austrian Centre, 134–36

exile: Austrian Centre, 1, 134–38, 141–44, 146, 148, 155; Austrian Centre and Young Austria in, 133–38, 135; 144; Austrian Communist Party in, 132–43; creating new homes abroad, 4–5, 174–80; education after, 148, 149–50, 150n76; employment after, 147–50, 167–89; expectation encounters reality after, 144–47; forced emigration and, 4–5, 7, 13, 31–35, 236; gender and, 174–80; gentiles and returnees from, 147, 151–54, 178, 232–34; home after, 2, 5, 147–54, 238–42; housing after, 147–50, 186–87; identity and, 128–29, 174–80; Jewish returnees from, 9–10, 143–54, 169–80; lands of, 37–41; male refugees in, 174–80; in Palestine, 169–70, 173–76, 180–81, 185; political activity in, 126–30, 132–43; political home and, 127–30, 141–43; reestablishing lives after, 147–50, 171–74; returning to Vienna after, 143–54; in Shanghai, 38, 190–96; Social Democratic Party in, 132–43; in United Kingdom, 1, 32, 34, 39, 133–34, 232–33; in United States, 164–65; World War II in, 132–43

FAM (Free Austrian Movement), 138–41, 144, 155

familial home, 4, 7, 8–9, 37, 228–29, 238–39; for concentration camp survivors, 86, 95, 123–24; gender and, 168, 180, 195

family and friends: during Habsburg Empire, 41–42; searching for, 55, 82, 94–97

fascism: antifascism and, 68, 106, 127, 155–57, 197–98, 216, 221. Austrofascism, 8, 24–25, 127; Catholic, 8, 24–25; in Italy, 23–24

Fatherland Front, 23–24, 25, 29, 29n42, 131

FAWM (Free Austrian World Movement), 158

Feldsberg, Gerda, 16

Figl, Leopold, 68–69, 197–99, 206, 240

Fischer, Ernst, 159, 160

Fischer, Frau, 179–80

Fischer, Hannah, 130, 147–48, 151–52

Flight from the Reich (Dwork and van Pelt), 38

FÖJ (Freie Österreichische Jugend), 149

food scarcity, 1, 20, 43, 56, 61, 93, 97, 117–18, 144, 147

footwear, 61, 152–53

foreign organizations and Jewish community, 32, 64, 73–76, 108, 113, 159, 207. *See also* American Jewish Joint Distribution Committee

Förstergasse: cellar, 43–45; massacre, 44–45, 53n43

Fraenkel, Frieda (Frau), 210, 210n71, 233–34

France, 13, 41n88, 131, 132, 136, 146. *See also* Paris

Fräser, Kurt, 172–73, 172n21, 211
Free Austrian Fighting Unit, 140
Free Austrian Movement (FAM), 138–41, 144, 155
Free Austrian World Movement (FAWM), 158
"freedom fighters" designation, 204
Freie Österreichische Jugend (FÖJ), 149
Freud, Anna, 148, 179
Freud, Sigmund, 12–14
Freundlich, Elisabeth, 188
Friedjung, Prive, 131, 148
Friedman, Towiah (also Tuviah), 78, 173–74
furniture and home goods, 57–58, 210–11

Geiringer, Gerda, 146–47
Geller, Jay Howard, 76n113
Gemeinde (magazine), 69–70
gender: Anschluss and new roles of, 35–37; exile and, 174–80; familial home and, 168; German culture and, 36; identity and, 174–80; Jewish returnee's gendered experiences, 174–80; mixed marriages and, 50–51; professional home and, 168; victim myth relating to, 178–79
gentiles, 9; antisemitism from, 99–103, 151–54, 177–78; "Aryanization" and, 27–29; disappointing responses from, 151–54; distrust of, 58–59; exiles and, 147, 151–54, 178, 232–34; housing for, 100; identity and, 232–34; interacting with, 99–103, 151–54; Nazis and, 3; Polish, 103; support from, 100–101
George, Manfred, 76
German nationalism: antisemitism and, 18; Austrian Nazi Party and, 22–23; Christian Social Party and, 23; Habsburg Empire and, 18–19, 21–22; Pan-German Party and, 17–18
German National Socialist Workers' Party (Deutsche Nationalsozialistische Arbeiterpartei or DNSAP), 22–23
German Revolution, 1848–1849, 18
Gestapo arrests, 25, 48, 48n21, 108
Gorbach, Alfons, 157
Gottschalk, Hans Ludwig, 176

Great Britain. *See* United Kingdom
Greenleigh, Arthur, 193
Grossmann, Atina, 75–76

H., Theresia, 108–9
Habsburg Empire, 7–8, 15–19, 33, 165, 182; Austrian identity after, 21–22; dissolution of, 20–21; German nationalism and, 18–19, 21–22; Jewish family life during, 41–42
Hacker, Iwan, 69
Hahn, Franz, 99, 102–3, 102nn65–67
Hakoah, 72, 76
Hartwich, A., 184
Hausner, Gideon, 78
Heilman, Lucia, 46–47, 46n15, 54, 57, 59
Heimat, 11–12, 191
Helmer, Oskar, 157, 200, 218, 219, 220, 222
Herz, Helen, 19
Herz, Peter, 122
Herzog, Kurt, 101
Hirschmann, Max, 121
Hitler, Adolf, 8, 22–23, 25, 78, 129, 145, 146, 230
Hitler Youth, 142–43, 232
Holocaust survivors: definition of, 12; elderly, 91–93, 119–20
Holzer, Anni, 84–85, 90, 91, 96, 99
Holzer, Edith, 84–85, 90, 91, 96, 99
home: concentration camp survivors' arrival at, 93–103, 123–24, 239; creating new, abroad, 4–5, 174–80; after exile, 2, 5, 146–54, 238–42; familial, 4, 7–9, 37, 86, 95, 96, 123–24, 167, 168, 174–80, 195, 229, 238–39; identity and, 4, 128–30, 228–31; political, 4, 7, 9, 127–30, 141–43, 161, 238–39; professional, 4, 7, 9–10, 164–69, 174–85, 195, 239–40; women and, 37, 168, 174–75
homelessness, 56–58, 98, 100, 112, 171, 187, 208
hospitals, 49, 70, 72–73, 80, 96, 99, 114, 115–23, 171, 185, 211, 214
housing: assignments, 97–98; after exile, 147–50, 186–87. 194; finding, 56–58, 97–99, 119, 147–48, 186–87, 202, 208, 232; furniture and home goods, 57–58, 210–11; for gentiles, 100, 107; IKG and, 98, 112, 115,

housing (*continued*)
159, 211–12; reclaiming property ownership and, 207–15
How We Lived (*Wie wir gelebt haben*; Eckstein and Kaldori), 15–17, 15n1, 41–42
Hungarian Uprising of 1956, 154–55, 161

identity: Austrian, 4, 9, 10, 13, 21–22, 23, 59, 66, 68, 104, 105–6, 152–53, 155–59, 185, 188, 196, 197–201, 205–7, 214–17, 227, 230, 234–35, 238, 240–41, 242; clothing and, 152–53; employment and, 229–30; exile and, 128–29, 174–80; gender and, 37, 174–80; gentiles and, 232–34; for Habsburg Jews, 19–20; home and, 4, 128–30, 228–31; for Jewish returnees, 3–4, 228–34; politics relating to, 128–29; religious and political, 236–38; Viennese, 4, 19–20, 227–35, 241–42; Viennese Jewish, 10, 73, 166, 169, 196, 227–35, 238, 240–42. *See also* Jewish identity
Israelitische Kultusgemeinde Wien (IKG), 3n6, 27, 44n6, 52, 65, 69, 70, 92, 94–5, 123, 157; Ältestenrat, 45–46, 49, 51, 70, 115, 211; Communist Party and, 154, 159–60; concentration camp survivors and, 95, 98, 112–23; controversies surrounding, 76–81; "denazification" of, 76–81; Eichmann, Adolf and, 29–31, 77; emigration and, 8, 30–35, 39, 40–41, 79, 92, 133; employment with, 2, 40, 43, 49, 99; foreign organizations and, 73–76, 108; housing and, 97–98, 211–12; Jewish identity and, 20–21; KZ Rückkehrerheim at Seegasse 9, 115–23; leadership, 29, 31, 40, 41n87, 45, 81, 88; Löwenherz, Josef and, 29–30, 41n87, 45, 77–79, 88; member totals, 70, 85; Murmelstein, Benjamin and, 77–78, 78n121, 79; under Nazis, 29–35, 40, 48–49; in postwar reconstruction, 159–60, 160n105; provisions and communication through Kultusgemeinde, 64, 72–73, 113–14, 191; reconstituting, 70–71, 81–83; religion and, 20–21; restitution of Jewish community property, 72–73, 110–11, 115, 117, 122, 157, 200, 211–12, 214; at Terezín, 88, 116–17; surviving officials and families, 48–49
Italy, 24–25, 210, 210n71

JDC. *See* American Jewish Joint Distribution Committee
Jenseits des Krieges (documentary), 172n21
Jewish acculturation, 82, 228
Jewish assimilation, 19, 46, 82, 232
Jewish businesses, 57, 109–10, 111, 182–85; boycott of, 22; persecution and dismissals of, 27–29, 28; restitution of, 100, 196, 199, 210, 213, 226, 240. *See also* employment
Jewish community of Vienna. *See* Israelitische Kultusgemeinde Wien
Jewish identity, 19–21; IKG and, 20–21; as not "Austrian," 3–4, 230; prewar and postwar, 227–35; for returnees, 4, 228–34; as Viennese, 3–4, 19–20, 169, 227–35; Viennese Jewish, 10, 73, 166, 169, 196, 227–35, 238, 240–42
Jewish leaders, 40–41, 41n87. *See also* Ältestenrat leaders; Israelitische Kultusgemeinde Wien, leadership
Jewish Telegraphic Agency (JTA), 88–90, 198–99, 210
Jews: citizenship in Austria, 65–66, 67, 110, 162, 179, 198, 203, 204; citizenship and emancipation in Austria-Hungary, 17, 19; citizenship under Nazi law, 51; Dutch, 6, 6n11; German, 5–6, 36, 87; history of, in Austria, 15–26; Polish, 68, 103, 169; population statistics of Austrian Jews, 2–3, 3n6, 6, 22, 40, 40n86, 70, 91–92; post-Anschluss realities for, 26–29; "protected" status, 5, 40, 43, 48–53, 70, 239; remaining in Vienna, 1945, 45–53; *U-Boote*, 2, 5–6, 46–48, 48n21, 92, 167–68, 239; World War I supported by, 20. *See also under specific topics*
Jews, Germans, and Allies (Grossmann), 75–76
Jews, in hiding, 2, 6, 8, 12, 40, 54, 57, 59, 95; at Förstergasse cellar, 43–45; Gestapo arrests of, 48, 48n21, 108; *U-Boote*, 2, 5–6, 46–48, 48n21, 92, 167–68, 239

Joint. *See* American Jewish Joint Distribution Committee
journalists, 138, 164, 169
JTA. *See* Jewish Telegraphic Agency
Judenräte, 31, 77, 88
Jüdisches Echo (magazine), 82
Justice in Jerusalem (Hausner), 78

Kadmon, Stella, 180–81, 186–87
Kammerling, Walter, 150, 152, 161
Kaplan, Marion, 36–37
Karaganda, 38–39, 170–71
Kazakhstan, 38–39, 170–71
Kindertransport, 34, 39, 133, 196
Klaar, Paul, 81
Klein-Löw, Stella, 143, 148–49
Knight, Robert, 218
Kocsiss, Josef, 16
Koppe, Bertha, 50–52
Koppe, Fritz, 51–52
Körner, Theodor, 191, 200
KPÖ. *See* Austrian Communist Party
Kraus, Josef, 156–57, 200
Kreisky, Bruno, 128, 132, 161n108, 204, 236–38; as *Entlastungsjude* ("exonerating Jew"), 237
Kriss, Susanne, 88n252, 94–95, 102
Kunschak, Leopold, 67–69, 198
KZ Rückkehrerheime, 98, 112; at Seegasse 9, 115–23
KZ-Verband, 44n6, 47–48, 64–65, 107–8

labor camps, 38–39, 49, 87, 170–71
Lachs, Ernst, 158
Lamberg, Susanne, 123–24
Landesmann, Edith, 16
Langnas, Mignon, 96
language: dialect, 152; euphemism, 230; Nazi, 11–12
Last Waltz in Vienna (Clare), 81
law: Allied occupation forces and, 206; antisemitic legislation and, 22, 33, 49, 50, 51–53, 209–15, 217–22; Austrian neutrality, 240; Austrian War Criminal Law and war crimes under, 80–81; lawyers and, 183–84; mixed marriage and, 50–51; Nazi legislation, 33, 40, 109; Nuremberg Laws, 47, 65–66, 110, 116; politics and, 10; property ownership and, 209–15, 213, 217–22; race and, 29, 49, 64–66, 74, 184–85; restitution, 10, 56, 63–64, 100, 109–12, 119, 199, 207–15, 217–23, 224, 225–27, 235, 240; upholding Nazi legislation, 109; victim status and, 64–65, 106–9, 196, 202–5, 225–27; Victims' Welfare Act and, 64–65, 202–4
lawyers, 9–10, 168, 169, 182–84, 239
Lazarowitsch, Nicholas, 117, 117n119, 119, 121
Leavitt, Moses, 193
Leopoldstädter Tempel, 27–28
Lessing, Erich, 181–82, 231–32, 231n127, 232n128, 234
"Letters to My Grandchildren" (Segalman), 94n30, 160n105
Levinson, Nathan Peter, 74
Lingens, Ella, 108, 108n87, 109
London Bureau of the Austrian Socialists, 140–41
Lothar, Ernst, 13–14, 230
Löwenherz, Josef, 29–30, 45, 88; arrest of, 77–79; controversies surrounding, 41n87, 77–79
Lueger, Karl, 18

male refugees, in exile, 174–80
Mandl, Felix, 185
Mao Zedong, 194
Marshall Plan, US, 67
Matejka, Viktor, 158
Menasse, Eva, 13
Mirecki, Ruth, 54
"Mischlinge," 11, 40, 51–53, 74–75, 92, 226. *See also* "mixed" Jews
"mixed" Jews, 2, 6n11, 11, 46–47, 48, 51–53. *See also* "Mischlinge"
mixed marriages, 5, 11, 16, 40n86, 43, 44, 46–47, 49–51, 74–75, 76n113, 116, 232, 239; gender and, 50–51; law and, 50–51
Moscow Declaration (1943), 10, 59–60, 63–64, 106, 127, 129, 138, 162, 197, 206; FAM and, 140–41; reparations and, 106, 206; restitution and, 63–64; victim myth and, 59–60, 63, 106, 127, 141, 162
Moser, Gwyn, 47, 92

Moser, Jonny, 3n6, 35n64, 38n72, 39n80, 57–58, 92n26, 133n20
Moser-Pröll, Anne-Marie, 237
Murmelstein, Benjamin, 77–78, 78n121, 79
Musik, Irene, 91
Mussolini, Benito, 23, 24

National Socialists, 22, 49, 109, 127, 209, 219, 220. *See also* Nazis
Nazi hunters, 78, 81, 173–74
Nazi Party: banning of, 209; illegal Austrian Nazi Party, 8, 22–23, 25, 127, 172; legalization of, 25; postwar outcomes for, 105–6
Nazi propaganda, 69, 87, 125, 142–43, 155. *See also* propaganda
Nazis, 11, 111, 201; Anschluss and, 25–26, 127–28, 131–32; Austrofascism and, 8, 24–25; censorship by, 125–26; denouncing former Nazis, 101–3; fascism and, 8; gentiles and, 3; IKG under, 29–35; postwar amnesties of, 215; postwar Austrian government's reintegration of, 105, 112, 156–57, 199–200, 204–5, 214, 215, 227, 237; postwar Austrian political parties and, 10, 105, 106, 156–57, 199–200, 215–16, 226, 235; propaganda by, 125, 142–43, 155; racial laws by, 29, 65–66, 184–85; rise of, 22–24; Vienna taken by, 28–29
Nazi terminology, 11–12, 49, 52, 184
Nazi war crimes, 60, 62, 63–64, 66, 67, 173–74, 197–98, 199, 201, 209, 241; Austrian government on, 104–7; restitution and, 215–17, 218
Netherlands, 6, 34, 136n31
non-Aryan Christians, 29, 40, 48–49, 116
November Pogrom, 11, 27–28, 34–35, 39, 71, 73, 80, 96, 115, 192
Nuremberg Laws, 33, 45, 47, 51, 65–66, 110, 116, 183
nursing homes, 49, 72–73, 115–23, 214

Oberhammer, Hans, 220–21
Offenberger, Ilana, 30
Opferausweise (victim identification papers), 65, 202–3
Opferfürsorge, 47–48
Opferfürsorgegesetz (Victims' Welfare Act; 1945), 64–65, 202–3
Opole ghetto, 39, 41, 41n88

Palestine, 31n55, 37–8, 38n72, 42, 123, 131, 169–70, 173–74, 175–76, 180–81, 180n34, 183, 185, 194, 196
Palestine Liberation Organization (PLO), 236
Pan-German Party, 17–18; movement, 142
Paris, 127, 132, 146, 147, 164, 171, 182, 193. *See also* France
passports, 33–34, 91
Paul Lazarsfeld Society, 237
Paul Zsolnay Verlag, 181, 188
Perl, William, 82, 82n138
persecution of Jews: "Aryanization" and, 27–29, 33, 57, 99, 109–10, 152; beginning of, 26–29, 28; emigration and, 8, 33–35, 40–41; of "Mischlinge," 52–53; during November Pogrom, 27–29, 34–35, 71, 80, 115, 192; street scrubbing, 28, 28–29; "Vienna Pogrom of Spring 1938," 27–28. *See also* violence
Peter, Friedrich, 237
"phoney war," 136, 136n31
Pick, Anton, 183
Poland, 16, 41, 41n88, 63, 96, 123, 160n105; gentiles in, 103; Jewish population in, 103; Jews from, 103, 169; Nazi invasion of, 136n31; Opole ghetto in, 41, 41n88
political home, 4, 7, 9, 238, 239; exile and, 127–30, 141–43; preparing Austrian communists for return to, 141–43; Social Democratic Party and, 128, 161
politics: before Anschluss, 130–32; of Anschluss, 21–26, 127–30; Austrian government and reception of concentration camp survivors, 104–12; in Czechoslovakia, 131; "denazification" and, 67, 106, 184, 196, 199–200; disillusionment with communism and, 1, 154, 160–62; elections and, 67–69, 154, 155–59, 198–99, 215, 233–34; in exile, 126–30, 132–43; identity relating to, 128–29; Jewish identity and, 19–20; Jewish returnees' postwar political reality,

143–47, 154–63; Renner government and, 62–66, 104–6, 155, 197–205; restitution and, 199–201, 215–17; in United Kingdom, 134–43; victim myth and, 59–60, 66, 67, 138–41, 156–57; in Vienna, 21–22, 143–54. *See also under specific political groups*
Porges, Jeanette, 89
postwar, 10, 59–60, 67–69, 97, 98, 99–103, 151–54, 177–78, 185–86, 198–99, 211, 231–35
Potsdam Conference, 61
Prague Spring, 1968, 154–54, 161
professional home, 4, 7, 9–10, 164, 167–69, 181–82, 195, 239–40; familial home versus, 174–80
propaganda, 69, 87, 125, 142–43, 155. *See also* Nazi propaganda
property ownership: Allies and, 188, 207, 211–12; antisemitism and, 198–99; "Aryanization" and, 27–28, 29, 33, 109–12, 207–12, 214–18; Assets Transfer Agency and, 33; Austrian government on, 57–58, 64, 97, 109–12, 157, 199, 201; ban on Nazi Party and, 209; emigration and, 33–34; legislation, 10, 112, 119, 209–15, 213, 217–22, 224–27, 240; registration of assets gained through "Aryanization," 208–9; restitution of, 109–12, 198–99, 207–15; US Army and, 211–12
"protected" status (Jews), 5, 40, 43, 48–53, 70, 239
Protective Association for Parties Affected by Restitution. *See* Schutzverband der Rückstellungsbetroffenen
Prussia, 18–19
publishing, 181
Putschin, Gertrude, 58, 210–11

Raab, Julius, 68–69, 198
Rabinovici, Doron, 41n87, 81
Rabinowicz, Alexander, 90, 90n16, 94, 103
race: "Mischlinge" Jews and, 51–53; Nazi law and, 29, 49, 64–66, 74, 184–85
racism, 18. *See also* antisemitism
rape, 60, 85, 86, 91
Rattner, Anna, 175–76
Reclaiming Heimat (Vansant), 128–29, 230

Red Army, 2, 56, 67, 69, 77–78, 79–80, 82, 84–85, 88, 91, 93, 95, 106, 111, 150, 155, 160n105, 170, 201, 207, 221; in Baltic states, 38–39; housing in postwar Vienna and, 97; labor camps, 38–39, 170–71; rapes by, 60, 85, 86, 91; revenge and violence by, 60–61, 91, 206, 240–41; in Vienna, 8, 11, 42, 43–45, 53–55, 56–57, 59–62, 62–63, 66–67, 104, 117, 197, 239. *See also* Soviet Army
Red-White-Red Book (*Rot-Weiss-Rot Buch*), 106–7
refugees, 6n11, 12, 20, 22, 38–39, 41, 72, 118, 122; emigration and, 33n61, 34–35, 134–36, 164–67, 191–95; in exile, 125–27, 129, 132, 133, 134–38, 141–42, 145, 152, 162, 165; in exile (male), 174–80
Reich Flight Tax, 217–18
Reich Labor Service, 52–53
Reinprecht, Christoph, 207
Reisz, Wilhelm, 81
religion: conversion to Christianity, 19, 29, 47, 116; conversion to Judaism, 74; identity and, 236–38; IKG and, 20–21; non-Aryan Christians, 29, 40, 48–49, 116. *See also under specific religions*
Renner, Karl, 24–25, 62–66, 68, 93, 104–6, 155, 184; on property ownership, 110–11, 198–99, 209
Renner government, 67, 68, 93, 104–6, 111, 202, 210; antisemitism in, 198–205; "first victim" argument and, 197–201; rebuilding of Vienna and, 62–66, 104–6, 155
reparations, 106, 154, 199–200, 201, 218, 235, 240–41; Allied occupation and, 61, 67, 206–8, 211–12; Moscow Declaration and, 206; payments for, 206; victim myth and, 197–98, 220–21
repatriation, 69, 105, 144–45, 192–95; certificate, 89; transports, 87–90, 91–93, 117, 169, 170
restitution, 154, 196; Allies and, 188, 207; appeals, 219–20; Austrian identity and, 214–17; economy and, 224–25; Jewish exclusion from, 202–5; laws and legislation, 10, 56, 63–64, 109–12, 119, 207–15, 207–15, 213, 217–22, 240; list of Acts

restitution (*continued*)
for, 213; Nazi war crimes and, 215–17; opposition to, 217–27; organizations, 217–22; politics and, 199–201, 215–17, 235; problems, 207–18; of property ownership, 97, 109–12, 198–99, 207–15; rental agreements and, 119, 172; Schutzverband der Rückstellungsbetroffenen and, 217–27; *Unser Recht* on, 222–27; victim myth and, 157, 221, 226, 235

Revolutions of 1848–49, 17, 18

Roosevelt, Franklin D., 10, 122

Rosenkranz, Herbert, 3n6

Rosner, Robert, 149–50, 150n76, 172n21

Rosner-Jellinek, Elisabeth, 149

Rot-Weiss-Rot Buch (*Red-White-Red Book*), 106–7

Rozenblit, Marsha, 19–20, 241

Rubin-Bittmann, Josef, 80

"Rückkehr, Die" (Torberg), 166–67

Schaier, Martin, 44–45, 44n4

Schatzberg, Paul, 27–28

Schneider, Gertrude, 92n26, 99–100, 113, 114

Schneider, Max, 137

Scholz, Willi, 142

Schur, Heinrich, 70

Schuschnigg, Kurt, 23–24, 25–26, 28, 28–29, 127, 131

Schutzverband der Rückstellungsbetroffenen (Protective Association for Parties Affected by Restitution), 217–22; *Unser Recht* and voice of, 222–27

Schwartz, Joseph, 160n105

Seegasse 9, KZ Rückkehrerheim at, 73, 98, 115–23

Segalman, Ralph, 94, 95, 113–14, 160n105

Seitenstettengasse: Jewish community offices on, 29, 70, 73; synagogue, 71, 96

sexual violence, 60, 85, 86, 91

Seyss-Inquart, Arthur, 25

Shanghai, 7, 38, 122, 169, 170, 174, 190–96, 210, 214

Shoah (documentary), 78n121

Silber, Joseph (Josef), 169, 198

Silverman, Lisa, 166

Simon, Maria Dorothea, 179, 232–33

Slovakia, 6, 37–38, 41n88

Social Democratic Party. *See* Austrian Social Democratic Party

Socialism, 143

Soviet Army, 2, 56, 67, 69, 77–78, 79–80, 82, 84–85, 88, 91, 93, 95, 106, 111, 150, 155, 160n105, 170, 201, 207, 221; in Baltic states, 38–39; housing in postwar Vienna and, 97; labor camps, 38–39, 170–71; rapes by, 60, 85, 86, 91; revenge and violence by, 60–61, 91, 206, 240–41; in Vienna, 8, 11, 42, 43–45, 53–55, 56–57, 59–62, 62–63, 66–67, 104, 117, 144, 197, 239. *See also* Red Army

Soviet Union, 131, 132, 139, 196, 205, 209–10, 214, 236–37; Allied occupation and, 61, 66, 207, 214; in Czechoslovakia, 154–55, 161; as enemy, 20. *See also* Cold War; Red Army; Soviet Army

Sozialdemokratische Partei Österreichs (SPÖ). *See* Austrian Social Democratic Party

Spiel, Hilde, 152, 153, 153n88

SPÖ. *See* Austrian Social Democratic Party

Stahlecker, Franz, 30–31

Stalin, Joseph, 10, 61

stock market crash: of 1873, 17; of 1929, 182

Stux, Paul, 88

suicides, 81, 183

Suschny, Adele, 173

Suschny, Kitty, 174

Suschny, Otto, 173–74

Suschny, Siegfried, 173

Süss, Salomon, 88

Swedish Mission, 116–17, 121

Tante Jolesch, Die (Torberg), 165

Tate, Ralph, 118

Tauber, Lilli, 41n88

Tauber, Max, 131

Tausend-Mark-Sperre (Thousand Mark Tax), 22

Tausig, Franziska, 190–92, 194, 200

Tausig, Hansi, 1–2, 7, 12, 125–26, 146, 147–48, 150, 153, 155, 161, 161n108, 163, 190

Tausig, Otto, 125n1, 126, 146, 147–48, 190

taxes: credits to victims, 203; emigration, 32, 34, 50; Jewish community funding from, 74; Reich Flight Tax and, 217–18; tax relief to Jews, 65, 204; Thousand Mark Tax, 22
Terezín, 40, 77, 78, 84, 87–90, 89, 93, 93n27, 95, 96n39, 96n40, 98, 102, 102n65, 102n66, 116–17
Thalberg, Hans, 152
Theresienstadt, 87. See Terezín
Thousand Mark Tax (Tausend-Mark-Sperre), 22
Torberg, Friedrich, 164–67, 177–78, 229, 241
Trahan, Elizabeth Welt, 56–57, 57n51, 208
Tritt, Frances, 98, 98n48
Tuchman, Emil, 79–80
Tyrolean hats, 152–53

U-Boote, 2, 5–6, 46–48, 48n21, 92, 167–68, 239
Uhl, Heidemarie, 205
Ungar-Klein, Brigitte, 47, 92
United Kingdom: Austrian Association of Doctors in Great Britain, 176; Austrian Centre and Young Austria in, 1, 125–26, 133, 134–38, 135, 141–44, 146, 148, 155; Austrian Communist Party in, 126–28, 132–43, 155, 162–63; British Labour Party in, 138; emigration to, 1–2, 32, 34–35, 37, 39, 125, 133–34, 168, 176, 179, 181, 184, 232–33; FAM and, 138–41; internment of enemy aliens in, 136; Jewish community in, 134–38; Kindertransporte, 34–35, 39, 133, 196; London Bureau of the Austrian Socialists in, 140–41; Löwenherz postwar trial in London, 78–79; politics in, 134–43
United Nations Relief and Rehabilitation Administration (UNRRA), 38, 118, 191, 192
United States (US): emigration to, 13, 26n35, 37–38, 39, 74, 76, 79, 82n138, 97, 158–59, 168, 174, 179, 184; postwar intervention for Jews, 204, 221; Marshall Plan by, 67; postwar occupation zone, 113, 171; postwar politics, 66–67, 205, 214–15; refugee experience in, 164–65; return from, 169, 174, 179; Soviet Jews' flight to, 237

United States Forces–Austria (USFA), 66, 104, 110–11, 115, 117, 118–22, 207, 211–12
United States Holocaust Memorial Museum, 12
United States military: 113; Jewish refugees in, 39, 66, 82n138, 168, 171n19. See also United States Forces-Austria (USFA)
UNRRA (United Nations Relief and Rehabilitation Administration), 38, 118, 191, 192
Unser Recht (newspaper), 222–27
US. See United States
USFA. See United States Forces–Austria

van Pelt, Robert Jan, 32n59, 38
Vansant, Jacqueline, 4, 128–29, 230
victim identification papers (Opferausweise), 65, 185–86, 202–3
victim myth, 1, 3, 9, 240–42; Allies and, 67, 156, 205–7, 240–41; Austrian Communist Party and, 127–30, 137, 138–41, 143–44, 146, 162–63, 239; Austrian government and, 62, 66, 68, 104–9, 138–41, 146–47, 155–59, 162, 197–201, 202–5, 215–17; employment and, 172; FAM and, 138–41; "first victim" argument of, 197–201; gender relating to, 178–79; Jewish exclusion and, 202–5; Jewish returnees and, 10–11, 99–100, 146–47, 162–63, 172, 178–79, 185–86, 188; Moscow Declaration and, 59–60, 63, 106, 127, 141, 162; politics and, 59–60, 66, 67, 138–41, 156–57; reality of, 197–207; reparations and, 197–98, 220–21; restitution and, 157, 221, 226, 235; Social Democrat Party and, 127–30, 138–41, 143–44, 155–56, 162–63, 239
victim status (for official recognition and assistance), 154; Austrian citizens and, 9, 62, 106–9, 203, 204–5; Austrian government and, 106–9, 156–58, 159, 203–5, 226–27; defining, 106–9, 201, 202–5; Jews' exclusion from, 10, 64–66, 107, 156–58, 202–5; law and, 64–65, 108–9, 202–5, 225–27; taxes and, 204; women and, 108–9

Victims' Welfare Act (Opferfürsorgegesetz; 1945), 64–65, 202–3
Vienna, 2–3, 6–7, 12–14; Allied occupation and, 59–67, 82; battlefront, 43–45, 53–55; destruction of, 55–57, 93–94, 93n28, 181; exiles return to, 143–54; first Austrian elections and, 67–69, 155–59, 198–99, 233–34; Gestapo arrests of Jews in, 48, 48n21, 108; Jews in hiding in, 2, 5–6, 8, 12, 40, 43–45, 46–48, 48n21, 54, 57, 59, 92, 95, 167–68, 239; Jews remaining in 1945 in, 45–53; politics in, 21–22, 143–54; professional home in, 167–69; professionals in postwar in, 180–82; Red Army in, 8, 11, 42, 43–45, 53–55, 56–57, 59–62, 62–63, 66–67, 97, 104, 117, 197, 239; Renner government and rebuilding of, 62–66, 104–6, 155; restoring Jewish community, 69–83, 180–89; taken by Nazis, 28–29. *See also under specific topics*
"Vienna Pogrom of Spring 1938," 27–28
Vienna State Police, 79–80
Viennese identity, 4–5, 19–20, 241
Viennese Jews: acculturation, 82, 228; Gestapo arrests of, 48, 48n21, 108; in hiding, 2, 5–6, 8, 12, 40, 43–45, 46–48, 48n21, 54, 57, 59, 92, 95, 167–68, 239; poll of, 1946, 82; post-Anschluss realities for, 26–29; "protected" status, 5, 40, 43, 48–53, 70, 239; reemerging of, 53–59; remaining in Vienna, 1945, 45–53; World War I supported by, 20. *See also under specific topics*
Viennese Jewish identity, 166–67, 169, 227–235, 241–42
Vietner, Anna, 95
violence, 8; after Anschluss, 27–29, 34–35; under Austrofascism, 23, 156; Förstergasse massacre and, 44–45, 53n43; rape and sexual, 60, 85, 86, 90–91; by Red Army, 60–61, 91, 206, 240–41; after World War II, 59, 60–61
von Papen, Franz, 25
von Schönerer, Georg Ritter, 17–18
von Schuschnigg, Karl, 23–26, 28, 28–29, 68, 127, 131

Waldheim Affair, 233–34
war crimes: Allies' attitudes toward, 240–41; Ältestenrat trials and, 76–81; Austrian War Criminal Law on (Kriegsverbrechergesetz), 80–81, 209; legislation related to, 213; by Nazis, 62, 63–64, 66, 80–81, 105–8, 173–74, 197, 209, 215–17; of November Pogrom, 80–81
war memorials, 106, 216
weddings, 42, 96–97
Welcome in Vienna (film), 171n19
West, Franz Carl, 141–42
Western occupation powers, 59, 61, 62–63, 66–67, 82, 104, 106, 144–45, 201, 205–7, 209, 214–15
Wiesenthal, Simon, 81
Wie wir gelebt haben (*How We Lived*; Eckstein and Kaldori), 15–17, 15n1, 41–42
Windholm, Marianne, 86, 90–91, 93, 95, 98–99, 113
women: Anschluss and new roles of, 35–37; emigration for, 32, 36–37, 39; exile and, 174–80; familial home and, 168, 180, 195; gendered experience of women returnees, 174–80; gender roles and, 35–37; home and, 37, 168, 174–75; identity and, 37, 174–80; independent return and dangers to, 90–91; mixed marriages and, 50–51; rape and violence to, 60, 85, 86, 90–91; risk perceived by, 36; victim myth relating to, 178–79; victim status and, 108–9
World War I, 13, 16; antisemitism after, 7–8, 227; before, 18–20; Central Powers during, 7–8; Jewish veterans of, 15, 36, 45–46; Jews' flight to Vienna during, 16, 17; Jews' identity after, 21; Jews' migration to Vienna after, 182; Jews' support of, 20; Jews' support of the monarchy during, 7–8
World War II: air raids, 53, 55, 93n28, 100, 151–52, 232; Austrian citizenship after, 65–66, 198; Austrian Communist Party after, 104, 143–54; Austrian Communist Party during, 125–33; final days of, 53–55; navigating destruction after, 55–57, 93–94,

181; "phoney war" and, 136n31; Social Democratic Party after, 68–69, 110, 143–54; Social Democratic Party during, 126–30; violence after, 59, 60–61

Young Austria, 125–26, 142–43; in exile, 133–38, 135; founding of, 135; Jewish returnees and, 148–50; recruitment, 135–37

Zelman, Leon, 72
Zionism, 21, 72, 142, 160n105
Zsolnay, Paul and Zsolnay Verlag, 181, 188
Zubok, Vladislav M., 61

ABOUT THE AUTHOR

Elizabeth Anthony is a historian and serves as the director of Visiting Scholar Programs at the Jack, Joseph and Morton Mandel Center for Advanced Holocaust Studies at the United States Holocaust Memorial Museum. She received her PhD in history from Clark University and was coeditor of *Freilegungen: Spiegelungen der NS-Verfolgung und ihrer Konsequenzen, Jahrbuch des International Tracing Service, Bd. 4* with Rebecca Boehling, Susanne Urban, and Suzanne Brown-Fleming.

www.ingramcontent.com/pod-product-compliance
Lightning Source LLC
Chambersburg PA
CBHW021655230426
43668CB00008B/636